The Golden Age of Irish Art

The Golden Age of Irish Art

The Medieval Achievement

600–1200

PETER HARBISON

Thames and Hudson

First Published in 1999 by Thames & Hudson Ltd, London.

First published in hardback in the United States of America in 1999
by Thames and Hudson Inc., 500 Fifth Avenue,
New York, New York 10110

British Library Cataloguing in Publication Data

A catalogue record for this publication is available
from the British Library

Library of Congress Catalog Card Number 98-61896

ISBN 0–500–01927–4

Printed and bound in France

Contents

Preface

■

MORE THAN THREE DECADES HAVE PASSED SINCE ZODIAQUE
published Françoise Henry's three-volume *L'Art Irlandais* (1963–65), which
quickly became – and has since remained – the standard work on the subject. The
English edition appeared in 1965–70. It was the culmination of a lifetime's work
devoted to her adopted country, and many of her ideas had already developed there
in the 1930s, when Europe was still in the grip of doctrinaire nationalism. The basic
structure which she erected over the years has remained solid, but some of the pieces
of scaffolding supporting it have had to be changed around in the meantime, and
others have fortunately been added to it. It would be foolhardy to try to emulate,
let alone surpass, her achievement, and space does not allow me here to repeat the
depth of her documentation. It is better to take it as read, and cover the same
material in less depth but with the hindsight of new discoveries and subsequent
research. The names of many of the scholars who have contributed to the re-framed
picture are mentioned in the text, and their works will be listed selectively in the
bibliography. Without them, and without Dr Henry's pioneering studies, it would
not have been possible to write the present work. An effort has also been made to
fit the story of early medieval Irish art into the political and religious background
which helped to determine its course.

I

Prehistoric Forebears

■

THE IRELAND THAT ST PATRICK, AND his predecessor Palladius, came to christianize in the fifth century was a country which already had a long and artistic tradition behind it, stretching as far back as the Stone Age. Had an ancient European been able to see that island from the top of an Alpine peak, he would have considered it as being a very remote bastion, facing the full force of the Atlantic waves and acting like a *Finis Terra* at the north-western end of his continent. But, for prehistoric peoples who frequented the seaways of the western European coast, Ireland lay midway on the maritime route between Spain and Scandinavia, and was therefore, in a sense, at the very centre of Europe's Atlantic littoral – as the Vikings were to find out for themselves during the course of the ninth century AD. Thus it comes as no surprise to discover that Ireland's first artistic expression survives on a type

of Neolithic tomb which finds echoes in the Orkneys to the north, as well as in Brittany and – to a lesser extent – on the Iberian Peninsula further south. It takes the form of carving on large stones in and around Passage Graves of *c.* 3000 BC which are scattered throughout the countryside, but the most highly decorated examples are concentrated in the County Meath near the east coast, north of Dublin. Best known of these is Newgrange where, at the winter solstice, the rays of the rising sun penetrate along a 20m passage to the very centre of the tomb. In front of the doorway is one of the finest carved stones to survive from prehistoric Europe – a large boulder decorated with diamond-shaped designs, undulating lines and a triple spiral which one could see as the cradle for Ireland's predilection for the spiral form that lives on under many guises into the medieval period.

Entrance stone to the Passage Grave at Newgrange, Co. Meath.

Elsewhere in County Meath, at Sliabh na Calliaghe, Loughcrew, the presence on the carved stones of small circles with radiating lines would suggest a representation of the sun — doubtless the nature god worshipped by those who built the tombs. If this indeed be a sun-symbol, one may well ask: what do the other motifs represent which are found in Passage Grave art in Ireland and elsewhere — the diamond-shape, the zigzag, or a shield-like motif? These must have been potent symbols for Stone Age man and woman, but nowadays we can only hope to discover their meaning and significance with the aid of our imagination. They were signs to give hope and comfort to those buried in the house of the dead, together with those who survived them and, given that stone is usually the last in a long line of materials to receive the results of artistic creativity, we could envisage these same motifs having been applied earlier to the homes of the living on media which have long since disintegrated — carved wooden surfaces or perhaps even woven fabrics which might have served as wall-hangings.

It would be a mistake, however, to think of Passage Grave art as purely symbolic, for it can be representational even if in a rather stylized way. The chamber at Newgrange bears a carving which looks very like a fern and, elsewhere, there are also interesting occurrences of the human figure. Perhaps the most appealing is the little smiling man in the tomb at Fourknocks, Co. Meath, and another appears on orthostat 49 of the western tomb of the largest treasury of Passage Grave art in Ireland (or anywhere else in Europe) — the mighty tumulus at Knowth, about a mile away from Newgrange. It was in the other, eastern, tomb chamber there that the most outstanding piece of mobile Passage Grave art was found — a spirally-decorated flat macehead (Pl.3) which must surely be understood as a stylized representation of the human face.

The subsequent discovery and utilization of metal provided the craftsman with new materials on which to practise his skills during the Bronze Age (*c.* 2000–500 BC) – not only bronze itself, but also gold, of which Ireland seems to have had the richest resources in the whole of north-western Europe. The metal surfaces were embellished with geometrical ornament – often triangles and zigzags on the earlier, wafer-thin, lunulae, but with more frequent use of concentric circles when the gold became ever more abundant during the later Bronze Age, *c.* 700 BC. While the men were occupied with incising or punching in their geometrical ornament into metal, the women were producing highly sophisticated patterns on pottery which was placed in graves during the earlier Bronze Age around 1500 BC.

It is perhaps during the Bronze Age period that we should envisage the earlier population groups being augmented slowly but surely by the arrival of some Indo-Europeans who spoke a language ancestral to the Gaelic which lives on in parts of the west of Ireland today. Just when these Celtic speakers first arrived no one knows, but they had begun to make their artistic mark on the northern half of the country by at least the third century BC. This was a time when, on the European continent, Celtic La Tène art had entered an already developed phase with the Waldalgesheim style, which was practised with great originality and brilliance from the Marne to Moravia. Its genius lay in the adaptation of motifs derived from the classical art of Greece and Etruria, but stylized in such a way as to leave the original components disarticulated and disguised in the background while creating a whole new set of designs which played visually with the contrast of positive and negative. In addition, they possessed a studied asymmetry which frequently kept the eye fixed upon a series of ingenious, never-ending, swirling curves and undulations. The rejection of classical forms appealed to the Celts, who preferred to leave to the Greeks or Etruscans the naturalistic and idealistic reproduction of the human figure and Mediterranean vegetal motifs; their predilection, instead, was to engage the mind in seeing nature enriched in a novel, vibrant and stylized form. Practised in their ultimate perfection on metal-work, these wonderful Celtic skills proliferated over much of central Europe and spread across the English Channel to England, where they were to take on new vigour and sheer inventiveness of pattern. Designs on sword-scabbards executed, for instance, in eastern Gaul, and as far east as Hungary, also found their way to the north-eastern tip of Ireland. How they came there, and even when, is a question difficult to answer, but it is likely that around the third or second century BC a workshop associated with Celtic warriors was active in the area around the lower river Bann in producing bronze sword-scabbards (Pl.6) which are among the most intricate examples of early La Tène art in Ireland. With only a few ingenious strokes, the craftsmen could evoke a face-mask on a bronze horse-bit from Attymon, Co. Galway (Pl.5) and, when geo-metrical compass-drawn designs became common in the centuries bracketing the time of Christ, bronzesmiths applied them with eye-catching effect on objects like the box-lid from Somerset in the same county (Pl.7), and masterfully combined them with stylized bird-heads on the unprovenanced 'Petrie Crown' (Pl.8), a bronze object of unknown use dating from around the first century AD.

The discovery of bone plaques with compass-made designs (Pl.4) in a much older Passage Grave at Loughcrew, Co. Meath, suggests the thought that the love of geometric ornamentation and the stylization of the human face found on Irish La Tène material was a conscious continuation from the art of the megalithic tombs of the Stone Age, but such is unlikely to have been the case.

The La Tène decoration found in Ireland is certainly derived ultimately from its continental Gaulish counterparts, filtered through Britain, yet nevertheless with a high-calibre quality of its own which gives it a very honourable place among the objects decorated in the La Tène style throughout Europe. In Ireland, the La Tène-decorated objects cannot be closely dated, and may be spread loosely over half a millennium or more from 300 BC onwards. The question is: how much more? Sadly, the problem has no ready solution, yet it is a matter of considerable importance because of the latent La Tène element which makes itself felt in the earliest of Ireland's surviving manuscripts dating, in all probability, from the period between 575 and 675 AD.

Stag incised on a bone plaque from Loughcrew, Co. Meath (National Museum, Dublin).

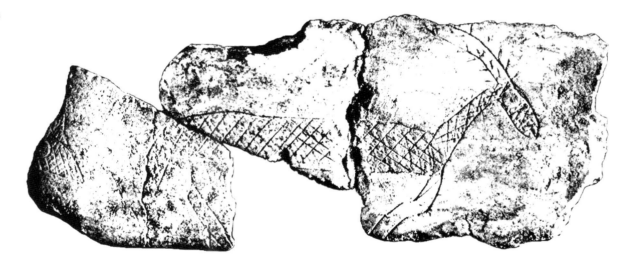

2

Early Christian Rebirth

■

T HE CENTURIES LEADING UP TO THE
appearance of the first surviving manuscripts in
Ireland were doubtless turbulent, though we know
all too little about them. The Romanization of
Britain, increasing in intensity from the time of
Christ, was not replicated in Ireland which, at first,
became more isolated from its erstwhile Celtic
neighbours as a result. The well of inspiration
which had come from the heartlands of Celtic
Gaul, and then through England before Caesar's
conquest, began to dry up. Gradual Roman
dominance of the Atlantic sea-routes in the early
centuries after Christ must have restricted the
mobility of Irish seafarers accustomed to bringing
with them new ideas from France and England.
Yet this did not mean that the two sister islands
were not in contact with one another. On the
contrary. It may well have been Romanized
Britons who deposited gold coins and ornaments

around the mound at Newgrange, which continued the tradition of ritual sanctity that must
have made it into one of the tourist wonders of
the barbarian world at the time. A lead seal and
other artefacts of about 300 AD, found on the so-
called 'Rath of the Synods' on the symbolically-
rich Hill of Tara, Co. Meath, certainly suggests
links with the Roman world. But while this can be
interpreted as Roman Britons being present on
what was once one of Ireland's most sacred royal
sites, it could also reflect the return of Irish
people who had been to Roman Britain and
beyond. There is, indeed, reason to think that Irish
mercenaries may have enlisted in the Roman army,
and objects found on the island of Lambay and
on the adjacent mainland of Loughshinny in
north County Dublin indicate the possible
presence of Roman Britons (settlers or refugees?)
during the second century AD. The Roman writer,

Tacitus, reported that his father-in-law, Agricola, had given hospitality to an Irish prince who had been driven from his kingdom by rebellion, and who had doubtless come to seek Agricola's help in reconquering it, as Diarmaid MacMurrough was to do with disastrous consequences 1100 years later. It gave rise to Agricola's remark to his son-in-law that a Roman legion and a few auxiliaries could easily conquer Ireland, and that it would be to Britain's advantage if Roman arms were in evidence on every side 'and liberty vanished off the map'! His views may have been naive, but they show that the Romans had considered the conquest of Ireland, yet had not pursued the matter further, presumably for reasons of expediency more than fear.

However, though never conquered by Rome, Ireland was much in her debt, for it was through the Roman Empire that Ireland became literate. The earliest form of writing known in Ireland is the Ogham script, a cipher or alphabet consisting of nineteen letters (and one diphthong) divided into four groups of five, one of which contained the vowels AOUEI. It is generally agreed that the Ogham alphabet, though different from the Latin in being made up of a number of notches placed on, diagonally across or on either side of a central line, must nevertheless have been developed with a knowledge of the Roman alphabet in mind. While originally practised on wood and metal, the earliest surviving Ogham inscriptions come down to us on stones starting no later than the fourth century, continuing in popularity until the sixth or seventh, and used sporadically afterwards until even as late as the nineteenth century. Ogham inscriptions commemorate individuals, whose

names have yet to be equated satisfactorily with personalities recorded in historical or genealogical sources, but they do help to put some flesh on the meagre skeleton of what we know about the peoples of Ireland up to the later sixth century AD, the period before the earliest surviving Irish manuscripts came to be written. Paradoxically, this Roman-inspired alphabet that developed in Ireland was brought back to Roman Britain when Irish emigrants settled in Wales and Cornwall in the fifth century, and was utilized on stones which also bore Latin inscriptions with a similar message.

But it is more to Roman Gaul than to Roman Britain that we should look for the greatest gift that the late Roman Empire was to bestow upon Ireland – namely Christianity. Our first record of Christianity in Ireland is a statement by the Aquitanian chronicler Prosper that a certain Palladius, having been ordained by no less a person than Pope Celestine, was sent by him as the first bishop to the Irish believing in Christ. This reveals to us that there were Christians in Ireland before Palladius arrived in 431, and we can only surmise that they were scattered over the east and south-east of the country. They must have been sufficiently numerous to have had their request for a bishop taken so seriously that it was granted – the first known instance of this happening outside the bounds of the Roman Empire. The Palladian mission has been overshadowed by that under-taken subsequently by St Patrick, simply because those interested in expanding the cult of St Patrick in the seventh century suppressed details of Palladius who – they thought – might detract from the perceived achievement of their hero having christianized Ireland in the course of a few decades. Palladius, a Gallo-Roman aristocrat, came from Auxerre which, at the time, was the centre of the Gallican church, and Ireland can thus be seen to have received its religious organization from the very fount of Gallican church orthodoxy – but precisely what form that organization took is difficult to ascertain. We first hear of Irish bishops a century and a half after the arrival of Palladius, so that we know next to nothing about how he structured the church in the country to which he came as a missionary.

The ecclesiastical authorities who sent Palladius have left us no details of his mission, but we do know more about St Patrick who, in contrast, seems to have undertaken the further christianization of Ireland on his own initiative, having received the call through a dream. He was a humble man, with a deep belief in God as his guide and helper, and his autobiographical *Confessio* tells us how he grew up in Roman Britain, and was taken by Irish raiders as a slave. But he later found his way back home and, having heard the voice of the Irish calling on him to return, he did just that and spent the rest of his life among them before dying probably in 493, rather than the more usually accepted death date of 461. But of his own missionary activity he tells us little, and much of what we think we know about it comes from adulatory hagiography written two centuries after his death.

We cannot be sure that St Patrick set up a network of bishoprics of the kind we know existed in the land of his birth, but it seems quite likely. However, he must also have looked benignly upon the monastic life, for he tells us that some of his converts became monks and nuns. Monasticism had developed in Egypt and the East, and was introduced into Gaul through the small island of Lerins, not far from the French Mediterranean coast near Nice. Palladius would have been well acquainted with monastic institutions in Gaul, and it was from France – possibly through intermediate stations such as Whithorn in Galloway or St David's in Wales – that the idea was gradually implanted in Ireland. There, during the course of the sixth century, it was to transform the country and build up an ecclesiastical system that seemed strange to people like the Venerable Bede in Northumbria. He was surprised to note that Iona, a monastery founded by an Irishman on an island in the Inner Hebrides in 565, always had an abbot as its ruler to whom the province, including the bishops, were subject. His observation brings out clearly the remarkable change which the Irish church had undergone in the sixth century, from a presumed diocesan system in which the bishop is the authority, to one where individual monasteries take over religious leadership from the bishops who, nevertheless, continue to play a significant sacramental role, for instance in the ordination of priests. This arrangement set Ireland apart from the rest of Europe, and was retained until the twelfth-century church reform finally brought the country back to conformity with the normal episcopal system.

From early on, some monasteries were more eminent than others. One of these was Clonard, Co. Meath, where St Finnian's foundation became a 'nursery of saints', numbering among its graduates those who were later destined to found notable monasteries elsewhere themselves.

3   Neolithic flint mace-head found in the Passage Grave at Knowth,
    Co. Meath, and fashioned in the form of a human face (National
    Museum, Dublin).

4   Iron Age bone plaques from Loughcrew, Co. Meath, decorated with
    compass-drawn designs (National Museum, Dublin).

5   Stylized head on a bronze horse-bit from Attymon, Co. Galway
    (National Museum, Dublin).

6   Incised La Tène ornament on a sword-scabbard from Lisnacroghera,
    Co. Antrim (British Museum, London).

7   Eye-catching round shapes on a box cover from Somerset,
    Co. Galway (National Museum, Dublin).

8   The so-called 'Petrie Crown' featuring elegant bird-heads in relief
    (National Museum, Dublin).

9   *The Cathach* manuscript in the Royal Irish Academy, Dublin: initial Q
    with 'fish' and cross on Fol. 48a.

10 *The Cathach*: the initial letter M on Fol. 21a may have been inspired
    by La Tène metalwork.

11 Seventh-century bronze penannular brooch from near Athlone, Co.
    Westmeath, decorated with spiral ornament (National Museum,
    Dublin).

12 Bronze latchet, probably once decorated with red enamel
    (National Museum, Dublin).

13 Panels of a small seventh-century house-shaped shrine from the
    river Blackwater at Clonmore, Co. Armagh (Ulster Museum,
    Belfast).

14 Metal-framed enamel escutcheon from the large hanging-bowl
    found at Sutton Hoo in Suffolk (British Museum, London).

15 *Millefiori*-decorated penannular brooch from Ballinderry,
    Co. Westmeath, and two 'hand-pins' (National Museum, Dublin).

16 Three basic motifs used in early Christian Irish art – interlace,
    spirals and animal ornament – are assembled together in concentric
    bands around a central rock crystal on the underside of the Ardagh
    Chalice (National Museum, Dublin).

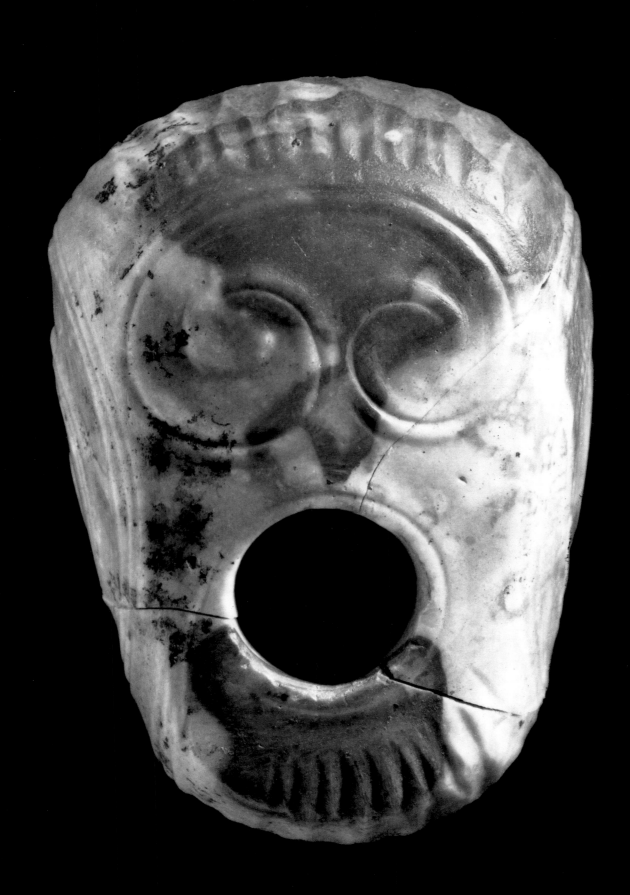

3

4

5

6

8

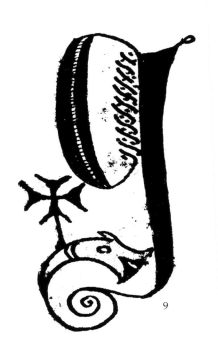

9

10

14

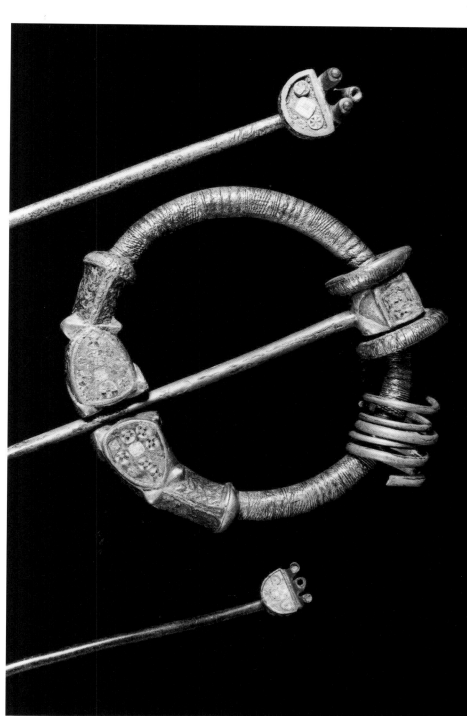

15

16

Among them may be cited Ciarán of Clonmacnoise, Brendan of Clonfert (the great navigator), Colum of Terryglass and, one of the greatest of them all, St Columba of Derry, Durrow and Iona. We shall be meeting some of these places again as centres of artistic production and, because the monasteries were usually associated with important dynasties and families in their respective localities, they had the wherewithal to provide artistic patronage and to encourage learning within the monastic community. For some centuries after the foundation of these monasteries, the church and monks' quarters – and possibly standing crosses as well – were made of wood and have, consequently, vanished through exposure to centuries of Irish weather. Nothing remains of Clonard, and, as we shall see, the monuments surviving in stone on other sites such as Glendalough (Pl.2) are mostly later than 800, and thus many centuries later than the days of the monastic founders.

The rules of these monasteries in the decades after their foundation were extremely harsh and ascetic, and the human deprivation to which the monks subjected themselves were the natural continuation of the spirit of the founding fathers of the Egyptian desert. A novel form of self-denial came in the form of voluntary exile, not just on a temporary basis, but for life, which involved leaving one's country and going on *peregrinatio*, pilgrimage, which involved praying, practising a harsh daily regimen, and spreading the gospel of Christ to the heathen. One of the first to follow this path was St Columba, a remarkable scion of the royal Uí Néill dynasty in the north-west of Ireland, who founded

monasteries such as Durrow in the midland county of Offaly and that on the island of Iona, where he died in exile in 597. It was some monks from this last-named monastery who just over two hundred years later fled to the inland safety of Kells in County Meath, bringing with them relics of their founding saint including, some think, the famous Book of Kells. It, the Book of Durrow and the Book of Lindisfarne (written in a daughter-house of Iona), can also be seen to have been associated with the *paruchia* – or family of monasteries – associated with St Columba, whose significance for insular art is, therefore, of inestimable importance.

The Cathach and Other Early Manuscripts

One other manuscript which has often been associated with St Columba himself is that known as the Cathach, an Irish word for Battler – a name given to the codex because it was carried into battle as a talisman by its then owners, the O'Donnells, the family to which St Columba belonged. Now preserved in the Library of the Royal Irish Academy in Dublin, the Cathach was, for centuries, contained in a shrine (p.263). This was opened in 1813, and found to contain the rather damaged pages of the manuscript which have since been excellently conserved. The earliest of the important insular manuscripts to survive, it is an incomplete text of the Psalms following St Jerome's original correction of the Latin Psalter known as the *Gallicanum*, though with a small

Initial E with fish on Fol. 22a of the *Cathach* of St Columba.

Initial D(eu)S on
Fol. 19a of the *Cathach*.

admixture of Old Latin readings. Described by E.A. Lowe as 'the pure milk of Irish calligraphy', and executed by what H.J. Lawlor saw as a 'penman of more than average excellence', the Cathach is written in a clear Irish majuscule script which bears little or no relationship to those used on the European continent during the Late Antique era. The Cathach shows us that, by the time it was written around the year 600, the Irish had already evolved their own style of writing, and we can only presume that there were generations of earlier manuscripts now lost in which the Irish would gradually have developed their own characteristic script from the books that earlier missionaries may have brought to them. For a people who had first learned to write in a language (Latin) not their own, they succeeded remarkably well in swiftly nurturing an individual style of writing. This is suggested by a set of Psalms written on wax tablets that were found at Springmount bog in County Antrim, and which may be even older than the Cathach.

The same generations of manuscripts that had developed the writing style had also, presumably, been making the first faltering steps in decoration which, in the case of the Cathach, is seen in the first letters of each Psalm. These opening letters in the Cathach (Pl.9–10) present us with an already mature ornament dominated by the well-tried traditional Celtic La Tène motifs of trumpet spirals, demonstrating not only the retention of traditional pagan patterns but also showing how far the Irish scribe had advanced in distancing himself from Late Antique manuscripts on the Continent. No longer was the initial letter using the same base as the other letters of the first line; instead, it could take up the height of three lines of text, and the immediately ensuing letters would be gradually reduced in size until they were of the same height as the normal text letters. In this way, the initial letter takes on a new emphasis hitherto unknown. It becomes a decorative motif stressing the important beginning of a sacred text, with which it is organically united by the gradually decreasing size of the letters following it. Drawn in brown ink and sometimes surrounded by red dots, the initials — probably penned by the same scribe who wrote the text — seem to breathe in and out, allowing for an expansion or contraction of the line of the letter, while the ends of these lines can expand into spirals, spherical triangles, trumpet-spirals — and even a fish or cross, both of which are combined on fol. 6a. The fish is probably an Irishman's idea of a dolphin, and suggests that this is an element in the Cathach's decoration which derives ultimately from the Mediterranean world.

But through which channels did the dolphin swim to reach Ireland from the Mediterranean? Many scholars believed that it — and certain other decorative features of the Cathach — may have come about through Ireland's first really important direct contact with the artistic world of Mediterranean Christianity — the foundation of the monastery at Bobbio in the foothills of the southern Alps in northern Italy by the Irish missionary, St Columbanus, shortly before his death around the year 615. Of the rare manuscripts surviving from the first decade of the monastery's existence, one in particular (Milan, Biblioteca Ambrosiana MS. S 45. sup.) is associated by inscription with Atalanus, the first successor of Columbanus as abbot, who died in 622. Because two out of the four scribes who worked on the Atalan codex wrote in a style closely resembling that of the Cathach, some scholars believe that Bobbio was the intermediary in passing on Mediterranean ideas to Irish writing schools, thus providing a date for the Cathach of after 614 – the year that Bobbio was founded. A comparison of detail between the Cathach and one of the hanging bowls (Pl.14) in the Sutton Hoo ship burial of *c.* 625 led David Wright to speculate that the Cathach could even be as late as the 630s. Although one of the earliest surviving Irish manuscripts, the Cathach, is, as we have seen, probably by no means the first, and the mature style of its writing and decoration are likely to have been the result of gradual scriptorial development over many decades. The discovery of sixth-century Mediterranean pottery in both Britain and Ireland shows that the contacts between the Mediterranean and the insular world of north-western Europe had already been active long before Bobbio was ever founded, thus making an earlier date for the Cathach possible. There is an old tradition associating the writing of the Cathach with St Columba himself, who died in 597, and while there is little likelihood that there is any link between our manuscript

and one which St Columba is said to have copied illicitly before 563, it is nevertheless palaeographically possible that the manuscript could belong to the late sixth century, and not inconceivable, therefore, that it was written by the hand of St Columba.

The equal-armed crosses with expanding ends on folios 6a, 48a (Pl.9) and 50b of the Cathach are clearly modelled on metalwork crosses of the kind well known from the eastern Mediterranean and Italy at the time. A similar cross is present on another early Irish manuscript known as the Codex Usserianus Primus [Trinity College Library, Dublin, Ms. A. 4. 15 (55)], which may be marginally earlier than the Cathach and shows us that metalwork must have played a significant role in the incipient formation of Irish manuscript ornament. This is also in evidence among the

Detail of Fol. 6a of the *Cathach* showing the diminuendo effect of the capitals reducing in size until they match the height of the text letters.

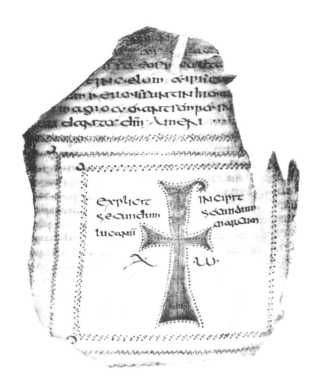

Celtic spirals and trumpet patterns seen so clearly on the initial M of fol. 21a of the Cathach (Pl.10), where the small lentoid feature betrays a background in the bronzesmith's workshop. This leads us on to the thorny problem of which metalwork stood as model for this ornament — and where it was made.

Metalwork up to *c.* 650

Although the evidence is slight, it would seem that the Celtic La Tène tradition of metalworking had been kept alive in Ireland during the centuries of the declining Roman Empire with the production at least of simple pins for personal adornment. But the break-up of the Empire in the fifth century AD gradually led to the development of new styles in jewellery and, consequently, in metalworking. The heads of pins took on the shape of the knuckle of

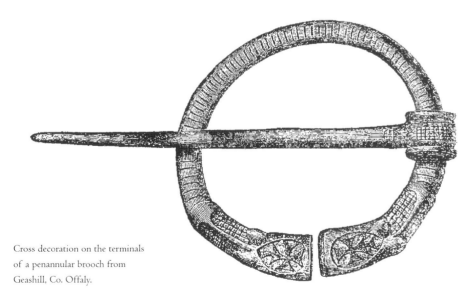

Cross decoration on the terminals of a penannular brooch from Geashill, Co. Offaly.

a clenched fist (Pl.15), and were decorated with the old La Tène style of pelta ornament, heightened in effect by the use of red enamel. The same combination of Celtic ornament with red enamel is present also on the most decorative example of an enigmatic type of object known as a latchet (Pl.12), which may date from the sixth or seventh century. But more significant for the future of early medieval metalwork was the adoption on both sides of the Irish Sea of a Roman brooch type that was round, though not forming a complete circle — hence the name penannular — and which was fixed to the garment by means of a movable pin. This suggests the adoption of late Roman clothing fashions in Ireland, where the terminals of the brooches take on the shape of a stylized animal head. By about 600 — the period of the Cathach — these terminals had expanded to accommodate pelta-type decoration in the La Tène style (Pl.11) and often filled with red enamel. The brooch from Ballinderry, Co. Westmeath (Pl.15), shows us, too, the emergence in Irish jewellery of the addition of a new kind of glass ornament known as *millefiori*, consisting of numerous strands of different-coloured glass fused together into a long rod, pieces of which are sliced off like a chopped cucumber and set into place. The pelta-like decoration on brooch terminals suggests further metalwork sources for the Cathach initials, and it is interesting to note, too, that at about the same period – say around 600 – some brooches, including one from the Hunt Museum in Limerick and another from Geashill in County Offaly, began to be decorated with a cross motif on the terminals. These crosses are equal-armed and, though not identical with those in the Cathach, they do make it likely that by this time the Irish Church was already beginning to take a serious interest in metalwork, and showing signs of becoming a fosterer and benefactor of the metalsmith's art. Even clearer evidence of this comes from two separate sets of bronze plates from around the first half of the seventh century, one recently discovered in the river Blackwater at Clonmore, Co. Armagh (Pl.13), and the other re-discovered at Bobbio. Both are decorated with assured peltae and curvilinear designs of various kinds, and Late Antique comparisons for the concave ends of the plates suggest their use as 'house'- or 'tomb'-shaped shrines. They represent another early example of insular ornament being applied to types of objects derived from the Continent, and suggest furthermore that Bobbio's influence on Irish art may not have been confined solely to manuscripts.

Another potential indicator of the Church's early involvement in metalwork was in the occasional appearance of crosses on bronze vessels known as hanging-bowls, which were probably already in production by the end of the sixth century. These bowls, made of a thin copper alloy, are decorated by three or four handles, known as escutcheons, which were soldered on and had a chain attached to them for suspension. The escutcheons are bearers of a richly-varied style of La Tène-type ornament with the sporadic admixture of dolphins, presumably of Roman/Mediterranean origin, and it is these escutcheons that are sometimes the bearers of the Christian crosses, suggesting a possible ecclesiastical function. The bowls have been the subject of much discussion for more than half a century, not only because of the enigma of their purpose, but also because of the mystery of where they were made. Many of them have been found in pagan graves in the east and south of England dating from the

Hanging-bowl escutcheons showing Celtic spiral and trumpet patterns.

period 550–650, but their Celtic ornament makes it unlikely that the bowls were originally made for heathen Saxon burials of the kind encountered at Sutton Hoo in Suffolk, where two examples were found among the grave-goods of a ship-burial. The mere handful of escutcheons and the lack of the usual round-shaped bronze bowls in Ireland, when compared to nearly one hundred examples found in Britain, would not appear to favour the claim that hanging-bowls with enamelled escutcheons were produced mainly in Ireland in the late sixth and seventh centuries. But Michael Ryan strengthened the case by finding a virtual identity in style between the frames surrounding the escutcheon on the large hanging bowl buried at Sutton Hoo around 625 (Pl.14) and a half-cylindrical length of grey metal, apparently unfinished and therefore probably of local manufacture, discovered in the crannog (man-made island) of Ballinderry II in County Offaly. The same site also produced a bird-shaped escutcheon which could create an additional argument in favour of partial production in Ireland around 600 AD. In contrast, however, another enamelled escutcheon found in the river Bann in Northern Ireland may well have been imported from the land of the Picts in northern Scotland, because a mould for making just such an escutcheon was excavated at Craig Phadraig in Inverness. One particular group of escutcheons, not hitherto found in Ireland, bears Celtic scroll and trumpet pattern ornament expanding from a central whorl. Its origin remains obscure, but it would be of advantage to find out – if one could – where it was manufactured, as this ornament becomes one of the chief elements of early medieval insular metalwork, and also erupts upon the manuscript scene in the Book of Durrow, which gives the old pagan pattern a whole new lease of life in a Christian context.

3

The Seventh Century

■

THE CATHACH SUGGESTS THAT, BY around 600, the Irish monasteries which had been founded in the preceding century had already reached a degree of sophistication in the writing of manuscripts and, in the course of the seventh century, they attained a very high reputation, too, for the learning contained in other, undecorated, manuscripts which they produced. Ludwig Bieler pointed out that, in matters of Latin learning and intellectual culture, Ireland had caught up with the rest of the Roman world by the year 600 and, in the following hundred years, 'her Latin culture was remarkably superior to anything that could be found in Saxon England, Lombard Italy, or Merovingian France'. Suddenly, Ireland came to the fore in producing exegetical works on the Holy Scriptures, grammatical treatises, computistical tracts and also – unusually for the period – *Vitae*, or lives of the local saints. The Venerable

Bede, historian of the early medieval English church and people, tells us that, before 664, there were many members of the English nobility and lesser folk who had gone to Ireland for religious studies either in a single monastery or travelling from one to another, and receiving there hospitality, books and instruction free, gratis and for nothing. These Irish monasteries, therefore, must have been hives of activity and, we may presume, not just in the world of learning but also in the field of manuscript illumination and metalworking as well.

Two monasteries which had risen like cream to the top of the milk were Armagh and Kildare. At the start of the seventh century, Armagh was still very much a bishopric, which it proclaimed as a foundation of St Patrick but, as the century proceeded, it developed an increasingly monastic character wanting to extend the physical bounds of its hill-top church further down the slopes to make it into an extensive *civitas refugii* – a place of refuge for pilgrims and the sick, as well as for widows and orphans. But its horizons expanded, too, in wishing to incorporate into its *paruchia*, or family of churches, not only those which had traditionally been associated with St Patrick, but also independent churches, some associated with Palladius, and others in areas where it sought influence in the Midlands, in Connacht to the west, and Leinster in the east. In fact, as we have seen, it was Armagh that strove to dismiss the pioneering work of Palladius in order to incorporate it into the legend of St Patrick, whose cult Armagh was interested in promoting.

The rival in this expansionist programme was Kildare on the plains of Leinster, a foundation with a somewhat shadowy early history associated with St Brigid. Where Armagh sought to propagate the biography of St Patrick, Kildare got to work creating not one, but three *Vitae* of St Brigid and – like Armagh – it claimed to provide sanctuary for pilgrims, the poor and the needy, not on a local but on an all-Ireland basis. It countered Armagh's propaganda by building a large wooden double church for its community of monks and nuns (p.192), and showed off its riches by enshrining the remains of St Brigid and her bishop Conlaed in two sarcophagi decorated with gold, silver and precious stones, and with a crown of gold and silver hanging overhead. These had probably all been commissioned by the Uí Dúnlainge, the dynasty of local potentates. Sadly, nothing remains of their artistic patronage today, but one may well wonder if the sarcophagi bore any similarity to the stone versions preserved in the crypt of the French abbey of Jouarre, and if the crown had any resemblance to surviving Visigothic examples like those from Guarrazár in Spain. Not only for Armagh and Kildare, but also for the lesser foundations as well, the seventh century saw the growing importance of the ruling political families in the governance and affairs of the individual monasteries which, in most instances, they had been involved in founding.

But the seventh century also saw the expansion of two other monasteries of importance which, subsequently, were to play a considerable artistic role. One of these was Clonmacnoise in County Offaly, the cross-roads of Ireland where the main east-west road crossed the river Shannon – the vital north-south traffic artery in the centre of Ireland. From the middle of the seventh century onwards, Clonmacnoise became an important burial place for the kings of Connacht who lived west of the Shannon, and it was doubtless their patronage which contributed to its fame as a centre of artistic excellence. The other really significant foundation was St Columba's monastery on the island of Iona which, though Scottish, remained in close contact with the homeland of its founding father, from whence many of its abbots came. It had a considerable influence on Ireland, including the writing of its history, for its annals which chronicled important Irish events were kept up to date in Iona until around 740, after which they were continued and expanded in Ireland to form the basic chronological framework for the writing of the country's medieval history. Iona, thus, has a significance which goes far beyond its own important *paruchia*, the family of churches which had been founded by St Columba or incorporated into it. Indeed, though very much on the periphery of Britain, Iona played a very valuable role in its artistic development which came about through Iona's missionary activity. This had included work among the Picts of Scotland during and after Columba's lifetime, but further seeds were sown when King Oswald of Northumbria asked bishop Aidan of Iona to come and preach the word of God among his subjects who, as Bede noted, spoke four languages – British, Pictish, Scottish (i.e. Gaelic) and English. One fruitful outcome was Aidan's foundation of the monastery of Lindisfarne on an island off the Northumbrian coast. It formed one of the main spring-boards for the christianization of the English, another arm converging in a 'pincer movement' from its southern base in Canterbury, where it was managed by continental personnel directed by Rome. These two movements had the same godly goal, but they came into conflict with one another over the date on which Easter should be celebrated, and also about the type of tonsure to be worn by the monks. Matters came to a head at the Synod of Whitby in 664, when the Roman party's more up-to-date method of calculating Easter was given preference over the older and more traditional method used by the Irish. The Irish camp retired from Northumbria and went, first to Iona, and then back to Ireland, though Irish influence still persisted in Northumbria. Aidan, abbot of Iona, subsequently won over many of the northern Irish churches to the Roman system of calculating the date of Easter, though his own community on Iona was not finally convinced of its advantage until 715.

The combination of the many English people described by Bede as coming to Ireland for study in the first half of the seventh century, and the many Irish who went the other way to assist Aidan's mission in Northumbria between the foundation of Lindisfarne in 635 and the Synod of Whitby in 664, helps to explain the cultural cross-fertilization which took place between Ireland and Northumbria. Its impetus was so widespread that the two areas became so mutually interlinked and culturally indivisible that the artistic developments which proceeded in tandem in both areas were described in non-committal terms as 'insular' or 'Hiberno-Saxon' simply because scholars could not satisfactorily differentiate between products of the two areas. Yet, even after the Synod of Whitby, the Irish seem to have been leaders in the writing of manuscripts, for E.A. Lowe, the great American expert, had to admit that, in insular manuscripts of the late seventh or early eighth century, 'the palaeographer finds himself unable to say whether they were written by an English or an Irish scribe since at that period the English were still the imitators, following closely the methods of their Irish masters'. One of those masters must have been Ultán, an Irish scribe of the early eighth century who the Englishman Aethelwulf's ninth-century poem *De abbatibus* describes as 'one who could ornament books, decorate beautiful letters one by one, so that no modern scribe could equal him'. This is indeed high praise a century after his *floruit* but, for one so famous, it is surprising to find that not even the name of his monastery – near, but not at, Lindisfarne – is revealed in the literary sources.

Though no products of Ultán's pen and paint-brush have been identified among historical documents, Dáibhí Ó Cróinín has suggested that he may well have been the illuminator of the manuscript A.II.17 in the Library at Durham, a fine Gospel-book whose artist was deemed by English scholars to have also decorated the great Echternach Codex Ms. 9389 in the Bibliothèque Nationale in Paris. Ó Cróinín has also suggested that the tradition of both of these manuscripts may be linked to an English foundation in Ireland, Rath Melsigi, mentioned by Bede, though not yet satisfactorily localized (County Carlow?). The same scholar believes that Rath Melsigi was where the scribe of the Calendar of Echternach's founder Willibrord learned his trade around 700, and that his distinctive flourishes used in that manuscript (Paris, Bibliothèque Nationale, Ms. lat 10837) are identical to that in the Book of Durrow, the first great insular painted (as opposed to merely penned) manuscript, to which we must now turn.

The Book of Durrow

Bearing the number A.4.5 (57) in the Library of Trinity College, Dublin, the Book of Durrow is a set of the Gospels written on calf vellum and of comparatively slight dimensions (245 × 145mm) when compared to its larger and more magnificent counterparts, the Books of Lindisfarne and Kells. It is one of the — if not *the* — first completely preserved illuminated de luxe manuscript of western civilization, and one which laid down the guidelines for the coherent organization, layout

and design of later manuscripts. Its expert calligraphic majuscule forms long lines in the Irish manner, rather than the bi-columnar system preferred in Northumbria. The Gospel text is a pure copy of the Vulgate version of the Holy Scriptures as translated by St Jerome, but the evangelists' words are preceded by a number of preliminary notices which are, in contrast, in the pre-Vulgate, Old Latin version. These, and their placing before the Gospels, connect the Durrow manuscript with the Book of Kells, in contrast to the Northumbrian system which places them between the Gospels. Among these preliminaries, the interpretation of the Hebrew names used in the Gospels connect it with a family of Irish Vulgate texts, including the Book of Armagh.

The preliminaries — which also include the canon tables — take up the first sixteen text folios, and the remainder give the Gospels in the Vulgate order: Matthew, Mark, Luke and John. Each of the Gospels is preceded by the symbol of the relevant evangelist, but the Book of Durrow follows the pre-Vulgate interpretation of Irenaeus in presenting us with the lion as emblem of St John and the eagle as that of St Mark, rather than the other way round, as is more usual. Each of these symbols is preceded by a so-called carpet page, a full page of ornament which has been likened to the provision of an outside cover for each of the separate gospels. The beginning of each Gospel is also decorated with an ornate initial letter and, in addition, the first mention of Christ's name in Matthew — as it were, a tribute to the Word itself — is specially emphasized with a further decorated initial, while others appear in the preliminaries.

The decoration of the manuscript opens on the very first page (fol. 1v) with a double-armed cross surrounded by interlace. Both of these features may be derived from Coptic or eastern Mediterranean practice, as reflected in the Glazier Codex, a Coptic text of around 400 AD now deposited in the Pierpoint Morgan Library in New York, where a cross, derived from the ancient Egyptian Ankh-symbol, is decorated by interlace within its contours. Carl Nordenfalk retracted his suggestion that the origin of the double-armed cross might be sought farther to the east in a so-called Diatesseron or Gospel narrative, ancestral to a sixteenth-century Persian example in Florence, and which could conceivably have been brought to Iona by the shipwrecked Arculf in the seventh century. Opposite this carpet page is one (fol. 2r) with a series of diamond shapes enclosing a framed cross with interlacing, and having evangelist symbols above and below the arms which, if read clockwise, accord with the Vulgate order of the Gospels and, if viewed anti-clockwise, agree with the Old Latin order – perhaps an intentional ambivalence in a manuscript which combines both traditions. The symbols are stylized, all except the eagle seen frontally, though the lion thereby presents difficulties of identification to anyone who did not know which animal was meant to be represented. Fol. 3v (Pl.17) shows how full-page illustrations get the name of carpet pages, for its spiral decoration in a frame surrounded by interlace could well be taken for the design of a modern rug. No other manuscript shows off more dramatically those spirals which are likely to have been inspired by the art of Celtic metalwork as found on the

hanging bowls, and which find later echoes in the presumably Irish bronze plaques in the Musée des Antiquités Nationales in St Germain-en-Laye (Pl.84). Tightly coiled like the springs of an old watch, the spirals have their own harmonious hierarchy one above the other in the centre (each with two sets of differing spirals ticking over inside, yet having no centre themselves), and one at each corner within the frame (where spirals emanate from a central whorl) – all joined together into a very lively pattern by connecting tangents expanding from six major spiral roundels.

Each evangelist symbol is also given a separate page to itself before the appropriate Gospel, and there they stand out clearly and are given plenty of room to breathe within an interlaced frame. They, too, show clear signs of being derived from metalwork designs though, as David Wright pointed out, the metalwork influence fades further into the background as the pages progress, so that when the artist reached the last symbol, the lion on fol. 191v (Pl.18), he was thinking more in terms of a painted page than of a metalwork model. The feathers of the appealing eagle on fol. 84v (Pl.20) have been likened to the cloisonné work of Anglo-Saxon jewellery of the kind found in the Sutton Hoo boat burial of *c.* 625, while the symbol of *Homo* on fol. 21v (Pl.21) – a human figure representing St Matthew, statically monolithic unlike his lively frame – has a poncho-like body garment lined horizontally and vertically to resemble a chess-board with squares of red and yellow, as well as cross-motifs, which are clearly copied from the enamel and *millefiori* designs on contemporary metalwork. It has been suggested, though without any convincing evidence, that the figure's centrally-parted hair may reflect the tonsure worn by the early Irish monks who lost out at the Synod of Whitby. The calf, symbolizing St Luke, has spiral ornament on the shoulders, a feature also found on Pictish stone carvings in eastern Scotland. The one page which offers something totally different is fol. 192v (Pl.22, left), where the accustomed interlace in a central roundel cradles an equal-armed cross at its centre and contains a trio of discs patterned like the enamelled metalwork bosses we shall meet again later. This grouping is surrounded by a framework of animals interlacing with one another in four horizontal and two smaller vertical panels, which add immense vivacity to the normal range of interlace found elsewhere in this manuscript. These animals have been compared with some justification to those on Anglo-Saxon metalwork, but Günther Haseloff, one of the great experts on Germanic animal ornament, has pointed out that the interlacing Durrow beasts are more naturalistic than their metalwork counterparts, and should be seen as showing a combination of Mediterranean and Germanic traits. The page also introduces us to one of the examples of the possible use of number symbolism in the decoration of the Book's pages, in that the three discs surrounding the central cross may symbolize the Trinity, the inner horizontal panels, each containing eight animals, perhaps reflecting a number taken anciently to represent the Resurrection, while the ten animals interlacing with one another on the top and bottom panels might point to St Augustine's perfect number.

The Incipits, or Gospel beginnings, fit the initial letters beautifully into the text, becoming more expansive and elaborate as the Book progresses (e.g. Pl.19), culminating in fol. 193r (Pl.22, right), which is the most lavish of them all, extending the full height of the page. Here, spirals jump into action to enliven the more strait-laced panels of interlace, even blossoming out like bouquets from above and below the stems, and acting like a complicated set of cog-wheels in the generous and lively diagonal links joining the vertical parts of the I and the N of *Initium* and *In Principio*. The particular treatment given to the letters XPI, the first letters of Christ's name in Greek, on fol. 23r, shortly after the start of St Matthew's Gospel, is perhaps the earliest representative of a design which Irish and other manuscripts were to reproduce with the numerous variations for up to five centuries following the production of the Book of Durrow. More reduced in size are the capital letters of the individual sections of the text which adopt the same graceful diminuendo effect already seen in the Cathach, whereby the characters after the initial letter become gradually smaller until they correspond in size to the remainder of the text, though the diminuendo in the Book of Durrow seems to submit itself to more regulated geometrical principles. These diminishing letters are frequently accompanied by red dotting found also in the Cathach and in the Codex Usserianus Primus (p.29). Additionally, they occasionally show a feature of ultimate La Tène art known as the developed trumpet pattern which, once more, probably derives from metalwork designs.

The Book of Durrow gives new life to the idea of a purely ornamental carpet page, already present in the Coptic Glazier Codex, but also practised on what may have been an intermediary manuscript, the Bobbio Orosius (Milan, Biblioteca Ambrosiana Ms. D.23.sup.), produced in the Bobbio scriptorium not long after the monastery's foundation in 614. The interlace used in the Book of Durrow was not a novelty either, as it had been used to good effect some considerable time earlier in the manuscript A.II.10 in the Durham Cathedral Library though, in Durrow, it is more loosely woven like the Coptic interlace, as Françoise Henry pointed out. However, among surviving early manuscripts, the Book of Durrow is full of innovations other than that of the presentation of the Chi-Rho (XPI) letters already alluded to above. Prime among these is the new organization of the manuscript as a whole, introducing the use of non-textual ornamental pages before the start of each Gospel as well as a symbol for each of the evangelists preceding his own particular Gospel, and a page containing all the symbols together. It demonstrates a wealth of the two major forms of line ornament in the shape of interlace and spirals, but only tentatively does it make an effort to integrate the two together. An interesting interplay is, however, observable between the frame and the framed, the former — with few exceptions — seeming to emerge as surprisingly more important than the latter. The book is, nevertheless, remarkably successful in gathering ideas from various sources as far apart as the eastern Mediterranean and Anglo-Saxon England and combining them into one aesthetically unified whole. All the elements are put together in a clear and orderly way, and with a technical mastery uniting text and decoration. The successful blend of so many novel elements can be seen in the opening of folios 192v and 193r together (Pl.22) where, for the first time in insular illumination, we find the introduction of an animal interlace which must be rooted partly in the world of Anglo-Saxon metalwork, but which in itself has no true parallels or descendants. Another startling factor in the ornament of the Book of Durrow is the extent to which metalwork and its decorative additions play a role in the patterns used throughout the manuscript. The craft of the smith was already reflected in the Cathach but here, in the Book of Durrow, the art of the enameller and the glass-worker proved fruitful sources for the designs on the garment of the *Homo* symbol of St Matthew on fol. 21v, and certainly added to the colourfulness, metallic brilliance and the exactitude of the ornament. Both human and animal figures show a stylization which helps to define an insular from a classically-inspired manuscript, but the dotted stubble on the face of the *Homo* figure does help to bring in a degree of realism. Similarly, the animals on fol. 192v, though zoologically indefinable, do show a greater degree of naturalness than do their counterparts in Anglo-Saxon interlace. In contrast to the monochrome Cathach, the colours introduced earlier in the Durham Gospels are heightened here into contrasting oranges, reds and yellows with the occasional addition of green.

The date of the Book of Durrow has been a source of debate for generations, with suggestions ranging from around 600 to the early eighth century. The majority of scholars have opted for a middle course, preferring a date in the third quarter of the seventh century because they see the Book of Durrow as a preparatory stage in the development of the Book of Lindisfarne, tentatively assigned to the years 698–721 on the basis of a colophon added more than two centuries later.

But it should be realized that the Book of Durrow is a rare and fortunate survival of what must once have been generations of manuscripts now lost, any one of which could have acted as a closer preliminary development to the Book of Lindisfarne. There is no necessity to see the Book of Durrow as being in the *direct* line of development to the Book of Lindisfarne. Durrow has a life of its own, and Dáibhí Ó Cróinín's suggestion that a certain vertical flourish on fol. 124 is identical to one in the Calendar of Willibrord dating from around the first decade of the eighth century could suggest a date for Durrow in the period around 700 or even into the very early eighth century. Such a dating is not new, but it could be seen as being supported by one small detail on the very first page of the manuscript (fol. 1v), namely the conjoined T-shapes at the centre of the squares in the middle of the double-armed cross. Metalwork analogies bearing such designs in cloisonné enamel are notoriously difficult to date, but comparisons such as the belt-buckle from Lough Gara in the National Museum in Dublin are more likely to belong to the eighth than to the seventh century. An early eighth-century date for the manuscript would put it much closer in time to the Book of Lindisfarne and the great Echternach Gospels in Paris, and would correspondingly increase the gap between the Cathach and it to roughly a century, which was doubtless filled with generations of manuscripts now all sadly lost to us.

But such a comparatively late date could cause difficulties in ascribing the Book of Durrow to a Northumbrian origin, which some authorities have suggested. We do know through an inscription on the lost *cumdach* or cover of the manuscript, recorded in 1677, that the manuscript must have been in Ireland during the reign of the High King Flann Sinna (879–916). If it came from Northumbria, the best explanation how it found its way to Ireland has normally been to connect it with the retreat of the Irish party from the Synod of Whitby in 664 – hence the dates clustering around this time normally proposed for the manuscript. It would be less easy to find a reason why it should have been brought to Ireland if it is dated around 700 – unless it could have come, not from Northumbria, but from Iona. An increasing number of scholars are tending to locate its origin there, where its many elements of Celtic and Anglo-Saxon metalwork as well as Pictish animal ornament could easily have coalesced. But the good Irish parallels for the T-shapes on fol. 1v, and Ó Cróinín's linkage of fol. 124 with the scribe of Willibrord's Calendar who seems to have been trained at Rath Melsigi, could be seen to plead for an Irish origin. If so, the presence of English people in Rath Melsigi might help to account for the Anglo-Saxon similarities of the animals on fol. 192v, though Rath Melsigi is almost certainly not the scriptorium which produced the Book of Durrow. A colophon, re-written later, asks a prayer for the scribe Columba, and its origin is likely to have been associated with one of the monasteries in the *paruchia Columbae*. Iona fits into this category – but so does Durrow itself, a monastery sufficiently important for the Venerable Bede to have mentioned its founding by St Columba, and therefore worthy enough to have produced the manuscript. The Book was certainly there in the seventeenth century, but how many centuries before that sadly no one knows. Purely objective criteria for an attribution of the Book of Durrow to Ireland, England or Scotland may never be forthcoming, and on present evidence it is impossible to be certain where the Book was created. While all options ought to be kept open, chauvinistic sentiments set aside and dogmatic pronouncements avoided, an Irish provenance for the Book of Durrow is certainly worth considering much more seriously than in recent decades.

Cross-Decorated Stone Monuments – Seventh Century and Later

The ribbon interlace with a broad central band and narrow borders which, as we have seen, decorates the Book of Durrow is also found on stone monuments, including a rather hetero-geneous group centred on Donegal in the north-west of Ireland. The most striking example of this group is a tall pedimented stele almost 3m high standing in a graveyard at Fahan, where we know that St Mura founded a monastery in the seventh century. Standing out magnificently in relief against a framed background on one face (Pl.24) is a Latin cross with expanding flat-ended arms. This has an interlace tightly-woven on the stem but loosening as it winds its way into the upper

part of the cross, where it forms what is almost a pointed triquetra in the arms on either side of a central boss. The lower part of the head has a horizontal oblong shape, and the surfaces between it and the lower end of the arms are deepened so as to give the impression of the segment of a ring.

Within the interstices of the arms there are raised circles best compared to draughtsmen. Under the pediment are two opposed birds with their beaks intertwined as their claws rest on the head of the cross. The other face of the Fahan stele (Pl.25) is also decorated with an interlaced cross. But here the interlace on the stem tightens upwards towards the head, where an interlaced cross is interwoven within the cross-head, thereby providing undulating terminations to the cross-arms – and creating the possibility that the different strands were originally coloured, as in manuscripts.

This interlacing stands out in strong relief from a background cross, and the relief is more restrained on the stem which branches out left and right along the bottom of the frame, supporting two long-robed figures. Apparently long-haired with D-shaped heads, they bear inscriptions on their garments which have never been satisfactorily deciphered. The sculptor's uncomfortable treatment of these stiff figures contrasts with the confident and vigorous way he carved his interlace, which makes a bold statement as if wishing to expand beyond its constricting frame – an impression strengthened by the arm-shaped stumps which project outwards from the narrow side of the monument. Beneath that on the northern side is a Greek inscription, reading downwards:

18

19

20

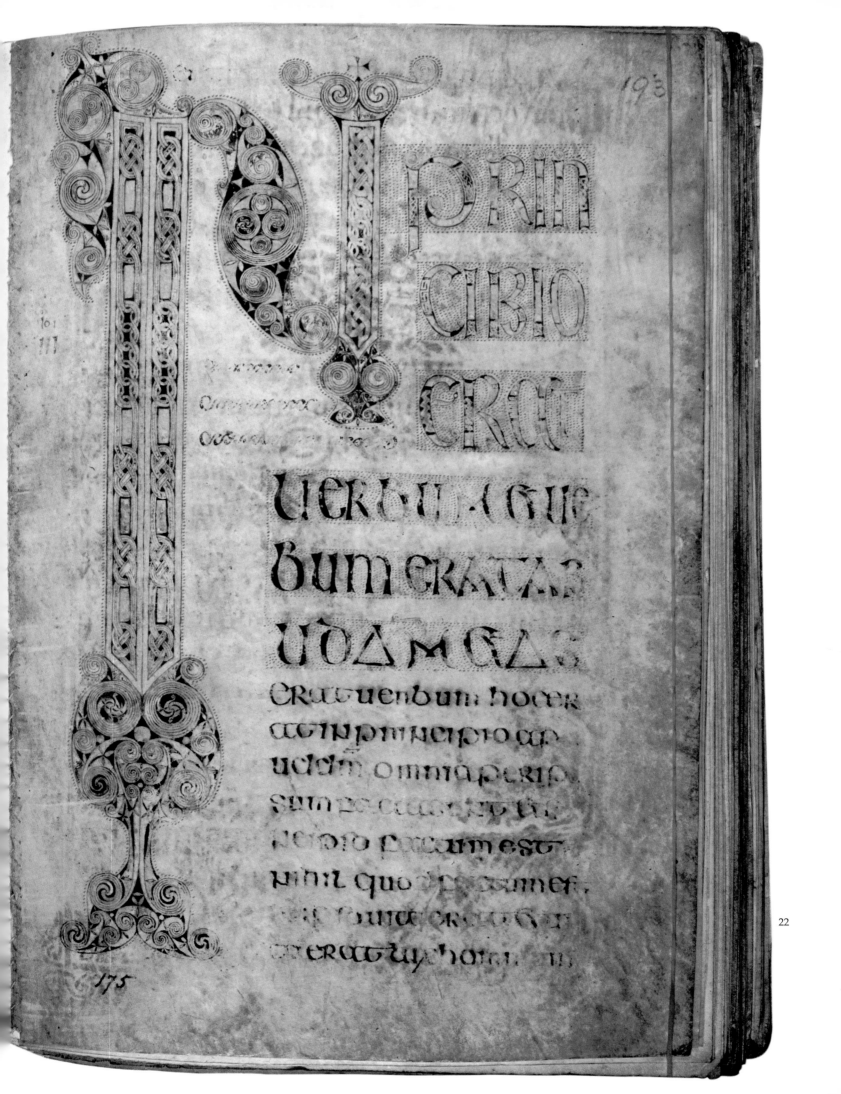

IN PRIN
CIPIO
ERAT

VERBU AGUE
BUM ERATAB
UDAMGAS

erat uerbum hoc er
at in principio ap
ud dm omnia per ip
sum fca ccaa sp sic
nep fca caum est
nihil quod fca cumest
ipso uua erat a
uta erat uix hona tu

24

25

ΔΟΞΑ ΚΑΙ ΤΙΜΕ ΠΑΤΡΙ ΚΑΙ ΥΙΩ
ΚΑΙ ΠΝΕΥΜΑΤΙ ΑΓΙΩ

and which may be translated as 'Glory and Honour to the Father, Son and Holy Spirit'.

Through the addition of the words 'and honour' to the normal doxology of the Gloria, the inscription follows the text formulated in 633 by the Council of Toledo which was presided over by none other than Isidore of Seville. The inscription has been used to ascribe the Fahan stele to the seventh century, but the Bollandiste Père Grosjean warned against too facile an acceptance of this dating because the formula was used in Ireland until 800, and probably much later. The stone's pediment shape is reminiscent of the equally large and impressive Pictish cross-decorated stones in Scotland (e.g. Glamis), which are normally dated to the eighth century. The birds with crossing beaks have counterparts on the cross at Dupplin in Perthshire, recently dated with probability to the late eighth or early ninth century on the basis of an inscription. Comparisons with manuscript interlace in the Book of Durrow and the triquetra in the Durham manuscript A.II.10 have both been used to argue for a seventh-century date for the Donegal stele, but the presence of a similar double-edged ribbon interlace in the ninth century Book of Macdurnan (Pl.137) must make us wary. Furthermore, the comparable interlace on the oldest part of the metal reliquary known as the Domhnach Airgid, in the National Museum in Dublin, is accompanied by a fretwork pattern which, while *sui generis*, is unlikely to be earlier than the eighth century, and is more probably ninth. If we date the Book of Durrow to, say, sometime shortly after 700, then it would seem acceptable to place the Fahan stele in the eighth century or towards 800, as it shows the same stylish accomplishment as the manuscript in its interlace patterning and change of rhythm, its respect for breathing space for the central subject within an upright frame and the overall demonstration of a carefully thought-out design. The Fahan slab testifies to the talent of the Irish stonemason in forging a visually appealing unit out of inspiration coming from different media – manuscripts, probably metalwork and possibly wood as well – and from various directions – possibly Spain (for the inscription), ultimately the eastern Mediterranean (for the interlace) and Scotland, where the pedimented form of such a tall and imposing monument is most at home.

The mystery of the identity of the two figures on either side of the cross on one face of the Fahan stele recurs on another decorated stone at Drumhallagh in the same county (Pl.23), less than five miles distant across the Swilly estuary. Here, there is a figure above and below each arm of the cross, the two upper ones apparently seated and licking their thumbs, one of them at least having spiral ornament on what looks like a triangular garment, but which may be shorthand for an angel's wing. Each of the figures beneath the arms bears a staff or crozier, that on the left with a crook, the other with a T-shaped head of the kind used as the emblem of St Anthony the hermit in later medieval art. Each wears a voluminous cloak expanding downwards towards spiral decoration above the hem, giving both the look of well-nourished clerics – that on the right being much more a portrait than the face with caricature nose

East face of the
Carndonagh Cross.

Pillar at Carndonagh with
(?) The Multiplication of
the Loaves and Fishes.

on the left. The cross on the other face bears a large boss at its centre and smaller ones in the arms, obviously imitating a jewelled metal cross which must have stood on a pedestal to judge by the square box on which this stone copy is placed. As at Fahan, there are large circular bosses helping to fill the gaps above and below the arm-pits.

Carndonagh, a mere five miles north-west of Fahan, has a number of monuments which make up further members of this very varied assembly of early stone carvings in Donegal. One of these is a cross having one face covered with double-edged ribbon interlace, and the other (Pl.28) bearing an interlaced cross on the head above a Crucifixion scene on the shaft. Its reputation as coming at the start of a direct line in the development of the Irish High Crosses may be unjustified, as it seems to stand very much on its own without having any obvious successors. Displayed beside it are two small pillars carved partially in high relief and bearing spiral ornament, a bird clawing a fish, and a number of human figures — one with a harp presumably representing David and another with bell and (pilgrim's?) staff, while a third may be an unusual portrayal of the Miracle of the Loaves and Fishes. But on the other side of a wall, in the Protestant churchyard, there is another interesting upright rectangular pillar decorated on the top of one face (Pl.30) with a marigold pattern forming the top of a *flabellum* — a liturgical instrument used in medieval times as a swatter to keep flies away from the chalice on the altar. The stem of the *flabellum* is ornamented with Greek meander ornament and, below, it branches out into two loops which — on the model on which the carving was presumably based – were probably leather thongs on which it hung when not in use. As one of St Columba's known relics was a *cuilebaidh*, the Irish word for a *flabellum*, this object on the Carndonagh slab may well be a copy of the actual relic, in which case the two figures standing on either side of it could be interpreted as pilgrims doing reverence before the relic, as the right-hand figure wears a travelling bag and carries what may be a pilgrim's staff in his hand. Both bear a facial resemblance to the figure on the Fahan slab, though their garments are shorter and they stand on a four-pointed interlace in a circle, of a kind found on Merovingian carvings in Poitou. If the interpretation of these two Carndonagh figures as pilgrims be correct, it could perhaps also be applied in the cases of the Fahan and Drumhallagh figures as well. The other face of this Carndonagh stele (Pl.29) bears two more primitive figures marked with crosses, presumably the thieves Dysmas and Gestas as they stand beneath a cross with expanding terminals which bears the crucified Christ in a long colobium – his large head being emphasised by expanding into a noticeable hump on the top of the stone. The Christ figure was probably copied from a metal prototype, like those on Byzantine pectoral crosses, but here Christ's cross stands on a further cross with interlace gone horribly awry. It cannot be established that these Donegal monuments are even roughly contemporary, but a date in the eighth or early ninth century is probably more likely than in the seventh.

The larger of these Donegal monuments are among the most decorative and imaginative examples of the many cross-decorated stones found particularly along the west and north-west coast of Ireland, whose origins (in wood?) may go back even earlier. One notable instance is the tallest of the stones at Reask (Pl.27), an early ecclesiastical site on the Dingle Peninsula in County Kerry. Its sculptor carved his designs on the uneven surface of the stone, perhaps to create interesting effects of light and shadow. Here, an equal-armed cross of arcs enclosed in a circle stands on a stem with a pelta-shaped foot and flanked by a symmetrical set of interlinking spirals. Their similarity to the spirals on a bronze brooch of around 600 found in Lough Neagh prompts consideration of the first half of the seventh century as the earliest possible date for this stone. Tom Fanning's excavation of the site in the 1970s brought to light examples of a type of pottery known as E Ware, which was imported – conceivably as wine jars – into Ireland in some considerable quantities during the seventh century, probably from the west coast of France. This was the period when 'le bon roi Dagobert' was spirited away to Ireland for a number of years and when many came from England (and probably also from the European continent) to study the Scriptures in Ireland, as was the case with the Parisian

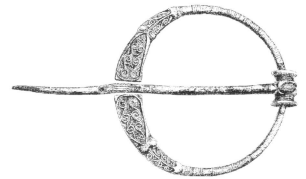

Bronze brooch from Lough Neagh.

Agilbert whose alleged tomb is one of the sculptural treasures in the crypt of the abbey of Jouarre. Already in the first half of the seventh century, the Irish were among the very first and most enthusiastic to receive and play with the *Etymologies* of Isidore of Seville who, as we have seen, presided over the Council of Toledo which formulated the Greek inscription found on the Fahan slab. We do not know if the erudite Spaniard's work came to Ireland directly or via Italy and Gaul but, following in the footsteps of Isidore's scholastic learning, the Irish Glossary of Cormac written about 900 explains one meaning of the word *Gall* as 'a high stone pillar, called *Gall* because the Galli first set them up in Ireland', the Galli being further glossed as the old Frankish tribes of Gaul. The Reask stone might well have

been set up in the wake of this Gaulish inspiration, and its compass-made cross-of-arcs might well be a reflection of that origin. But we should be wary of applying generally such an early date to cross-decorated pillars along the west of Ireland because another example of a cross-of-arcs found on one face of a stone on the island of Duvillaun More off the coast of Mayo has on the other face a representation of the crucified Christ with bare legs and features which suggest a date no earlier than the ninth century. Cross-shaped stones bearing no decoration, like that at Glendalough (Pl.26) are, of course, virtually undatable. In its simplest form, the cross of arcs in a circle can be seen on stones such as those at Kildun, County Mayo (Pl.31) and Faha, County Kerry (Pl.38), but on an upright stone at Ballyvourney, County Cork (Pl.35), it has the felicitous addition of a jaunty figure which walks upon the surrounding circle, carrying a crook and sporting the same tonsure as the *Homo* figure in the Book of Durrow. Because the cross-of-arcs is a motif found decorating reliquaries which once contained the relics of a revered saint, this happy walker may well be a pilgrim on his way to venerate a relic of the local saint, in this case Gobnait, patroness of bee-keepers and one of the more important female saints of early Ireland. The same motif is found on other stones near the west coast of Ireland – one, at Caherlehillan, Co. Kerry (Pl.I), with the addition of a bird, and another on Caher Island, Co. Mayo, with what seem to be two dolphins, which suggest ideas coming from further south. The alpha and omega on a standing stone at Loher, Co. Kerry, finds an interesting parallel in the Vendée, and another Christian

The two faces of the slab on the island of Duvillaun More, Co. Mayo.

symbol which could have come to the south-west of Ireland from the same area is the Chi-Rho, the first two letters of Christ's name in Greek which, on the ten or so Irish stones where it occurs, is indicated by a little extra curve at the top right-hand corner of the cross. Like the cross-of-arcs, this Chi-Rho is found along the west and north coasts of Ireland, and penetrates up the Shannon, perhaps reflecting the story of Gaulish merchants coming up river to offer St Ciaran some wine at Clonmacnoise on its eastern shore.

If these designs were introduced from Gaul, they were adapted to Irish tastes, and had native spirals grafted on to them, as can be seen on the Reask stone and on another nearby at Kilfountain (Pl.33). A further pillar from the Dingle Peninsula was discovered at Ardamore (Pl.37). It bears a cross form with arms branching out into pelta ornament which is a more attractive and complicated version of that found at the foot of one face of a pillar far away inland at Kilnasaggart, Co. Armagh (Pl.32). This latter bears a number of different cross-shapes, together with an inscription naming a Ternoc Ceran who may be identical with the Ternoc son of Ciaran whose death the *Annals of Tigernach* report in 716. If correct, this identification would make the Kilnasaggart pillar the earliest monument in Ireland datable by inscription. But it also shows that early-looking cross-inscribed pillars should not necessarily be dated to the sixth or seventh century on the basis of Gaulish inspiration, but might carry on to the eighth century or even later, as there is in the present state of our knowledge no realistic way in which they can be anchored to any one particular century.

Two dolphins supporting an encircled cross decorate a stone on Caher island, Co. Mayo.

If the Gauls provided the inspiration for erecting stone pillars in Ireland, did the Irish follow the Franks in applying the sculptured motifs largely to funerary monuments? Where inscriptions occur on Irish monuments in the earliest Irish Ogham script which records personal names, the written text never indicates specifically that such an Ogham stone was set up as a funerary monument. The pillar at Reask on the Dingle Peninsula bearing the Roman letters DNE – presumably an abbreviation for the Latin invocation *Domine*, meaning 'Lord' – was located close to what seems to have been the grave of an important or revered personage and may have been intended to mark the location of an important relic, if not acting as a gravestone in the normal sense. Kathleen Hughes has pointed out that the word *dominus*, 'Lord', is also used in the sense of 'abbot', so that the *DNE* on the Reask stone could refer to a founding abbot buried

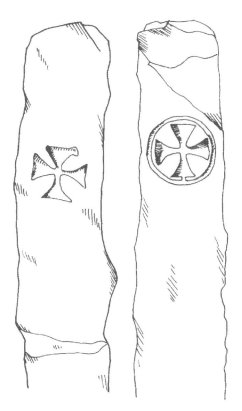

The two faces of the pillar at Arraglen, Co. Kerry.

nearby. Many of the other cross-decorated stones stand in what are once likely to have been religious or monastic enclosures, but that at Arraglen, which combines an Ogham inscription naming 'Ronan the priest' with a Chi-Rho cross and an equal-armed cross in a circle, is situated at a height of around 2000 feet up the side of a pilgrimage mountain, Mount Brandon, and can scarcely be interpreted as a burial marker. The comparison of the cross copied from a metal prototype on the back of the Drumhallagh slab to those on some Italian altar-screens brings up the unanswerable question whether at least some of these early cross-decorated pillars were always out in the open air, or whether they could have stood close to the altar in some small wooden church long since

disintegrated. This suggestion finds support in some of the decorative features on the Christ-bearing stele at Carndonagh which have been compared to a ninth-century or older altar-screen at Hirsau in southern Germany. But no matter what purpose these cross-decorated pillars served, or when they were first erected, they show us how the early centuries of Christianity in Ireland were capable of producing a remarkable testimony to the strength of Church patronage of the Irish stonemason's art, which was to last for many hundreds of years. But the stone-working tradition which it created particularly along the Atlantic coast of Ireland is probably separate from that which created the great stone High Crosses further east in the ninth and tenth centuries, to be discussed in a later chapter.

In seeking grave-markers among the cross-decorated stones, we are perhaps on firmer ground with those slabs bearing a memorial inscription requesting a prayer for a named person (using the formula $\overline{OR}\ DO$, 'pray for') which are found on a number of old monastic sites, even though there are no instances where it can be proved unequivocally that they did act as grave-markers. Probably originally laid flat in the ground, they are found in greatest numbers at Clonmacnoise, where a workshop must have been busy for centuries manufacturing stones of this kind (Pl.34 and 36). Perhaps the earliest datable example was found not far away at Athlone, bearing the inscription *Ailill aue Dunchatho*, the name of a king of Connacht who died in 764. It bears an equal-armed cross with a circle around its centre and enclosed within a square frame filled with a Greek meander. By the ninth century, and continuing at least into the tenth, Clonmacnoise had a series of stones bearing the usual formula accompanied by a Latin cross with circular centre, and arms and feet expanding into a half-circle usually decorated with geometrical designs. Variants of this popular type are also found at other sites, including Inishcealtra and Durrow, but one particularly fine, if rather unusual, example comes from the lesser-known site at Tullylease near the northern tip of County Cork. The name Berechtuine inscribed on it cannot give an absolute date for it (eighth or ninth century?), but its cross design resembles a page in the Book of

Lindisfarne, though scarcely directly inspired by it. One unusual group of stones, probably though not certainly recumbent, came to light at Carrowntemple, Co. Sligo, in the 1970s. They have no inscriptions, and only a few are decorated with crosses, but they do bear competently-executed spiral and interlaced ornament. The most unusual stone of the group, which must have stood vertically, bears a stylized human figure with lowered arms showing the palms facing forward, back to back with a more confidently-designed interlaced cross of three strands.

Memorial inscriptions on two slabs from Clonmacnoise, Co. Offaly.

27

28

29

30

31

32

34

35

36

4

The Eighth Century – an Apogee

■

IF THE IRISH CHURCH HAD COME OF age in the seventh century, it succeeded in going through a further stage of consolidation in the eighth. It accommodated itself to native Irish society, and a collection of older Church canons, compiled around 725, shows how Church law and native pagan legal custom merged and fused together to form a compromise acceptable to both traditions. Church leaders – not necessarily all in major orders or even celibate – had their status aligned with the secular social ladder, the celibate bishop being on a par with a local king, of which there may have been about 150 throughout the whole island. But it was the abbots of monasteries who really wielded power in the Church; they were the administrative authorities, with their own monastic clients bound to them as in the secular world around them. They increased their wealth by getting dues from subservient churches – often located some distance away, and at times even beyond the provincial boundaries. This expansion they furthered by allying themselves to local political dynasties, who used the monasteries as family burial places, and who vied and fought with one another for more secular power. The Uí Briúin were dominant in Connacht, the Uí Dúnlainge in Leinster, and in Munster it was largely the Eóganachta who were in control. But the most powerful of all were the Uí Néill who, in their various manifestations, held sway over the midlands and the north. Suppressing local kings to ensure Uí Néill supremacy over territory, they may even have been creating a rudimentary government structure, and perhaps using the model of their Frankish counterparts in the process. As throughout the remainder of medieval Ireland (and Europe), the secular world was a wearisome series of struggles for dominance and, in the important midlands area, the Clann Cholmáin branch of the Uí Néill succeeded in gaining power over their rival kinsmen, the Síl nAedo Sláine, to become not only the most ambitious Irish provincial kings whose tide few could stem, but also important artistic patrons in the period between 750 and 950.

But the same squabbles that characterized the secular scene also broke out among the richer churches as their wealth increased and, by 760, instances are recorded of monasteries such as Clonmacnoise and Durrow going to war with one another, and leaving hundreds dead upon the battlefield. Yet, for all that, it was the increasing prosperity of the major monasteries which led to their aristocratic abbots becoming patrons of learning and the arts. During the course of the eighth century, they oversaw the compilation not only of legal codices but also of commentaries on the Old and New Testaments, usually in Latin but increasingly also in Irish. It was equally their patronage of the arts which helped Ireland to go far beyond what the scholars achieved, and produce glittering objects to grace church altars, including some of the most inspired artistic metalwork to survive from the whole of eighth-century Europe. However, the very flamboyance of these works of art shows the Irish abbots turning their backs on the simple ascetic ideals of their monastic founders in favour of the brilliant ostentation of an established church. Legally and academically, the Irish church had come of age; artistically, it was now to reach greater heights than ever before – or after. The contact which the Irish church had with Northumbria even after the Synod of Whitby must have exposed it to further

Mediterranean influence and opened its eyes to the quality already achieved by Anglo-Saxon metalsmiths in southern England. But this is not enough to account for all the complex elements involved in the superb Irish craftworking which erupted on the scene in the late seventh and early eighth century, as a parallel to the Book of Durrow, if the date for it suggested above be accepted. No obvious explanation is forthcoming and, as with the rise of many world cultures, it probably resulted from the inspiration and creative activity of a few gifted and anonymous individuals. The presence of seventh-century Anglo-Saxon jewellery at Dunadd, Strathclyde, suggests that Scotland probably played an intermediary role and, while going its own independent way in the design of brooches, for instance, Scotland nevertheless long continued to remain Ireland's partner in artistic development to such an extent that it is often difficult to decide from which side of the North Channel a particular masterpiece may have come – as instanced by the Book of Kells.

Perhaps reflecting a further increase in the social status of the craftsman already enshrined in old Irish law, the late seventh and early eighth century saw his use of long-established materials being transformed from the pedestrian to an absolute mastery of new techniques. These produced dazzlingly polychrome effects hitherto unknown in Ireland on objects where function was almost overwhelmed by overall ornamental display. The Irish craftsmen showed their brilliance in the harmonious combination of ornamental patterns coming from widely differing sources, neatly presented together in copy-book fashion on the underside of the Ardagh Chalice (Pl.16), where they can usefully be grouped under three headings:

1. Spiral designs and pelta motifs of a kind which go back to the prehistoric Celts and which had managed to survive long enough in Ireland and elsewhere to be given a new vigour and revitalization in the Book of Durrow and in the secular and religious art of the seventh and eighth centuries. It experienced one of its last glorious gasps in the Book of Kells at the end of this period, before expiring with little more than a whimper.

2. Interlace of Mediterranean origin (perhaps less Coptic than has been thought) and transmitted by Italy to north-western Europe, it was already encountered on the Durham manuscripts A.II.10 and A.II.17 and in the Book of Durrow, though vellum was not necessarily the sole medium which brought it northwards. Metalworkers were quick to adopt and adapt it, revelling in the hundreds of variations it offered – each with its own individual shade of meaning, such as perhaps helping to ward off evil, though today it is difficult to penetrate the symbolism of such geometrical motifs.

3. Animal ornament of Germanic origin, consisting of stylized fabulous and zoologically indefinable beasts, having genes sufficiently different not to be derivable directly from their earlier Anglo-Saxon counterparts, and thus of undefined geographical origin.

The last two of these elements were to remain part of Ireland's artistic repertoire for centuries, providing inexhaustible variations which never seem to repeat themselves. But, even though the animal ornament could form an interlace within itself, these three ornaments were normally kept separate where they appeared on one and the same object. However, the motifs had become sufficiently digested by the end of the eighth century to fuse into a coherent whole in masterpieces like the Book of Kells. Irish art of the Golden Age cannot be described as a unified style as was the prehistoric La Tène ornament, because it is an amalgam, a compendium of totally different types of decoration very different in origin, yet often placed contrastingly next to one another in ordered spaces. Each of these pattern types pleaded with the eye to look its way, demanding attention and respect. What all of these decorations have in common is their linear, abstract nature which – perhaps as a conscious reaction to the victory of the Roman party at the Synod of Whitby in 664 – sets out to be a totally anti-classical art. Even its one-dimensionality is the antithesis of the high relief of Roman art, and the Celt tended to eschew naturalistic representations of humans and animals, preferring stylization and schematization. What never fails to amaze is the miniature, not to say minute, scale of the execution of the motifs by master smiths who were doubtless concerned more with their art than with the strain on their eyesight which must have ensued. These craftsmen had grown up with the traditional methods of bronze-casting, engraving and adding colour through the application of red enamel. Now the colour range was to be extended to include yellow, blue and green. Polychrome glass studs were made more striking by the addition of complicated geometric patterns in metal, while gold was introduced not only as a basic material but also for gilding and the making of filigree and granulation. Novel effects were created with the die-stamping of silver foil, and with *Kerbschnitt* — the facetting of surfaces to provide contrasts of light and shade in imitation of the Germanic art of chip-carving. Some or all of these novelties were applied to a small number of top-quality objects of an ecclesiastical or sometimes secular nature. Many of these would have been made by specialist smiths in a monastic milieu, as suggested by excavations in Armagh. That this was not always the case, however, was shown by John Bradley's discovery of moulds for metalworking on the site of a crannog at Moynagh Lough, Co. Meath, which lacks any obvious religious connotations.

The Tara and Hunterston Brooches

The first of these high-quality items is the so-called Tara brooch, found beside the sea at Bettystown, Co. Meath, in 1850 and now in the National Museum in Dublin. Made of gilt silver, it differs from its simpler predecessors in being not a penannular brooch, that is, one with a break in the ring, but what is described as a 'pseudo-penannular brooch', for here the gap has been filled so that the ring forms a complete circle. The penannular brooch allowed the pin to pass from one side of the brooch to the other, thus enabling it to be used to join two pieces of a garment together and lock them into position. Blocking the gap, as here, meant that the brooch became just a stick-pin with a ring more for show than for utility, but it did create more space for ornament to be applied — an opportunity which the metalsmith avidly exploited. Indeed, one of the most remarkable characteristics of the Tara brooch, in addition to its sheer technical perfection, is how — with a diameter of only 8.7 cms — so much of its surface is packed with decoration on an incredibly miniature scale, that can be seen to be faultless even when magnified.

The back of the brooch (Pl.41) is relatively flat so as not to get snarled up in the wearer's garment, but where the upper and lower halves of the brooch meet, there are two domed glass studs in a grille of patterned silver. The latter material dominates the two trapezoidal panels in the lower part of the brooch, which were cut away within to create spiral ornament of La Tène type originally radiantly red from the copper base beneath, though now turned black through long exposure. Their smooth silver surface acts as a foil to the restless activity of the golden animals surrounding them — be they upright quadrupeds facing each other in the centre, or birds flying in a gently curving formation around the brooch's rim.

The front of the brooch (Pl.39) is much more dramatic — the relief of the studs is higher, and the individual panels of decoration are highlighted by darker glass frames. Here the studs — with gold 'nest-egg' insets — are not only of glass but also, in certain instances, of amber, a material probably imported from the Baltic or the North Sea. Many of the panels have, sadly, long since disappeared, but those remaining consist largely of interlace designs executed in gold filigree on a gold sheet base. The one notable exception is the animal in the sole-surviving trapezoidal panel. It, too, is made of filigree — gold granules, and beaded and twisted wire, applied in relief to a flat background — and showing only two of its presumed four legs as its body contorts itself behind the elongated neck, and its hind paw ends up in the back corner of the panel. To us, the animal seems to be upside down, but the wearer, viewing it from above, would have seen it the right-way up. In contrast, the animals on the free-ranging pin — either the full beast in the central triangular panel, or the cast head with rolled snout and horns looking down the narrow part of the pin — were meant to be seen the correct way up by the beholder, perhaps to ward off evil from the wearer. The animal heads (some with attenuated bodies) emerging from the rim of the brooch, and frequently interlacing with one another, ought possibly to be understood in a similar fashion as, Cerberus-like, they seem to act as guardians for the whole inner decoration of the brooch. Also emerging from the side of the brooch is a fragment of meshed wire known as trichinopoly, which may have been somehow attached to the foot of the pin so as to keep the whole brooch in place, though none is visible on the brooches worn by some of the figures sculpted on the Irish High Crosses. The animal head at the top of the trichinopoly chain is flanked by the only two human heads on the brooch, both made of blue moulded glass. In its exquisite beauty of design and virtuosity of technique, this brooch can have found few equals in Europe. Stylistically,

this would have been roughly the period of the Book of Lindisfarne (698 – 721), which is as much the aristocrat of contemporary manuscripts as the Tara brooch is of jewellery. Nevertheless, not far removed from it in quality is the Hunterston brooch in the National Museum in Edinburgh which, though found in south-western Scotland, may have come from Ireland, as its manner of closing the gap in the ring follows more Irish than Scottish fashion. Robert Stevenson, who envisaged an Anglo-Saxon prototype for both brooches, recognized a cross-shape in the central panel of the Hunterston brooch which he thought might have had some Christian reliquary as its model. This idea makes us look afresh at the central panel on the front of the Tara brooch, where the glass and amber studs around the rhomb-shaped central stud could be seen to present a cross-shaped arrangement, while the pellets set in a wire frame on the rhomb actually form a cross themselves, thus raising the question as to whether the Tara brooch may have been designed originally to adorn a liturgical vestment rather than a secular cloak.

Reconstruction of the central panel on the Hunterston brooch.

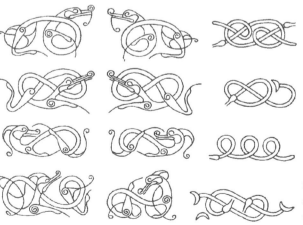

Drawings of filigree animals and interlace on the Hunterston brooch.

The Lough Kinale Book-shrine and the Steeple Bumpstead Boss

Among the remarkable pieces of eighth-century metalwork which have recently been brought to light is a book-shrine dredged up from Lough Kinale, Co. Longford, in 1986, and now in the National Museum of Ireland (Pl.45). By far the earliest known Irish example of its kind, it was essentially a wooden box covered with a framed metal cross having domed bosses at the end of each arm, and a larger one at the centre. The bosses were topped by an amber stud, and decorated with spirals in the La Tène tradition, those on the central stud ending in bird-heads. A lively spiral scroll runs around outside the tubular frame and, within the cusped arms of the cross, there are panels bearing animals with hatched bodies related to those on the Tara brooch. Though lacking the brooch's finesse and finish, it may give us a taste of what the world lost when the shrine of the Book of Kells was stolen in 1007 but, unlike the manuscript it contained, never recovered. E.P. Kelly's preliminary publication of this important shrine showed that its manuscript, too, had been removed before it was consigned to the waters, as the shrine was both incomplete and dismantled when found. Though just the right size, the Lough Kinale book-shrine cannot have been designed to contain the Book of Kells, as it is anything up to a century older. The domed bosses on the Lough

Kinale shrine suggest a possible function for an isolated example which, though found deep in Anglo-Saxon territory at Steeple Bumpstead in Essex, is likely to have been manufactured either in Ireland or northern Britain. Now in the British Museum in London, this gilded dome is divided horizontally into two levels by a raised rib, and vertically into quadrants by four remarkable animals in high relief, with their paws facing forward. Susan Youngs, who has studied the boss in detail, considers them to have been (protective) lions, created by the lost wax or *cire perdue* process. Though only 3.6cm high and 12.8cm in diameter, the boss, like the Tara brooch, packs in a great deal of ornament on to its surfaces. Both the dome itself and the flat flange used for attachment are divided up into panels bearing animals and spirals. The animals – either single or in pairs turning their backs on one another without interlacing – have hatched bodies and spiral joints resembling those on the Tara brooch, but not close enough to them to have been produced in the same workshop. The spiral ornament also finds its parallel in the Tara brooch, but its end-twists also show it to be related to the Book of Lindisfarne, with which it must be roughly contemporary. In addition to its use of amber, this boss has one technical peculiarity which was to become more popular in later centuries – the use of a black substance known as niello, into which decorative silver wire was laid. When first noticed early in this century, the boss ornamented a church door – almost certainly not its original function – but another recent discovery demonstrates what splendid door-furniture Irish churches of the eighth century really did have.

Details of animals with hatched bodies decorating the Steeple Bumpstead boss.

 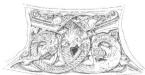 

The Donore Hoard

In 1984 drainage works at Donore, Co. Meath, brought to light a hoard of nine metal objects which are among the most fascinating Irish finds of recent years. They include two discs and a square plaque of tinned bronze, as well as a superbly cast animal-headed ring handle which prompts the interpretation of the whole hoard as fittings for a door, presumably of a church, though none is known in the immediate vicinity. The discs, with a diameter of just over 13cm, are each very different in design. The more complete example (Pl.83), with a square perforation in the centre, has two concentric bands of extraordinarily lively decoration, the outer one consisting of ten interlinked circles pirouetting around the perimeter. They derive their energy from internal tripartite spiral motifs which betray no hint of duplication or symmetry, and allow the eye to follow the pulsating roll of ornament emanating from a central vortex. They bear comparison with the spiral patterns inside the rim of the Lough Kinale book-shrine, while the Tara brooch and the Steeple Bumpstead boss offer parallels for the ribbon bodies and hatched snouts of the trio of paired animals which fill the inner band. Each pair of these beasts cross their necks and front paws, as their intertwining tails fill out any unoccupied space. The other disc (Pl.44), though incomplete, can be reconstructed to show one of the most sustained pieces of Celtic inventiveness in the whole of medieval Irish art. The circular hole at its centre is the focus for tightly-packed triads of circles decorated with marigolds or spirals (the latter creating triangles of three or six units,

depending on how you view it), and all creating a centrifugal tension which relaxes into larger-scale pelta and trumpet patterns towards the perimeter, where the background of carved hatchings add their own movement to the incomparable rhythm of this composition. It may be noted that, selectively, there is an emphasis in the discs of threes and their multiples – three pairs of animals on the first disc, and three marigold circles and nine La Tène-ornamented spirals on the second – all of which raise the question whether this number symbolism is related to the Trinity. An exception are the ten circles in the outer band of the first disc, which would have had a very different meaning, and closely link the number combination with that on fol. 192v of the Book of Durrow (p.38).

As if these two discs were not triumphs enough, the most astounding item of this Donore hoard is the handle in the form of an animal-head holding a movable ring at the back of its jaws (Pl.83). Both of the pieces must have been cast together in a *tour-de-force* of the bronzesmith's art. The under part of the animal-head is flat, and the teeth which stand out in low relief from both jaws seem harmless. All the action is to be found on the upper part of the head where we find further examples of the Ultimate La Tène spiral ornament, with (again) three elements rotating within – two are placed on the snout, and a pair each behind and in front of the ears. The hairs of the snout are formed of S-shapes cast in false relief, and the eyes are of a luminous amber staring out animatedly from their bronze surroundings. In his initial publication of the hoard, Dr Michael Ryan pointed out that the handle is probably earlier

39

41

43

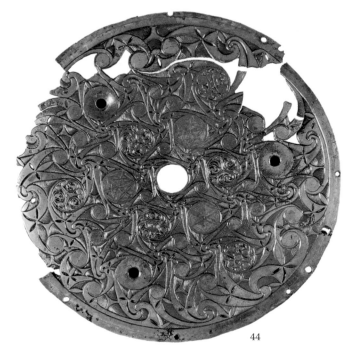

44

45

46

47

than its most famous counterpart, the *Wolfstür* (Wolf door) door-knocker in Charlemagne's Palatine Chapel at Aachen. While the abstract form of the head may go back to more naturalistic forebears in the Mediterranean area, the closest comparisons for the spiral ornament he found to be on the Tara brooch and in the Book of Lindisfarne (particularly noticeable in the feature which looks like the turned-down beak-end of an albatross), which would place the hoard firmly in an eighth-century context, and more probably in its first half. We know nothing of the church which these pieces once adorned, but it is an enticing thought to imagine that its altar-vessels might have included a chalice of matching quality, of which two highly decorative examples are known from early medieval Ireland.

The Ardagh Chalice

The Ardagh Chalice was found along with a smaller example and four later brooches (Pl.40) when a boy was digging potatoes in a circular earthwork or rath in West Limerick in 1868, and is now one of the most important items on display in the National Museum in Dublin. A *calix ministerialis* used to distribute wine to the faithful and dating perhaps from around the middle of the eighth century, the silver chalice (Pl.47) stands to a height of 17.8cm. Riveted on to the bowl beneath the rim are two semicircular cast handles (Pl.43), decorated with panels of red and blue enamel separated by grilles of stepped and other patterns, and sunken areas of interlace designs

executed in gold filigree on the background plate of gold. Beneath the handle is a triangular arrangement of domed red and blue enamelled bosses framed by silver grilles, and manufactured by the same complicated process as those used on the Tara brooch.

Just a little beneath the rim of the chalice the handles are linked by a band of ornament consisting of horizontal intricate filigree patterns of interlace panels, and interlacing animals standing out in relief from the gold background, all punctuated by a series of twelve silver-grille enamelled bosses. Placed centrally beneath this band on each face is a circular medallion decorated with a cross-of-arcs animated by S-spirals in filigree, with a similar enamel boss at the centre, and studs, partially of blue glass, on the perimeter. Running around the chalice beneath the band with gold filigree is an incised inscription giving the names of the twelve apostles all in the genitive case, except the last two – Thaddeus and Simon – who are in the nominative case. Why this should have been so is difficult to determine, though the incorrect spelling of *Piliphi* for *Philippi* may suggest that the engraver could craft better than he could spell. The letters are large capitals resembling those found in the Book of Lindisfarne, while the stippling used as a background reflects the use of the same technique in the Book of Durrow.

Unexpectedly, the Ardagh chalice is also richly decorated on the underside of the foot (Pl.42). Around the central piece of rock crystal which hides the bolt joining bowl and foot, three concentric bands of ornament (Pl.16) provide us with *the* classic example of three main types of ornament used side-by-side in various

manifestations of early medieval art in Ireland (see p.68–9) – interlace on the outside, spirals of Ultimate La Tène type in the middle, and animal ornament on the innermost band, in this instance animals running around in a circle back-to-back, or trying to bite each other head-on. Another remarkable feature of the chalice is the decoration on the rim of the base. Top and bottom are a number of almost rectangular flattened studs of blue glass, enriched with red and yellow enamel, and interspersed with trichinopoly (woven wire) and *Pressblech* silver panels with embossed crosses and interlacing. The unusual use of trichinopoly, together with the similar grille bosses and type of spiral ornament, shows a very considerable affinity between this chalice and the Tara brooch, suggesting reasonable closeness in techniques, though we need not assume both to have been products of exactly the same workshop, particularly as they were found over 100 miles apart.

The exquisite execution of the details of the gold and enamel work in particular, the technical mastery of the various ornament types, the grace and elegance of the bowl, the effective contrast between undecorated areas of the silver bowl and the high relief ornament around the handles and beneath the rim, make this into a masterpiece of the metalsmith's craft in the service of the Church. The comparison of the lettering with the Book of Lindisfarne suggests artistic contacts with Northumbria (which led one commentator to suggest that the chalice had actually been made there), but the shape of the vessel demonstrates influence from farther afield. For the two handles in particular – rare features among early medieval chalices – the nearest parallels outside Ireland would appear to be on a sixth-century (?) example from Resafa in Syria, now in the Museum of Fine Arts in Boston. Such far-flung comparisons need not, of course, imply any direct connection between the Byzantine East and Ireland. Instead, one could imagine Rome as being a possible link in the similarity of design, as Rome has always been a melting-pot for ideas in religious art, and a city which gave a warm welcome to peoples from East and West. The Ardagh chalice differs from all the non-Irish two-handled examples in having no knop at the junction of foot and bowl and, while most European chalices are likely to be derived ultimately from Roman prototypes, the decoration and style of the Ardagh chalice shows its creators to have digested a whole range of influences before they imbued it with an unmistakably Irish stamp.

The Derrynaflan Hoard

Any doubts which may have remained in the minds of those who supported an English origin for the Ardagh chalice must have been swept away with the discovery in 1980 of yet another very remarkable hoard of early medieval altar plate, including a chalice, at Derrynaflan, Co. Tipperary. This hoard, one of the most important from the early medieval period in north-western Europe, was discovered on an island in the middle of a bog, the site of a monastery concerned with church reform in the eighth and ninth centuries, and under the protection of the ascetic king-bishop of the southern province of Munster,

Feidlimidh mac Crimthainn. The hoard (Pl.49) consisted of a chalice, a paten and its stand, and a strainer ladle, all covered by a basin of copper alloy. Though probably buried together some time during the ninth or tenth century, the individual objects themselves were not necessarily all made at the same time – the chalice being among the latest. Its lesser quality suggests that it may have been manufactured considerably later than the Ardagh chalice and probably after 800. In contrast, the paten and its stand (Pl.46) can be added to that distinguished gallery of metal masterpieces discussed above as being assignable probably to the eighth century. In complexity and quality, the paten is only matched by the Ardagh chalice. Its striking beauty was revealed when it was cleaned in the British Museum Conservation Laboratory, its true magnificence residing in the decoration around the rim of the gently convex silver dish of the paten (Pl.50). In the upper surface of this rim, a concentric ring of intermeshed silver and copper wire (trichinopoly) flanks a circle of most intricate gold and polychrome enamel ornament. The enamel is in the form of 24 studs of the same kind as those already encountered on the Ardagh chalice and the Tara brooch but, if anything, with more complicated patterns in the dome-shaped metal grille and a greater interplay of the red, yellow and blue colours. Each of the studs is placed in a different circular setting, and between each of them is a panel with spirals and interlace, and containing filigree designs enriched with gold strips and beaded wire. These designs include kneeling men placed back to back, an eagle, various beasts as well as interlace, spiral and trumpet designs.

The outer face of this hoop surrounding the rim of the Derrynaflan paten also has patterned enamel panels, but this time they are flat and rectangular in shape. There are a dozen of these, suggesting a number symbolism related to the apostles, in which case the twenty-four studs on the top of the paten rim could be connected with the elders of the Apocalypse seated around the throne of God. Between the twelve studs are thin rectangular gold foils die-stamped with remarkably fine interlace and trumpet patterns. When taken apart in the British Museum laboratory, the paten was discovered to have incised letters and symbols, suggesting that its components were carefully assembled to a preconceived plan. The Derrynaflan paten is not the only one known from Ireland – Tirechán records in the seventh century having seen some examples traditionally said to have been made by St Patrick's silversmith, Assicus, and another from the later Middle Ages, once thought lost, was illustrated in the nineteenth century. Nor is it unique in a wider European context. Michael Ryan, who has given a preliminary account of the Derrynaflan hoard, pointed to other patens from the Byzantine world as seen, for instance, in the treasury of St Mark's in Venice, and he suggested that the origin and iconography of the filigree men and animals must probably be sought in Late Antique Roman silver, even though they appear here in a typically stylized Celtic version. The Derrynaflan paten has a circular support made separately, but sharing with it the delicate die-stamped interlace and spiral patterns, and the flat rectangular enamel panels, one of which, unusually, contains spiral designs. Here, the

number has been reduced to eight, but it is not known if this number symbolism is related to that of the paten, as the stand may have been made later for the paten, or in a different workshop.

The largest piece of the Derrynaflan hoard other than the copper alloy basin which covered all the objects is aesthetically the least pleasing. This is the silver chalice (Pl.48) which is larger than that from Ardagh and stands on a taller, stepped foot. Like the Ardagh chalice, it has small rounded handles above an escutcheon; it, too, has the ornamental frieze running all the way round a little below the rim. But the tautness of the filigree designs on the Ardagh chalice and the Derrynaflan paten has begun to disintegrate, just as the elements of Hellenistic coins did at the hands of Celtic moneyers in Gaul almost a thousand years earlier, but here this development goes hand in hand with a decline in technical skill coupled with a more extensive use of amber. The Derrynaflan chalice may not come well out of a close comparison with Ardagh, but this is not to deny its qualities, including its interesting use of animal ornament – though not animal interlace. Some of the animals may descend from classical lions, others have bird heads, and human heads also appear separately. But it is the backward look of some of the filigree animals comparable to those on ninth-century brooches (e.g. Pl.145) which suggests that the differences between the Ardagh and Derrynaflan chalices are not merely one of workshop, but of chronology as well, and thus making the chalice later than the paten.

5

Manuscripts of the Eighth and Early Ninth Centuries

■

THE POLYCHROME EFFECT, ACHIEVED by the enamel and other decoration visible on the metalwork just discussed, must have been even more in evidence in the manuscripts which would have gone hand in hand with them. Yet one of the curious twists of fate in the preservation of the Irish heritage is that we know all too little of the nature of illuminated manuscripts emanating from Irish monastic scriptoria between the earliest and the latest decades of the eighth century – just the period when the greatest pieces of decorative metalwork are likely to have been produced. It would look as if we have lost most of the fruit of two generations of master illuminators. The survival statistics of manuscripts is somewhat higher in Britain. If we are to believe a colophon written two centuries later, the eighth century was ushered in there by the creation of one of supreme masterpieces of early medieval book

illumination, the Book of Lindisfarne, Cotton Ms. Nero D.IV. in the British Library in London. With dimensions of 34 × 24cm, it is larger than the codices discussed earlier, and it is conceivable that all of its 250 folios could have been decorated by a single man – the Eadfrith named in the colophon – who may have been master scribe and illustrator all in one. If so, he was a man with a most orderly and tidy mind, who could lay out his page with mathematical precision and brilliance, and decorate it with wonderful combinations of Ultimate La Tène spiral and trumpet ornament, ribbon and animal interlace, as well as birds and fantastic animals running after or facing one another. His pensive evangelist figures, guarded above by their symbols and portrayed in the act of writing, are shown with flowing robes and with a certain freedom of movement and gesture which bespeaks a

southern origin. The text, too, is graceful and well-mannered, and easy to view at a glance, with each section carefully dovetailing into the next, and into the ornament provided.

This manuscript was written in Northumbria and may have contributed to the creation of another important example which shows what treasures we have lost among the products of Irish monastic scriptoria around the second quarter of the eighth century. This is the Book of St Chad in the Cathedral Library at Lichfield, a volume almost as large and sumptuous as the Book of Lindisfarne. Its colours were not always as muted as they are today, though its yellows and blues do stand out brightly on certain pages. It expands the ornament of Lindisfarne, and for each Gospel it probably had an evangelist portrait, a four-symbols page and one with a decorative initial letter. The evangelist figures here, however, look straight out at the beholder, and the folds in their garments, as well as their hair and ears, are more Celtic than classical. The spiral ornament of the Book of Lindisfarne is still playing an important role, but fretwork motifs have come to dominate the frame of the pictured pages. If evidence is insufficient to claim the Book of Lichfield for Ireland, its use of linear geometrical ornament in the frames is a feature which it shares with a group of smaller manuscripts which help to fill out Ireland's eighth-century gap.

The Pocket Gospel-Books

These manuscripts are the pocket-gospel books which are likely to belong to the century after 750, though precisely where each fits within that span is difficult to say. The intimate form of the Gospel book, which would have been carried around by monks in their leather satchels, is one which is most likely to have developed in Ireland, because most, if not all, of the known examples are of Irish origin. Not the formal exercises in magnificence witnessed in the great Books of Lindisfarne, Lichfield and Kells, these are personal copies of the Gospels used for private reading and contemplation – and the Lives of Irish saints suggest that they could have been gifts from master to pupil or vice-versa. Typical features of these books, other than their size, is the desire to economise by writing in a miniscule script which quickly leads to an equally small cursive script, with frequent use of ingenious abbreviations – a style very different to the late classical volumes of similar size which use uncial or half-uncial letters. They also differ from their continental counter-parts in that each Gospel starts with an evangelist portrait as well as an *Incipit* page to mark the opening of the text. The Gospel books also omit all prefatory matter, the last of a Late Antique tradition to do so.

Probably the oldest of these is the Book of Mulling, Ms.A.I. 15 (60) in the Library of Trinity College, Dublin, which measures a mere 16.5 × 12 cm. The colophon on page 94 states *Nomen h. scriptoris mulling dicitur*, intimating that the manuscript was written by St Moling (or Mulling), who died in 697 and was founder of the monastery named after him at St Mullins in County Carlow. But this colophon is likely to have been copied from the model on which the Gospel book was based, as its style suggests a date scarcely earlier than the second half of the eighth century.

Included as part of the manuscript when it was found in the book-shrine long in the possession of the Kavanagh family in County Carlow were eleven leaves with canon tables and other matter which may be a little later in date. The initial letters are formed with long thin ribbons of animal bodies terminating in simple animal heads. The only elaborate example is Christ's monogram XPI of the *Christi autem Generatio* (Matthew 1,18) which, significantly, is absent in Lindisfarne but already developed in the Book of Lichfield, suggesting a link between the latter and the Gospel books.

The most characteristic features of the decoration of many of these Gospel books are the evangelist portraits, many of which, unlike Lichfield, have no accompanying symbol. While not comparable to the rich palette of the Books of Lindisfarne or Kells, they are painted in a variety of colours ranging from white, blue, green and yellow to ochre, brown, mauve, purple and cherry red. These evangelists are happy little men, their feet spaced apart, dressed in long garments to the ankle and covered by a cloak which contains stylized linear folds more visual than realistic. They hold a copy of the Gospels in the left hand, partially covered by a drape, and the right hand is placed across the cover of the book. In the portrait of St John on fol. 81v of the Book of Mulling, the evangelist looks straight out to engage the eye of the beholder, as his halo rises above the frame. The side frames have panels of interlaced animals accompanied by others decorated with spirals or interlace. In the Book of Dimma [Trinity College, Dublin, Library Ms. A.4. 23 (19)] – a manuscript probably emanating from a monastery in Roscrea,

Co. Tipperary – the evangelists (Pl.52–53) are very stylized, and the curious configurations of their garments make a derivation from enamel-decorated metalwork likely. Other Gospel books of the same period have comparable evangelist pictures, though with variations in colour and design, and generally without any indication whether the evangelist sits or stands, as in the British Library Ms. Add. 40618. The St John (Pl.58) of the Stowe Missal in the Royal Irish Academy (Ms. D.II.3, fol.11v) is identified by the eagle symbol hovering above his head like an umbrella, but here fretwork decoration dominates the frame – as in the Book of Lichfield. On the whole, it may be noticed that the drawing of the evangelists is more subtle and of a higher quality than the often humdrum decoration of the frames. On some of the text pages of the Gospel books – as on the initial page of a St John's Gospel fragment bound in with the Stowe Missal – the frames do, however, have an attractive combination of birds and beasts, together with fretwork, using yellow, brown, mauve, red and orange. One item of unique interest in the Book of Mulling is the apparent plan of a monastery, which may have been a later addition to fol. 94v. It shows a circle, presumably representing the surrounding wall, the sacred temenos as it were of the early monastery, and within it are crosses dedicated to Christ and his apostles, and the Holy Spirit; outside other crosses bear the names of Old Testament prophets and, towards the four cardinal points, the four evangelists. Efforts to correlate the plan with the site of the original monastery of St Mullins have not been successful, though some connection is not unlikely. The illustration,

53

54

55

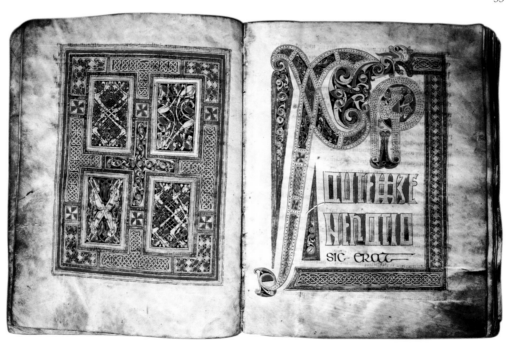

56

57

however, has been otherwise interpreted either as a reference to the baptistery in Ravenna, or a copy of a contemporary miniature from the Continent (possibly Tours) coupling the Old Testament prophets with the Evangelist. Such an interpretation would have the effect of providing the Book of Mulling with a not entirely implausible date in the second quarter of the ninth century.

The St Gall and Turin Manuscripts

The decoration of the Book of Mulling relates it to another manuscript which is one of a number preserved in the monastic library (*Stiftsbibliothek*) in the Swiss town of St Gall, a foundation which grew up around the tomb of the eponymous pupil of St Columbanus. Though not specifically an Irish foundation, St Gall nevertheless kept up its initial contacts with Ireland, and was a place where Irish monks were always welcomed. Some of these doubtless brought books with them, and a mid-ninth century catalogue gives a list of thirty books in the library which had been written by Irishmen – *libri scottice scripti*. One of these can probably be identified with the manuscript numbered 60, though some doubt has been cast on the Irish-style script having been actually executed in Ireland. Its decorated pages – the initial *In Principio* on page 5, and the portrait of St John preceding it – both show signs of hastiness, almost carelessness, in their execution, except for the interlace which the artist evidently enjoyed drawing. While the evangelist's head, facing the observer directly, is a simple and sympathetic portrayal, his formless and striped gown gives the impression that his head is growing out of a circus tent.

Though not included among the *libri scottice scripti*, the St Gall Library's most Irish manuscript is that numbered 51, a Gospel Book only marginally smaller than the Book of Kells (below, p.102), with which it has often been compared. It cannot compete with the Kells codex in variety of colour or in richness of inventive ornament, but it is nevertheless a minor masterpiece in its own right. Unusual among the larger Gospel books is the way in which not just single pages but a complete opening of two pages is presented as a harmonious whole, as when the evangelist figure appears on the left-hand page with a beautifully-decorated initial facing it on the right (Pl.55), or a carpet page is placed opposite the genealogy of Christ with his monogram XPI on the right (Pl.56) – or the two Christ illustrations to be discussed below. Each of their ornamental panels is – relative to the size of the page – on a much larger scale than in the Book of Kells, so that they stand out more clearly, as can be seen in the opening with the carpet-page and the XPI monogram on pages 6–7 (Pl.56). On the latter, the first letter X of Christ's name in Greek looks almost like a capital P, its body subdivided into panels of interlace, fretwork and animal interlace. In this, it shows its descent from the Books of Lindisfarne and Lichfield. The same page also brings out a number of characteristic features of the manuscript – the use of internal dotting, the unusual colour scheme involving pink, mauve, yellow and blue, and the incomplete rectangular frame which, instead of going all the way around the page, only completes half the course before terminating in a fierce animal head.

Because the manuscript is preserved in its entirety, the St Gall 51 Gospels have the advantage of retaining all the four evangelist portraits, which are of two different kinds. St Matthew on page 2 (Pl.55) and St Luke on page 128 have curious frames behind them, perhaps to make us believe that they are seated on thrones, and above them are their symbols, that for St Matthew being a charming winged genie with interwoven fingers and a benevolent cryptic smile. St Mark on page 78 (Pl.51) is accompanied by the symbols of all four evangelists, and he and St John on page 208 (Pl.54) have outsize faces, but less room than the other two, because the frames beside them are doubled in width and have an eye-catching diamond-shape or circle at the centre of the side. This doubling of the frame-width draws our attention to the fretwork, interlace, animal, spiral and geometrical ornament within its panels which must surely have had great symbolism for those who created it, but whose meaning is now sadly lost to us. Unlike classical art, where the figure subject is usually divorced from the frame, the evangelist portraits and their symbols in St Gall 51 touch the frames at a number of places — Saints Matthew and Luke have a part of the frame cut out top and bottom to allow room for the evangelist's symbol and feet respectively, which come into direct contact with the frame.

Perhaps the most striking images of all in the book — because also the most unexpected — are those making up the opening of pages 266–267 (Pl.57). On the left is the Crucifixion, the haloed figure of the Saviour placed against the background of the cross, his nailed hands and feet emerging small-scale from the mummy-like wrappings of Christ's body which, although only falling to a level just above the knee, are almost certainly derived from the oriental *colobium*, the full-length garment shown on most seventh- and eighth-century representations of the Crucifixion. Their folds emanate from Christ's shaven head, towards which Stephaton raises a pole with a vessel on top to offer Christ the hyssop. As book-bearing angels look down upon the scene from above the arms of the cross, Longinus casts his lance into Christ's left armpit. Just perceptible as emerging from the wound is a zigzag line which falls on the face of Longinus, illustrating the apocryphal legend that the blood spurting from Christ's body at the Crucifixion cured the blindness of the man who pierced his side, a theme also illustrated on a mid-eighth century fresco in Santa Maria Antiqua in Rome and apparently also on the South Cross at Clonmacnoise. Facing the Crucifixion on the right is a scene divided into two registers, the lower one containing twelve figures (presumably apostles) gazing upwards towards the (now bearded) Christ in the centre of the upper register, where he is flanked by two trumpet-blowing angels. Christ bears a cross and a book, and blesses with his right hand. Though this scene has sometimes been interpreted as a Last Judgment, it almost certainly represents the apocalyptic Second Coming of Christ.

The same subject appears in another manuscript originally from Bobbio, the Alpine monastery founded by St Columbanus, and now bearing the shelf-mark O.IV.20 in the Biblioteca

Nazionale in Turin. Only four leaves of the manuscript survive – and miraculously so, as they had been removed for photography when the remainder of the manuscript perished in a disastrous fire in 1904. Though shrunk and discoloured nevertheless, the decorative scenes can be made out – an Ascension as well as a Second Coming, in addition to two carpet-pages. Round forms predominate much more so than in the St Gall manuscript – as in the circles encompassing the spiral-trumpet ornament of fol. 129 or the knotted interlace on fol. 128a, and in the frame of the Christ figure on the Ascension page, while ringed crosses – like those in stone on the High Crosses (p.151) – emanate from the centre of the frame of the Second Coming picture. The circles and circle-segments enclosing angels on the Ascension page, and the gallery-like range of twelve apostle figures beneath, give a strong impression of having been copied from a Mediterranean model, though the spiral and interlace decoration can only be the product of a scribe with 'insular' training. This Ascension page could provide grounds for thinking that this manuscript may have been written on the Continent, but by a scribe or scribes who had close connections with Ireland.

The suggestion has recently been made that some of the 'Irish' manuscripts in St Gall may also have been written in St Gall, rather than in Ireland. However, the evangelist portraits are close to those in the Irish Pocket-gospel books, though the layout of the letter L on the *Liber autem Generatio* on p.3 (Pl.55) is closely allied to those of the Books of Lindisfarne and Lichfield as well as the manuscript P.I.2 in the Cathedral Library in Hereford, hinting at English and Welsh links. The unusual piercing of Christ's *left* side by Longinus is a feature found on most, though not all, of the Irish High Crosses of stone, one of the few exceptions – Arboe, Co. Tyrone – by a curious coincidence providing by far the closest parallel for the Second Coming illustrated on p.267 of the St Gall manuscript. While it cannot be proven, the St Gall 51 manuscript has better claims to an Irish origin than does the Bobbio/Turin manuscript, but both introduce a whole new – presumably continental – element into insular manuscripts by illustrating biblical and apocalyptic events which (with the exception of the single Crucifixion page in the Durham Cathedral Library Ms. A.II.17) appear here possibly for the first time among surviving manuscripts of insular tradition, and which are also found in the Book of Kells.

The St Gall 51 manuscript can be seen to be in a line of development from the Books of Lindisfarne and Lichfield, to be related to the Hereford Cathedral Gospel book, to have close connections with the Irish Pocket-gospel books and to be a cousin of the Turin O.IV.20 codex. Because St Gall is seen as being a somewhat impoverished version of the Book of Kells, it has been presumed that it is later than it – an assumption which lacks proof. The great manuscript connoisseur Wilhelm Koehler spent more than half of his working life changing his mind about the relationship of the two codices to one another. He started by seeing Kells as earlier than St Gall, believing the latter to be the beginning of a downward path, showing an increasing impoverishment of the high standards set by the Book of Lindisfarne. Subsequently, his study of the decoration of the initials led him to the view that each represented a branch diverging from the Lindisfarne/Lichfield stem, with St Gall representing a decline and Kells a refinement. However, further study of the figural painting made him think that Kells depended on St Gall, and that Kells was not too far distant in time from the Book of Lindisfarne, which would make it much earlier than the date late in the eighth century which he had long presumed probable. Koehler's change of mind covers a span of ideas which have partially been reflected in other author's works over the last hundred years, where people have gone round in circles comparing one motif to another, manuscript to metalwork etc., without any clear consensus being reached. The likelihood is that all three manuscripts – St Gall, Turin O.IV.20 and the Book of Kells – belong, not necessarily in that order, within the period from the middle of the eighth century to the early years of the ninth century, without any great hope of ever confirming a more refined date for any of them, and therefore providing the correct order in which they came into being.

The Book of Kells

The Book of Kells is generally recognised as the zenith of 'Insular' manuscript production while being, at the same time, enigmatic in its origin, inspiration and date. This book of the four Gospels is now the greatest treasure in the Library of Trinity College, Dublin [Ms. A.I.6 (58)], to which it was given in the second half of the seventeenth century. In what is widely accepted as the first reference to the Book in historical sources, it was also described as a treasure, the *primh-mind* (most precious object) of the western world. This was when the *Annals of Ulster* reported under the year 1007 that the Great Gospel of Colum Cille was stolen from the western sacristy of the great church at Kells, the County Meath monastery which had been founded two centuries earlier by the monks of Iona, where St Colum Cille (or Columba) was buried in 597. Fortunately for us, it was recovered some time later, but without its gold covering (meaning, presumably, its book shrine). Through land charters recorded on pages originally left empty, we know it to have been in Kells in County Meath in the twelfth century, and it is extremely likely that the Great Book of Colum Cille can be equated with what we know today as the Book of Kells. The unfortunate theft almost a thousand years ago may have been responsible for the loss of a number of folios at both the beginning and end of the manuscript. At present, it consists of 340 folios (or 680 pages), but it is reckoned that there may have been up to thirty more originally – including possibly important decorated pages, some perhaps containing details of where (or even when) the manuscript was written, which might have saved the great amount of ink which has been spent speculating on solutions to these problems over the last century and a half.

Its first surviving page contains the last part of a section giving St Jerome's compilation of the Hebrew names occurring in the New Testament. This may well have been preceded by St Jerome's letter to Pope Damasus (known as the *Novum*

Opus) which is present in the Book of Durrow, whose contents are very close to those of the Book of Kells. The Hebrew names are followed by further preliminary matter in the form of Canon Tables which provide concordances indicating where passages recurring in different Gospels can be found in relation to one another. Ten folios are devoted to these Tables, followed by two more left blank at the time of writing, so that originally twelve would have been planned. But, in the Book of Kells, these Canon Tables were quite useless as the verse numbers they contain have no corresponding numbers in the Gospel text to which they could have referred. This is our first indication that the Book was not for everyday, or even practical, use, suggesting that it was something very special created more as a celebration of God and St Columba than as a manuscript for altar or other Gospel readings. But it is these same Canon Tables that introduce us to the superb skill of the illuminator's art for which the Book is famous. Their first eight pages consist of four or three arcades, framed by columns standing on round or hemispherical bases, and having their arches framed on top by one great tympanum which spans them all, and which has spandrels squaring off the upper corners of the decoration. The ornament of the columns, and their bases and capitals, includes much the same kind of La Tène-inspired spirals as found in the Book of Durrow, but here with many more variations of the basic theme. The same can also be said of the interlace motifs which show a much greater refinement and inventiveness than those in the Book of Durrow, and which are generally also on a much more miniature scale. But in the Book

of Kells they alternate playfully and are also intertwined with both bird and human forms — the latter being placed one on top of the other within the narrow confines of the columns, showing how the Celtic artist could neatly accommodate his motifs into the framework of a classical arcade. But even more attractive are the upper parts of the Tables where, either in the arcade arches or in the tympanum, or even in the spandrels, we find the symbols of the four Evangelists whose Gospels feature in the spaces beneath — *Homo*, or the man for Matthew, the lion for Mark, the calf for Luke and the eagle for John. Instead of each of these symbols being repeated in similar fashion, they are varied with great imagination of composition throughout the first eight pages of the Canon Tables. Nowhere can this ingenuity be seen to better effect than on fol. 5r (Pl.68), where the man of Matthew is given wings and a *flabellum* to create the unframed spandrel of the upper left-hand corner, balancing on the right (Pl.60) the equally winged eagle of John, which holds his Gospel with a human hand. Wings are also a feature of the lion and the calf in the tympanum, which touch each other gracefully as they avert their gaze from one another. The two arches which the tympanum spans are filled with animal or human interlace, and each is subdivided by a great lion-head which emerges from the column beneath and bites into the arch — the whole making one of the most lively and masterful compositions in the entire Book.

Even a detail of the upper part of this Canon Table (Pl.60) helps to show the considerable variety of colours used in the Book of Kells which was able to muster and assemble the whole range of colour materials known to have been available in Britain and Ireland at the time. Kells stresses blues and yellows more than Lindisfarne, some of the more striking blues being achieved by the use of lapis lazuli. This is a mineral known only from one source in the medieval period – namely Afghanistan, from whence a small amount must have reached the scriptorium of the Book of Kells which must, by inference, have been attached to a rich monastery. Another exotic oriental source in the form of the indigo plant may have provided other blue colourings for the manuscript. A Mediterranean plant *Crozophora tinctoria* may have been used to produce some of the mauves, maroons and purples, while a kermes red came from the pregnant body of the Mediterranean insect *Kermococcus vermilio*. Red lead was used for orange reds, and white lead for white, but the copper green had the disadvantage that it perforated the vellum when it was wet. For a manuscript of its magnificence, it comes almost as a surprise to realise that gold is never used. In its absence, an effort was made to create its wonderful effect by using a yellow arsenic sulphide known as *auripigmentum*, or golden pigment, many examples of which can be seen in the manuscript's pages. The illuminators sometimes applied a series of translucent washes one on top of the other to create a relief effect, though this was sadly diminished when the leaves were moistened for flattening in the last century. However, even today, this feeling of relief can still be experienced when the observer stands in front of the manuscript in the display cases of the Library of Trinity College, Dublin, but not on the printed page of a reproduction.

The Canon Tables change abruptly after fol. 5r, and, over the page, they drop the arcading system in favour of much simpler framed pages divided into various columns. Before launching directly into the individual Gospels, however, the Book continues with introductory material to all of the Gospels together, in contrast to the Book of Lindisfarne which places the relevant material at the beginning of each of the Gospels separately. The prefatory remarks comprise what are known as the *Breves Causae*, which are summaries of the texts that follow. St Matthew, the first of the Gospels, is introduced on fol. 8r with an ornamented page that includes a relaxed figure seated with an open book (Pl.76) and accompanied by a text referring to the Birth of Christ in Bethlehem in Judaea, and the Magi offering gifts. In an obvious reference to this passage – though noticeably without the three kings – is the magnificent icon of the Virgin and Child on the opposite page (fol. 7v). Icons are usually solemn and posed, and this one is no exception. The Virgin sits with her body shown frontally, her pendulous breasts indicated through her aristocratic upper garment, decorated with a diamond-shaped ornament or brooch, as suggested recently by Niamh Whitfield. Her legs are swung cautiously at right angles to the torso, and on her lap sits the child Jesus, his right hand placed lovingly on hers, and his other raised above her breasts. He looks up affectionately at her solemn face, but their heads are not quite close enough to equate the composition with the Byzantine *eleoussa* type of tender Virgin. For all its seeming static nature, the picture does have some feeling of movement – the raised left hand of Christ and the theatrical way in which the angel appears from behind the throne. There is, unusually for the Book of Kells, even a sense of depth, imparted by the wings of the two upper angels (Pl.61) passing behind the outer orb of the Virgin's halo and by the way in which what could be construed as two recessed legs of the chair or throne are seen between its two frontal legs. The ornamentation of the lower part of the throne seems to imitate enamel decoration, and an aggressive lion-head emerges from the top of the throne – a feature seen on furniture carved on the High Crosses at Moone, Co. Kildare, and Clonca, Co. Donegal.

The origin of this Virgin and Child representation has been much discussed, and at least there is general agreement that its closest analogy is found carved in wood on St Cuthbert's coffin in Durham, dated to around 698. While the essential elements are similar, there are differences, including the way Christ on the coffin-lid looks straight at the beholder, which would argue against the manuscript having directly copied the carving. An Eastern manuscript now in Florence, the Rabula Gospels of 586, does have an earlier representation of the Virgin and Child, though there she is shown standing. The Kells pair are the earliest known appearance of the Christ child with his mother in Western manuscripts, but who knows what other ones may once have existed to act as models, but have since perished?

Benedict Biscop is known to have brought a representation of the Mother of God with him from Rome to Monkwearmouth/Jarrow in Northumbria late in the seventh century, and icons similar to it may have been circulating in northern England at the time which could easily have served as models both for St Cuthbert's coffin and the Book of Kells. Without having to resort to Byzantium, Coptic Egypt or even Armenia, the city of Rome may well have provided the inspiration for these Marian images, as some examples from the period have survived in its early churches, though not necessarily showing all the characteristics of the Kells picture. The cult of the Virgin was already well-established in Ireland by the year 700, and the same almost certainly applied to northern England, so that the groundwork was well and truly laid for reception of her image in the Book of Kells, designed to encourage devotion to the Mother of God. One further small feature is worthy of comment. The Virgin and her attendants face the beholder, whereas Christ's head is shown in profile, but with the typical Kells eye represented full frontally. The same stylization occurs on the faces of six figures who interrupt the animal-interlaced frame to the right of the Virgin's knee and who, unexpectedly with their back to the Virgin, face towards the highly decorative *Breves Causae* page opposite them. The text there mentions the Magi, and it was Christ's appearance before the Magi which offered his first Theophany, his initial presentation to the world – and it may well be that the six small framed figures may represent the people of the world.

One of the features which sets the Book of Kells apart from all the other early medieval insular illuminated manuscripts is its richness in full-page miniatures, of which the Virgin and Child is only one of many. Two others may be introduced at this stage of the discussion, because they are among the few depictions in the Book

ui	fuit	zorim
ui	fuit	machat
ui	fuit	leui
ui	fuit	semeol˙
ui	fuit	iuda
ui	fuit	ioseph
ui	fuit	iona
ui	fuit	eliacim
ui	fuit	melcha
ui	fuit	mennan
ui	fuit	mathathia
ui	fuit	nathan
ui	fuit	dauid
ui	fuit	iesse
ui	fuit	obed
ui	fuit	boos
ui	fuit	salmon

61

65

66

70

71

73

74

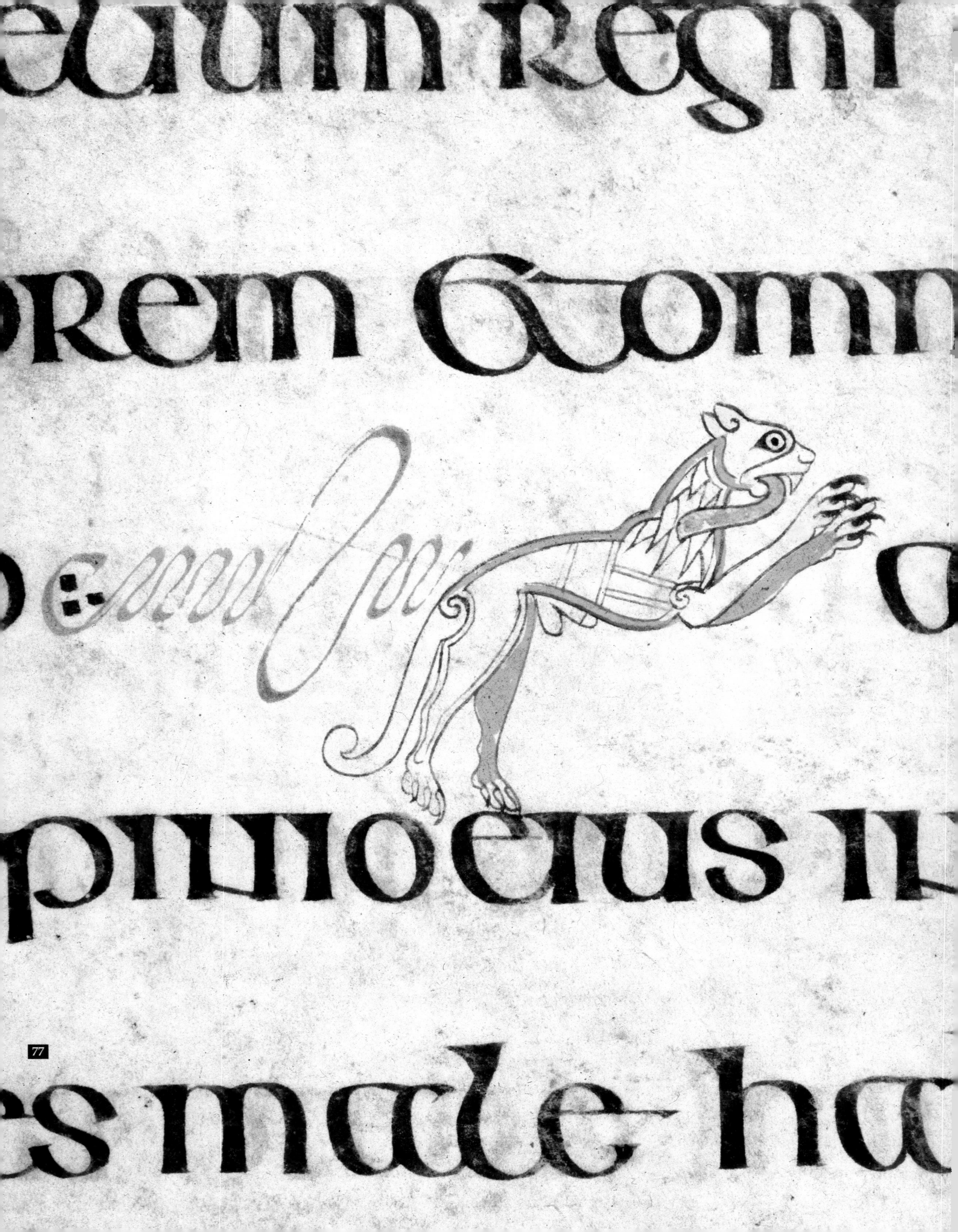

77

which illustrate narrative events in the life of Christ. One of these (Pl.63) is the Temptation of Christ in St Luke's Gospel (fol. 202v) when the devil brought Christ to Jerusalem and, in the words of the Evangelist, 'set him on a pinnacle of the temple, and said to him, If thou be the son of God, cast thyself down from hence. But Jesus was not to be tempted'.

This depiction, the earliest known representation of the scene and certainly one of the earliest surviving representations of Solomon's Temple in Western art, shows a benign and youthful, haloed Christ holding a scroll in his left hand and gesturing with his right hand towards a black and winged grimacing devil, which is among the oldest images known of the Evil One. The Temple is a building with sloping gables crowned by a finial formed of crossed animal heads. Above, Christ's shoulders and head form a neat triangle bringing the upward slope of the roof to a suitable climax, topped by two hovering angels who flank and protect the Saviour's halo. The animal-headed finials and sloping roof of the temple have understandably given rise to the comparison between it and the roughly contemporary house- or tomb-shaped shrines of metal (to be discussed below, p.133), but also to the suggestion that the temple gives us some inkling of the appearance of early Irish churches which — at the time the Book of Kells was written — would have been made almost exclusively of wood. The cladding of the walls in the Temptation picture might be appropriate to the walls of a church, as its geometrical designs — largely though not exclusively symmetrical — look suspiciously like repetitive marquetry on the designs of inlaid wooden tiles. But they could equally well be imagined as having been copied from a tapestry, or forming the exterior ornament of an oriental tent. In the centre foreground of the Temple is a door that frames the bust of a youthful, haloed figure carrying two flower-headed staffs crossed on the breast in an Osiris pose, like that of the Christ figure in the Last Judgment scene on Muiredach's Cross at Monasterboice (p.162). Precisely who this figure is we do not know — Christ back on *terra firma* having successfully resisted the temptation of his ugly adversary, or even a reminiscence of the Old Testament builder of the Temple? Equally enigmatic are the many figures who stand as witnesses to the scene — nine on the left of the temple roof as we look at it, and twenty-five beneath the temple, standing on either side of what looks almost like a carpet leading up to the entrance. These are so similar to the individuals we have just seen in the frame of the Virgin and Child representation, and with the same profile image and expressions varying from the quizzical to the comic, that we might envisage them not as monks (as some have suggested), but the populace of the world to whom Christ is saying: 'Thou shalt not tempt the Lord thy God'.

The angels filling the stepped spandrels in the upper corner of the picture are accompanied by plants growing out of (and partially down from) vases — perhaps reinforcing the idea that this Temptation scene is to be located in the cultivated milieu of Jerusalem, though the resemblance of the building to a tent could suggest that the picture is a conflation of two of the Temptations to which Christ was subjected, one in Jerusalem and the other in the desert. Similar plants are found above the heads of the two figures flanking Christ in what is generally taken to be a depiction of the Arrest of Christ on fol. 114r (Pl.62). Characteristic of the Book of Kells, such plants are found in only one earlier insular manuscript, a copy of Bede in the St Petersburg Public Library (Cod. Q.v.I.18), written in Northumbria around 746, suggesting that such vegetal ornament may have come through northern England from some more luxuriant growth further south. In the so-called Arrest scene, the potted plants spread their tendrils almost like an octopus in the tympanum above the figure of Christ, and their stylized flowers hedge in the words, *Ymno dicto exierunt in montem Oliveta*, 'a hymn being said, they went out unto mount Olivet', leading Carl Nordenfalk to exclaim that here we have the earliest representation of landscape in northern art. Beneath, we have the figure of Christ, with tousled locks of hair and large soulful eyes which form the focal point of the whole picture. He raises his arms diagonally, in which position they are grasped by two black-bearded figures approaching from each side, normally interpreted as those who came to arrest the Saviour. The Arrest, however, is not described in the text until five pages later, whereas the text above the figures could suggest that this is a representation of Christ on the Mount of Olives. But the picture may have been located in advance of the relevant text to mark the beginning of Christ's Passion at this juncture, an interpretation strengthened by Christ's gesture pointing his hands towards the crosses at the bottom of the arch. Christ is not seen to stand on anything: the whole scene does, therefore, seem to be timeless

and somewhat removed from reality, for there is little movement in it except in the two flanking figures approaching from the side. Christ is being taken peacefully, stressing the voluntary nature of the Passion, and his serenity is underlined in that his clothing is symmetrical, contrasting with the restless asymmetry of those who have come to grasp his arms.

The Temptation and Arrest are the only two full page miniatures in the Book which actually illustrate scenes from the Gospels, though it has been prudently suggested that the blank left on the folio (123v) before St Matthew's account of the Crucifixion may have been intended to illustrate what follows, but (for whatever reason) Christ's death was not depicted in the Codex. Why should the two narrative scenes of the Temptation and Arrest have been chosen for illustration when so many other better-known biblical scenes could have been selected instead — or in addition? One suggestion is that both expressed Christ's exposure to the power of evil, when he did not use his own innate divine power to avoid or avert it, and warning those who look at the Book to avoid evil. Even more enigmatic is the question of the origin of these two narrative scenes. Parallels for the composition of the Temptation scene do not emerge until the tenth century on the European continent, and the 'Arrest' does not conform closely to other representations of the scene. While they make the Book of Kells probably the earliest surviving insular manuscript to illustrate biblical events other than the Crucifixion, they leave us with the puzzle what their origins are. Both, of course, could have been the original brainchild of the

Book of Kells illustrating team – and may not necessarily have been painted by the same hand.

These narrative pictures were the exception, but the planned norm did include a number of other full-page figures. The original decorational plan of the manuscript was probably to have a page of evangelist symbols and another bearing the portrait of the relevant evangelist before each Gospel, in addition to highlighting the initial letter of the first chapter (together with further decoration of minor initials). But the planning of the manuscript seems to have changed somewhat as the project progressed, so that what we have now may not entirely conform to the original plan. Following on the tradition of Books such as those of Durrow and Lichfield, each of the Gospels is preceded by a page bearing the symbols of the four evangelists – *Homo*, the man, for Matthew, the lion for Mark, the calf for Luke and the eagle for John. In addition, the very first surviving page (fol. 1v) has the four symbols turned at right angles, and holding up the Gospels with human hands, perhaps indicating the four authors whose works are co-ordinated in the Canon Tables which follow immediately. The Gospels of Matthew, Mark and John are each provided with a full page set of the four symbols, which are grouped around a cross formation that dominates the composition. All are enclosed by a frame made up of a number of differently-shaped panels decorated by spirals, as well as ribbon and human interlace, and emphasized by angular embellishments at the corners. The symbols preceding the Mark Gospel on fol. 129v (e.g. Pl.70) are placed in and around yellow halo-like circles, whereas those in St Matthew's Gospel

stand out vigorously from the parchment background in their upright rectangular frames. Rather different in style is that of the evangelist symbols before St John's Gospel on fol. 290v (Pl.67), where the central cross is a saltire with a diamond-shaped centre (perhaps representing Christ, the 'figure of light' in the Vision of Ezekiel), and the emblems like St John's eagle (Pl.65) are placed in what might be described as an M-shaped triangle. The design of the symbols varies too, with the lion and calf (Pl.66) sprouting unexpected wings, and while the lion is not always easily recognizable as such, all are individually the products of great fantasy and imaginative colouring. Fol. 187v, with a similar saltire arrangement, shows two of the evangelist symbols, but the portrait on fol. 28v at the beginning of St Matthew's Gospel brings up the question whether it is yet another example of an evangelist symbol in the form of *Homo*, St Matthew's symbol of the man. This portrait, one of a number in the Book, is placed in a T-shaped field dominated by a niche in the upper part, with lion heads on either side of the halo. Between an inner and an outer frame are the ends of a throne, above which the calf and the eagle are indicated, suggesting that this figure may be more the symbol of St Matthew than a portrait of the evangelist himself.

The only portrait which can be reliably identified as that of an evangelist is St John on fol. 291v (Pl.64). He sits holding up a copy of his finely-bound Gospel in his left hand, as his right grasps an extremely long pen which he is about to dip into an inkwell above his right foot. His bearded head, with large eyes riveted in a frontal gaze and with curly locks flowing over the forehead, is surrounded by an intricate halo. Concentric to it, but larger, is another circle which could be interpreted as an extension of the halo or as a very ornamental round head-cushion from which drapes fall onto the evangelist's throne, which has very enamel-like terminations. The figure is placed in a frame with equal-armed crosses right and left, and top and bottom. Outside these a clenched fist emerges on either side, together with a pair of feet below, and above it portion of a head which was badly mutilated by a nineteenth-century book binder. This disembodied figure, who is to be understood as being behind the whole frame, may be intended to represent Christ (or possibly even God the Father).

There is only one full page portrait of Christ himself, that on fol. 32v (Pl.72), where he is accompanied by four angels. Unexpectedly slim-figured compared to the other portrait figures, Christ sits on an understated throne, holding a book in a draped left hand as his open right hand holds the upper portion. Beside Christ's shoulders are two vases out of which plants grow, and above them are peacocks – symbols of eternal life. Christ stands in a key hole-shaped frame decorated with escutcheons – round with fretwork and square with spirals – which look like metalwork imitations, one of many such instances in the manuscript. Between the sides of the key-hole and the outer rectangular frame of animal interlacing there are two angels standing on each side, and from the centre of the arched top a cross descends to the figure's head, which helps to identify him as Christ. The justification for the Christ portrait in this position is the last piece of text preceding it on fol. 31v, which speaks of the fourteen generations from the carrying away into Babylon down to Christ, a passage which occurs in the first chapter of Matthew.

This part of the Gospel is, indeed, the most richly decorated section of the whole manuscript, for it contains not only a page of the four evangelist symbols on fol. 27v (e.g. Pl.71), the man or St Matthew (fol. 28v), a highly orna-mental *Liber autem Generatio* page (fol. 29r), and Christ on fol. 32v (Pl.72), but also the two most densely illuminated pages of the whole manu-script, the eight-circle cross on fol. 33r and the Chi-Rho page on fol. 34r. The precise significance of the cross of eight circles (Pl.69), and the exact reason for its positioning here, are difficult to determine, but it does probably relate to a page (fol. 1v) in the Book of Durrow where there is a double-armed cross with four others in a rectangular frame. The ebullient spiral ornament within the circles constantly changes and creates new tensions with every movement, and compar-ison with the Donore discs (p.73) shows how closely they are related to metalwork designs. Even if this ornament seems to be even more complicated than the workings of an old-fashioned watch, the clarity of its *perpetuum mobile* design can be contrasted with the seemingly impenetrable jungle of interlaced animals on the other panels of the page, where the individual snake-like creatures can, however, be unravelled or disentangled because each is colour-coded. Yet, for all its intricacy, this interlacing of animals is executed to perfection, with never a loop being missed and the whole design always superbly competent.

The same can also be said of fol. 34r (Pl.73), which bears the first letters of Christ's name in Greek – Chi Rho – which looks like an X with one leg extended, and a P followed by an I. They are used to illustrate the passage in Matthew I,18 describing the birth of Christ and introducing his name for the first time in the Gospel – *Christi autem Generatio*, and they were already the subject of a notable line of decoration on fol. 23r of the Book of Durrow. Both fol. 29r of the Lindisfarne Gospels and page 5 of the Gospels of St Chad in Lichfield Cathedral expand the three letters to cover one half or even more of a page, but the development reaches its zenith in the Book of Kells where the X alone takes up almost three-quarters of a page, and the P and I (Pl.74) make up a separate design in much of the remaining space, leaving scarcely any room for further text.

The gradual enlargement of this motif in these manuscripts shows clearly how Kells stands at the pinnacle of a lengthy development, though heaven alone knows how many lost manuscripts bearing the design may have contributed to the stage of development reached in the Book of Kells. The letters are the framework for an overall design which is broken up into many ornamental parts, all executed on a minute scale and with spiral and animal decoration. Microscopic examination shows it to be technically brilliant and, even without optical aids, it demonstrates a subtlety of asymmetry which brings the eye back for inspection again and again. There is constant rivalry between the individual animal and geometric elements, creating a tension which is heightened as rounded outlines battle for pride of

place with more angular and rectangular panels. In a composition which could only have been successfully executed by an inspired visionary who revelled in the perfection of minutiae to create the ultimate and indescribable, the artist has been able to introduce a number of unexpected elements – three angels who spread their protecting wings at right angles on the stem of the X, and human faces appearing in unpredictable places, including the innermost curl of the P, and the corners of the symbollically-significant rhombus at the junction of the limbs of the X.

But, most unusual of all, and the most commented-upon part of the page, are the small animals near the bottom – an otter catching a fish (a symbol of Christ throughout the Book) and cats and mice. Two large cats face one another, each having what seems to be a mouse on its back, and with two further mice between them, holding up a disc. This scene has given rise to a number of widely differing interpretations, allegorical, metaphorical or exegetical, usually with eucharistic connections. So much has been read into details like this in the Book of Kells that it is difficult to know how much the spiritual and exegetical studies of the monastic scriptorium are to be understood as having had an input into their creation, or whether we over-interpret in modern times, so that, in Swift's words

'... learned commentators view
in Homer more than Homer knew.'

For all we know, these cats and mice may have been intended as little more than comic relief in a page otherwise overladen with symbolism, and giving us a small but charming vignette of the smaller forms of life prancing around the scriptorium floor.

Part or all of some other pages have extensive decoration marking the beginning of specific important passages in the Gospels, as at the beginning of St John's Gospel on fol. 292r (Pl.75), and this is a feature which also occurs in the preliminary matter such as the *Breves Causae* of Matthew on fol. 8r. But the great majority of pages in the Book consist of text, and only two of those are undecorated. For the remainder, the initials of lines or chapters are decorated with wonderfully inventive letters, lively humans turning themselves inside out, animals fighting or interlacing acrobatically, or just geometric designs, all of which get little attention in comparison to the great decorative pages, but which are among the most constant delights in the Book. Scarcely

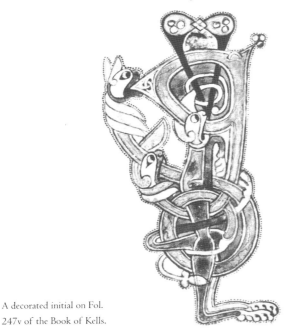

A decorated initial on Fol. 247v of the Book of Kells.

a single opening of the manuscript will fail to bring a smile of amusement and admiration to the viewer as one page after another is turned. Anticipating by half a millennium the drolleries of Gothic manuscripts, these decorations (e.g. Pl.77) are there to enliven rather than explain the text, though the hens and the cock on fol. 67r may have been intended to add an extra dimension to the parable of the sower and his seed which they accompany. The decoration seems to fit in so well with the text that the two must have been planned together. Though the beautifully-written text — 'a very masterpiece of calligraphy' in the words of E.A. Lowe — is fairly uniform, it has been suggested that at least three hands were involved in its creation, and at least three different artists have been put forward for the decoration of the manuscript, though scholars are not unanimous about which of them did what. There is also quite a possibility that some of the scribes and some of the artists may have been identical. We can at least presume that it was a closely-knit team which was involved in making the Book of Kells into the breath-taking performance that it is — and no amount of description or accolades will replace the experience of seeing the original manuscript and appreciating its magic. What that team created needs to be spoken of in hushed superlatives — an 'extraordinary wealth of decoration' (Nordenfalk), 'one of the great creations of western art' (Jacques Guilmain), with a 'richness and imaginative splendour' and 'astounding creative fecundity' (J.G.G. Alexander). For Françoise Henry, it towered above other manuscripts in profusion, variety, and perfection of minute execution. When compared to its nearest rival, the Book of Lindisfarne, the latter can be seen as a model of astounding inventiveness soberly controlled, whereas the Book of Kells has a contrasting wildness, a 'frenzy of excitement' in Margaret Rickert's phrase, a profusion of ornament which will not allow itself be repressed as it spills over into ever-new themes and variations. For all that, it has, too, a quality of mystery which has left us seeking answers, desperately and in vain, to the many questions it poses regarding sources and models, purpose, date and place of production.

For more than a century, scholars have been probing for the source of inspiration of the scriptorium which produced it. The text and preliminary matter, and even some of the spelling mistakes, seem to have been closely following the Book of Durrow, though at one or two removes. The decoration seems to owe something to the lead given by the Book of Lindisfarne, though not a product of the same milieu. Northumbria, the home of the Book of Lindisfarne, produced the Bede manuscript showing floral decoration before the Book of Kells, and offers another link in the form of the Virgin and Child composition found on St Cuthbert's coffin, now in Durham, though, as mentioned above, difference in detail would not suggest direct copying. Metalwork can be seen to have had its influence on the ornament, as seen for instance in the imitation of tronco-pyramidal enamelled metalwork bosses on the page of the eight-circled cross (Pl.69). Certain features of the Canon Tables, such as the filling of some of the spandrels, the full-length figures of the evangelist symbols in the tympanum, and the figures emerging from the top of the frame, as well as

Decorated initials on Fol. 253v of the Book of Kells.

Drawings enlivening the text of Fol. 201v of the Book of Kells.

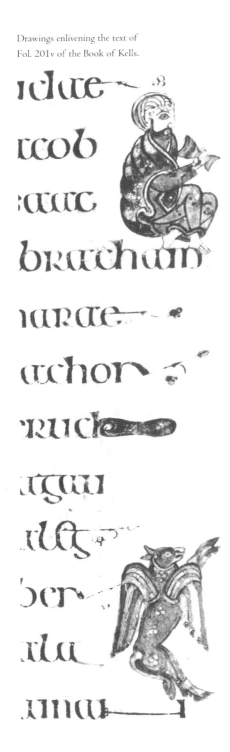

details elsewhere in the manuscript such as the drapery of the throne in the portrait of St John, have been invoked as characteristics which would scarcely have been possible without knowledge of the de luxe manuscripts of Charlemagne's court, such as the Harley Gospels, now in the British Library in London. The hunt for sources and parallels will doubtless continue, but the Book of Kells will be seen as a highly successful amalgam of influences coming from all quarters, north and south, yet moulding all into its own inimitable self, a zenith of insular production, never surpassed or even equalled.

It can be seen to be the high point of a development which can be traced back to the Books of Durrow and Lindisfarne, yet it had no followers which continued its tradition (though see below p.209). Were all the monks of its scriptorium – the best talent in all Britain and Ireland – struck dead by the Vikings, or could it be that the Book was not generally on view so that no one could copy its majestic style and decoration? Certainly, the manuscript could never have been used for study – the uselessness of the Canon Tables is sufficient proof of that. It was scarcely used for daily readings because its text, in the words of its present keeper, Dr Bernard Meehan, was written 'with a remarkable degree of inaccuracy'. Indeed, the textual carelessness, when compared with the exquisite perfection of the ornament, would suggest that it was not used for liturgical purposes such as readings from the altar, but was created for the beauty of its ornament, a one-off treasure made for a sacred occasion and then to be closed so that the eyes of the populace could not profane it – something like Verdi's

Requiem being composed for a single performance to honour the much-admired Manzoni. If a sacred cause were sought, it is most likely to be found in conjunction with the *persona* of St Columba, if not for the occasion of the 200th anniversary of his death in 797 (and we do not know if anniversaries were celebrated as early as that) – then perhaps for some translation of his relics. It is highly likely that it was seen as a Columban relic, if we can judge by the respect paid to it by the *Annals of Ulster* ('most precious object of the Western world') when it was stolen in 1007. In this context, it is significant, as Françoise Henry pointed out, that the manuscript was stolen not from the library at Kells, but from the western sacristy of the church (if that is what the Irish word *airdom* means), suggesting more a function as a sacred liturgical relic rather than a book for everyday use.

Of all the areas named as the most likely for the production of the Book of Kells – Ireland, Iona, Northumbria and Pictland in eastern Scotland – Iona is the one which currently finds most support. It was there that St Columba died and was buried in 597 and, by the eighth century at the latest, it had become a centre for learning and the arts. It was well endowed, wealthy enough to have had a herd big enough to choose 185 of the best calf-skins for use in the manuscript, and a capacity to maintain a scriptorium containing the finest artists and scribes integrated with well-read exegetes, as well as being able to muster the rare and expensive colouring materials necessary. It is more likely to have had all these accumulated advantages than the monastery at Kells, which was only a fledgling foundation in the early ninth

century and one to which the monks of Iona fled with some of their belongings when the Vikings made two devastating raids on the island monastery in 802 and 806. One of these raids took place in the same year as the death of Connachtach, 'a select scribe, and Abbot of Iona' in the words of the *Annals of the Four Masters*, and Françoise Henry thinks that he may have been one of the main scribes of our Codex. Paul Meyvaert noted that one figure in the Genealogy of Christ on fol. 201r (Pl.59) points to the word *Iona*, but was careful to remark that the island was known as *Í* and not Iona in the eighth and ninth centuries. But he did re-assure us, however, that in St Jerome's list of Hebrew names, Iona is glossed as Columba, the dove, which is the Latin name normally given to the saint who founded Iona, and whose Irish name is Colum Cille. Françoise Henry's predilection for what she called the Iona/Kells axis is still the most likely for the location of the scriptorium which produced the manuscript. If we could but discover the date, this would help to clarify the matter.

Apart from suggestions from the nineteenth century and earlier that the manuscript had been written by the hand of St Columba himself, a possibility which can now safely be excluded from the discussion, the date range proposed for the codex in recent times spans the century from about 725 to 825, with the greatest emphasis being placed on the period around 800. Many accepted A.M. Friend's argument, first published in 1939, that the break after fol. 5r in the Kells Canon Tables was copied from the late eighth-century Harley Gospels produced at Charlemagne's Court School because it showed a similar break in the same place. But this view was challenged for dating purposes when Patrick McGurk demonstrated that a mid-eighth century English manuscript also revealed a similar break many years earlier, though Guilmain rejected the 'faithful' copying of a faulty original as being the cause of the change in ornamental style between fol. 5r and 5v, suggesting instead that the decoration on the latter was executed by a later – and inferior – artist. Yet the features of the Canon Tables listed above, together with the drapery of St John's throne, are difficult to explain without having recourse to the notion that an illustrator of the Book of Kells had seen the Harley codex or some similar volume at the court of Charlemagne. Certainly, the lavishness of the Book of Kells, even when compared to the abundantly rich Book of Lindisfarne, suggests that the Book of Kells may have been seen by its creators and contemporaries as Northern Europe's answer to Charlemagne's munificence and magnificence. In richness of adornment, and in its profusion of full page miniatures, the Book of Kells certainly finds its best parallels in the Emperor's de luxe manuscripts, even if its style is Celtic and theirs classical. The comparison argues for a date for the Book of Kells of around 800, but that is not exact enough to decide the most likely place for it to have been created, presumably in a Columban milieu. If written before 804, when Kells was founded after the first of two destructive Viking raids on Iona in 802 and 806, then Iona is the obvious candidate but, if after 804, then Kells itself would have to be considered as a strong alternative.

To the other, smaller manuscripts which follow in the footsteps of the Book of Kells without even alluding to its existence, we shall return below (p.209).

A horseman on Fol. 255v of the Book of Kells.

6

Metalwork of around the
Year 800

■

'Tomb-shaped' Reliquary Shrines

The enshrining of relics was to play an important role in the development of religious metalwork in the later eighth and ninth centuries in Ireland. Probably as early as the 630s, the venerable city of Armagh had obtained from Rome relics of Saints Peter and Paul and these, together with the relics of St Patrick, were brought on a *commotatio*, a tour around the province, in 733, possibly in a leather satchel like that of some centuries later discovered by Dr Patrick Wallace in his excavation of the Viking city of Dublin. But, in preparation for such a journey, the relics must surely have been enshrined beforehand. In the year 800, Kildare – Armagh's great rival – provided a new shrine for the relics of bishop Conlaed, whose older sarcophagus (p.34) had been described in glowing terms by St Brigid's biographer, Cogitosus, in the later seventh century. The new shrine, which has

perished like its predecessor, was made of gold and silver, as was another prepared for the remains of Ronan, patron of Dromiskin, Co. Louth, in the following year. These instances may be symptomatic of a preoccupation with providing glistening reliquaries around the year 800, spurred on by the growing importance of relics which had manifested itself for a variety of reasons during the eighth century. A change in pilgrimage practice, first noticed by Kathleen Hughes, saw Irish pilgrims being discouraged from going overseas, and being presumably advised instead to go on pilgrimage to sites where Irish saints were venerated. Furthermore, the Second Council of Nicaea decreed in 787 that altars needed saints' relics before they could be consecrated. The most obvious place to find them was Rome, where the Catacombs had been heavily plundered for relics from the reign of Pope Paul I (757–767) onwards. This probably explains why two reliquaries of Irish or Pictish origin have recently been discovered in Italy, whither they were doubtless brought more than a thousand years ago to transport sacred relics back home. Others like them — somewhat larger successors of the Clonmore and Bobbio shrines mentioned above (p.31) — are known from Ireland and Britain, where they were made to contain relics of local saints, but also from northern Europe, where they were brought by Viking traders or looters from Irish or Scottish monasteries. Usually called 'house-shaped shrines', they are probably better described as 'tomb-shaped', as they presumably followed their continental counterparts (the *chasses*) in imitating the shape of a sarcophagus.

One of the two Italian specimens, that in the Tuscan monastery of San Salvatore on Mt. Amiata, still contains a relic. The other, empty, was discovered in the Museo Civico in Bologna by the Norwegian scholar, Martin Blindheim, who may well be right in considering it to have been made in Scotland. More probably Irish in origin are two shrines found in Norway, and now in the Trondheim museum, both characterized by a core of yew wood lacking in the Bologna example. One, from Melhus, bears round escutcheons with repoussé La Tène-style trumpet ornament and *millefiori* decoration on the side-hinges, as well as having a leather cord for carrying. The second, from Setnes, has rectangular escutcheons, but now deprived of their original decoration. Three shrines of similar type have been found in Ireland, all, curiously, recovered from water. One, from the river Shannon, is now in the National Museum in Edinburgh, while the other two, from Lough Erne

in County Fermanagh, are preserved in the National Museum in Dublin. The two Lough Erne shrines were found one inside the other, the smaller one measuring only 11cm long and 6.8cm high. Another shrine probably of Irish manufacture is almost as small — that known as the Emly shrine (Pl.80), now preserved in the museum of Fine Arts in Boston. It has round escutcheons decorated with deep green and yellow-coloured enamel set in T-shaped fields. This polychrome effect is heightened by the contrast between enamel and the background yew-wood of the casket, and the curious grille of gilded lead-tin alloy which has been let into it. This grille provides a stepped pattern, but its most striking feature is the recurrence of equal-armed crosses of arcs of a kind which, because carved in stone on a number of pilgrimage sites, may almost have been a 'logo' for relics associated with pilgrimage. This grille and the presence of an animal head on the end of the ridge pole relate the Emly shrine to that from San Salvatore. A detached ridge pole in the National Museum in Dublin has been shown by Raghnall Ó Floinn to have belonged to another reliquary, from Clonard in County Meath, where it was probably also rescued from the water.

The Moylough Belt-shrine

One early Irish metalwork reliquary of a very different kind is the belt-shrine (Pl.79) found during turf-cutting at Moylough, Co. Sligo, in 1945. Consisting of four gently-rounded parts, linked by hinges and with a buckle, it comes as no surprise to learn that, inside, it contains portions of a leather girdle. This doubtless once fastened the garment of a saint whose name is not recorded, but who must have been sufficiently important in the region for his relic to have been enshrined in such a comparatively opulent reliquary. The *Lives* of old Irish saints refer to such belt-shrines, and heap praise on them for the cures they brought about, but this is the only one of its kind known to have survived. The decoration around the buckle (Pl.82) shows off a variety of techniques at the master-craftsmen's disposal. On each side of the juncture there is a square or rectangular area framed with T-, L- or S-shaped fields of cloisonné enamels enclosing panels of silver foil die-stamped with spiral and conjoined bosses. From one side of the frame, animal heads with long snouts converge on, and bite, domed enamel bosses of a kind very similar to those encountered already on the Tara brooch and, more particularly, the Ardagh chalice, suggesting some link between the workshops which produced these two pieces. In the middle of the four fragments are circular medallions (Pl.81), some clearly showing the shape of the ringed cross which we shall meet again later, and these are decorated with enamel and *millefiori* glass. The bow of the buckle is formed by curved bird heads with long beaks. The style of the buckle has echoes of Burgundy in the period around 600, and the dates suggested for the belt-shrine have varied between the seventh and the ninth centuries. The die-stamped silver panels can certainly be compared to those found in a seventh-century Anglo-Saxon grave at Swallowcliffe Down in Wiltshire, but research showed that the Moylough panels did not fit

comfortably into their locations on the shrine, and may therefore have been re-used, thus making them unreliable for dating purposes. The use of an egg-and-dart motif on the surrounds of the die-stamped panels might — without any obvious proof — reflect Charlemagne's revival of classical Roman ornament during the 780s and 790s. While the style of the domed enamel bosses is reminiscent of those on the Ardagh chalice, they were also — *mutatis mutandis* — copied on the head of the west cross at Monasterboice which is scarcely earlier than the mid-ninth century. Robert Stevenson recently suggested a date early in the ninth century for the belt-shrine, and to see it as having been manufactured within a few decades on either side of the year 800 might not be too far from the truth. It is important, however, to recognize that the Moylough belt-shrine reflects continental styles of dress and ornament, indicating artistic contacts with the outside world at the time, as we have already seen in the Book of Kells.

Brooches

The same problem of dating faces us when we look to the splendid series of brooches which follow in the wake of the Tara and Hunterston brooches discussed above (pages 70–71), as they may belong to either the eighth or the ninth century, but at least we are on firmer ground in trying to establish the country of their origin through their shape. Unlike the Irish brooches, those from Scotland are truly penannular, that is, they do not form a complete ring, and the decoration is confined to the terminals and to a panel at the centre of the ring. In addition, the heads of the pins bear less ornament. We know from the old Irish laws that men wore brooches singly on their shoulders, in contrast to the women, who wore them on the breast. One fine illustration of a male wearing the brooch on the shoulder can be seen on one of the curious, stylized stone-carvings on White Island, Co. Fermanagh, which seem to be the products of a very individualistic school of masons operating on the shores of Lough Erne probably around the eighth or ninth century. The great stone Crosses, to be discussed below, also show examples of figures wearing similar brooches. One of these is the figure of Christ (Pl.103) in a Mocking scene on the west face of Muiredach's Cross at Monasterboice, suggesting that such brooches may have had a religious connection, and the 'Brooch of the Testament', the *Delg Aidechta*, was kept at Iona as a special relic of St Columba. In the series of Irish brooches of the later eighth or ninth century, the terminals — usually expanded into a roughly triangular shape — are joined by means of one or two bars, and are decorated with sunken panels of gold filigree. Critical junctions are frequently highlighted by the use of studs of glass, enamel and, increasingly, amber. Amber was becoming quite popular at this period, possibly coming from the Baltic along trade routes opened up by the Scandinavians long before the Vikings started descending upon Ireland in 795. Another material equally on the increase at the time, though not ultimately from the same source, was silver, from which many of these — and

subsequent — brooches were made. Unlike the fairly homogeneous Pictish brooches, the Irish examples — or what are taken to be Irish examples, as a number of them have been found in Britain — are much more varied and can only with difficulty be organized into groups.

One of the earliest of them, following after Tara and Hunterston, and dated by Robert Stevenson to around the second quarter of the eighth century, is a brooch found in a later (ninth century) Norse woman's grave at Westness on Rousay in Orkney, where the head is so small that the piece is normally described as a brooch-pin. It is decorated with a not very distinguished animal and interlace ornament in filigree of gold sheet, and with amber studs. Altogether more sumptuous is the so-called Londesborough brooch in the British Museum, whose provenance is sadly unknown, and which lacks filigree. But, for that, it has fine-quality animal, interlace and spiral ornament cast in gold, and the design is dominated by circular bosses divided into three or four parts topped with glass or amber. One of these bosses dominates each of the terminals, and the head of the pin. The hatched bodies of the animals hark back to the Tara brooch, but the appearance of fangs in gaping jaws looks more towards metalwork likely to date to the period around 800. Even more dominated by animal ornament is the brooch found on the Hebridean island of Mull, and now in the National Museum of Antiquities of Scotland in Edinburgh. The triangular panels of its terminals, as well as the cartouche at the top of the ring, are filled with contorting animals. Though found in Scotland, this brooch is almost certainly Irish. But other, probably Irish, brooches, such as the Cavan brooch (Pl.85), with circular ornament set in a trio of cusps on the terminals, show links with clearly Pictish brooches of a kind found in the Saint Ninian's Isle hoard in Shetland, but the use of human heads would argue for an Irish origin.

The combination of gold, silver and amber seems to dominate these brooches that may reasonably be ascribed to the early ninth century. The plain silver surfaces come into much greater prominence, as on the Loughmoe (formerly 'Tipperary') and Killamery (Pl.144–5) brooches and, to a lesser extent, the Roscrea brooch (Pl.78), all now housed in the National Museum in Dublin. The decoration becomes less refined, at times almost monotonous in its repetition, and the animal ornament becomes more stylized as it retreats further and further from its more recognizable forebears. The pin-heads turn from wedge-shapes into what are almost squares, as on one of the silver brooches found with the Ardagh chalice in 1868. A second brooch (Pl.90) from the same hoard might seem older in type, with

most surfaces on the front — including the stem of the pin — being decorated with variations of interlace in imitation chip-carving, but — unusually — the central meeting point of the terminals is characterized by three bird heads which stand out in high relief.

Shrine Fragments

This tendency towards animals emerging from the surface and rising in ever higher relief, which must have been developing certainly by around 800, is brilliantly shown on a gilt copper mount found at Romfohjellen in south-western Norway, but probably Irish in origin. Serpent-like creatures with hatched backs and snouts bite into one another after they uncoil themselves from hemispherical bosses of La Tène-type spirals (or from their own tails). The sense of irregular and asymmetrical motion created by the slimy snakes is reinforced by the seething and writhing of

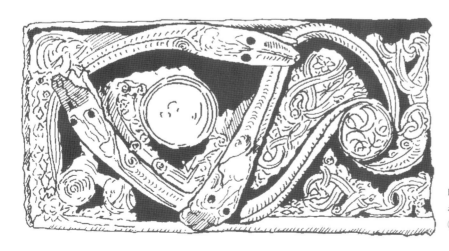

Reliquary fragment found at Romfohjellen, Norway (University Collection, Oslo).

79

80

81

82

83

84

86

87

88

89

similarly hatched animals which form the flat background from which the serpents rise. This remarkable composition, further enlivened with glass for the serpents' eyes and an amber stud, is one of the most animated of all early Irish pieces of metalwork, and must have decorated some highly-prized container – but of what we do not know. For its small size, it is impeccably executed, and its features are symptomatic of developments taking place in other, larger, specimens of metalwork, many of which are likely to be Irish – the most remarkable of which are the two bronze-shaped mounts preserved in the Musée des Antiquités in St Germain-en-Laye (Pl.84). Their surfaces on the front are covered with irregularly-placed high relief bosses uncoiling downwards from spiral or triskele ornament into hatched serpents which bite each other, or human heads also at the end of a coil. The background here is imitation chip-carving which, combined with human heads, is reminiscent of the Cavan brooch. Emanating from one end of the straight sides of these two St Germain mounts are sculptural animal heads which must have attached it to some object and acting perhaps, as John Hunt suggested, as the finials of a large sarcophagus, possibly resembling the twelfth-century stone example in Clones, Co. Monaghan, or, conceivably, as the terminals of a very large cross. The heightening of the relief may also have been going hand-in-hand with an increase in the size of metal objects (such as shrines) made in the period around 800, the approximate date of these two remarkable St Germain plaques. The flat spiral ornament on the back suggests that it was the side with the bosses which faced the public.

A more overtly religious object which also shows the tendency towards high relief in another way is the Antrim cross in the Hunt Museum in Limerick (Pl.86). This is an equal-armed cross, which may have been attached to the front of a shrine like the Romanesque example of St Manchan to be discussed below (p.295). It is ornamented with raised tronco-pyramidal bosses at the centre and at the end of each arm, probably signifying the wounds of Christ. The decoration of these bosses is traditional in some of its techniques, as instanced by the use of a fine blue and white cross-shaped *millefiori* in a quincunx formation at the top of the central boss. The use of yellow enamel is given variations in the form of interlinking angular fields of cloisonné, as well as arrow-shapes, and the form of the two animals on the central boss (Pl.87) could argue for a date for this cross of somewhere not too far removed from 800. A similar-shaped boss, but with angular fields of yellow enamel interspersed with blue and red, was found in the famous Viking ship-burial at Oseberg in Norway, which has recently been dated precisely to the year 834, thus providing us with a likely date *ante quem* for the Antrim cross without, of course, helping us to date it exactly. A unique bronze processional cross from Tully Lough in County Roscommon, partially re-assembled recently by E.P. Kelly in the National Museum, is also decorated with a tronco-pyramidal boss at the centre, but on the arms it has hemispherical bosses of the kind imitated in stone on crosses such as that at Dromiskin, Co. Louth. It also bears two openwork panels bearing a beast biting each ear of a mysterious standing figure with raised hands. The Oseberg ship-burial disgorged another insular piece of metalwork which shows us how these bright-coloured enamels must have proved attractive to the Viking eye in search of booty to bring back home from raids on Irish monasteries. This is a bucket bearing a handle-attachment in the form of a human figure seated in a Buddha-like pose, with crossed legs held by the hands. The body is a square dominated by a cross with blue and white *millefiori* inlay separating four squares decorated with interlocking T-shaped fields of enamel. Another Viking grave from Mykelebostad in south-western Norway produced a remarkably similar figure (Pl.91), also with the square torso, but subdivided in this instance into nine units decorated with *millefiori* and L-shaped cells of yellow enamel. The heads of both of these figures are mysterious, with a primitive strength in their features — mouth turning downwards, nose arching out into eyebrows in relief, and very protuberant eyes. The legs of the figures show the high relief in which they have been cast, and the prominence of the faces — together with their turned-down mouths — lead on to a consideration of one of the earliest clear representations of Irish religious figure sculpture in bronze or, more accurately, copper alloy.

The St John's (Rinnagan) Crucifixion Plaque

This is a plaque bearing a representation of the Crucifixion (Pl.89), found at St John's, Rinnagan near Athlone in the County of Roscommon, and now in the National Museum of Ireland in Dublin. Precisely what its purpose was is difficult to say. Rivet-holes at the corners show clearly that it was attached to something — but to what: a book-cover, a reliquary, or a piece of wood? Or could the bronze have served as an object to be kissed at the ceremonies of Good Friday? Whatever its original function was, it is one of the most remarkable pieces of Irish metalwork, and one of the earliest surviving to bear full human figures, albeit in a typically 'Celtic' stylized form which harks back to the evangelist symbol-figure in the Book of Durrow. Christ is placed against the background of his cross, which is only visible in the arms and in the top and bottom extremities. Resting partially on the indents of the arms are angels with tilted heads in high relief, and curving wings with interlace, herring-bone, spiral and fretwork decoration, against which can be seen a sword held by one of the angels' hands. The movement of the roundly-modelled legs of the angels show that they are moving towards Christ, in contrast to the figures of Stephaton and Longinus who seem to be statically frozen in time beneath the arms. Longinus pierces Christ's left arm-pit — the heart side preferred on most early Irish Crucifixions — while, opposite him, Stephaton (Pl.88) bears a pole on top of which is a chalice-like vessel seen in miniscule beneath Christ's chin as he offers the Saviour hyssop. These two flanking figures have their heads placed awkwardly and diagonally on their shoulders, looking as if they may have been copied from a manuscript. But this bronze Crucifixion is, curiously, a copy of another made up of a wooden core onto which a sheet of decorated metal was nailed. This is evident because the spiral ornament standing out in relief on Christ's breast and expanding outwards to form his arms can be seen to include small round bosses which can surely only be interpreted as copies of nail-heads used on the model to attach the high-relief bronze spiral ornament and arms onto what we can only presume to have been a wooden background. On that model, too, Christ's head would have been part of the wooden cross, rising more boldly from the background surface than any of the other features, while the ornament above his head and on the lower part of his long garment would have been carved into the wood. The age of this Crucifixion plaque is impossible to ascertain, the spiral ornament suggesting to many commentators a date not far from 700. But because the clean-shaven face of the Crucified Christ might be reflecting a fashion revitalised in the Carolingian renaissance, and as the decoration of the lower part of Christ's garment very closely resembles that on the South Cross at Clonmacnoise which may have been erected around the middle of the ninth century, we should consider a date in the later eighth or the first half of the ninth century for this captivating Crucifixion plaque.

7

Stone High Crosses of the Ninth and Tenth Centuries

■

THE GREAT STONE HIGH CROSSES for which Ireland is famous get their name from the Irish words *crois árd* found in the *Annals of the Four Masters* under the year 957, a fitting title for monuments which can reach a height of over 7m. The same *Annals* mention a 'Cross of the Scriptures' at Clonmacnoise, Co. Offaly, which is probably, but not certainly, the same as the main scriptural cross on the site which has been given that name in modern times, but otherwise the early historical sources provide us with no further enlightenment on the crosses. Since the middle of the last century, the High Cross – with its typical ring surrounding the junction of shaft and arms – has become one of the country's national symbols. Yet its origins are best sought outside Ireland and in other media. The earliest known ringed cross is on a textile of fifth–seventh century date

preserved in the Minneapolis Institute of Arts, but it is probably copying a metal model. Perhaps its earliest recorded use in Ireland is on the Ailill aue Dunchatho slab mentioned above (p.56) as dating from around 764. The ringed cross appears in metalwork on the Moylough belt shrine and, in manuscript, in the damaged Codex O.IV.20 from Bobbio, now in Turin, both undatable, but the earliest chronological fixed point for the form in manuscript is in the Dagulf Psalter of 783–795, Ms. 1861 in the National Library in Vienna.

The English were erecting stone crosses in Northumbria before the middle of the eighth century, and it has been argued that stone crosses on Iona belong to a later part of the same century. Yet there is no convincing evidence that any of the surviving stone crosses in Ireland were erected before 800 – though that is not to say that some of them might not be earlier, such as the fragmentary example at Toureen Peakaun, Co. Tipperary, with an as yet undeciphered inscription written in letters resembling those on the Ardagh chalice. For more than fifty years, it has been believed that the so-called Ahenny group of crosses in counties Tipperary and Kilkenny (see below, p.165–7) belonged to the eighth century on the basis of metalwork parallels, but doubt has been cast on the reliability of this chronology because, among other reasons, it is impossible to date the metalwork comparisons accurately. Inscriptions identifying historically-known kings come to our aid from the middle of the ninth century onwards, but one cross with inscription may be earlier, that at Bealin, Co. Westmeath. It bears the name Tuathgail which Françoise Henry equated with an abbot of Clonmacnoise named Tuathgall who reigned from 797 until 811, but as there is no evidence whatsoever to support her contention that the cross was brought to its present position from Clonmacnoise, the identification – and also the date of the cross – must remain uncertain. Nevertheless, the Bealin cross does belong to a group of related monuments which are centred on, and probably produced at, Clonmacnoise. This includes the North Cross and a pillar at Clonmacnoise itself, as well as two others – one also from Clonmacnoise and another from Banagher (Pl.97) nearby, which are both preserved in the National Museum in Dublin. Of these, Bealin is the only one to have a head, and the North Cross, being a shaft with a tenon on top for a missing upper part, may also have been an actual cross. But the remainder are pillars

undecorated on one face which may, therefore, have been placed against a wall originally, or have served a function similar to choir-screens, with only the decorated face and sides visible to the laity. The decorated faces and sides of each monument in the group are divided into panels of varying dimensions, bearing figure, animal and geometrical sculpture. Most striking is the single horseman, moving either to left or right, with hair curling noticeably at the nape of the neck and – in the case of Banagher – bearing a crook or staff. Also characteristic are the lions all proudly prancing to right or left, usually with foliate ends to their tails and doubtless inspired by classical images, but not necessarily from the Physiologus bestiary. The deer, bitten in the hind-leg by a dog at Bealin, and caught in a trap on the Banagher pillar, is probably also a motif borrowed from classical antiquity. While cross-shapes on the sides of Bealin and the Clonmacnoise shaft in the National Museum – clearly derived from metal-work prototypes – are the only clear indications of a Christian use for this group, the other characteristics already discussed are also likely to have had a religious significance – the riders may be 'saints on horseback', the lion probably a symbol of Christ, and the deer bitten or caught might have been intended to convey the idea of humankind being surrounded by evil. If so, the interlace of various forms (including human) which is part of the decorative scheme could also be taken to have had some symbolic significance, although at this remove in time we cannot say precisely what that may have been. Probably the finest impact in the whole group is made by the

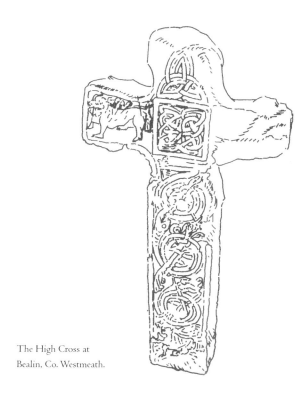

The High Cross at
Bealin, Co. Westmeath.

wonderful interlace of three superimposed, slender and long-necked birds on the east face of the shaft at Bealin, which is worthy of comparison with the Book of Kells. Leaving the inscription aside, it is that comparison which constitutes the most persuasive argument for an early ninth-century date for the cross and the whole group of Clonmacnoise monuments associated with it. Bealin is, therefore, likely to be among the earliest surviving carved High Crosses, and Clonmacnoise a credible candidate as the first focus for the development of stone High Crosses in Ireland. But before continuing with the story, it is best to look first at the political and religious background in Ireland before and after 800.

During the course of the eighth century, local kings and the Church were becoming more accommodating to one another, as reflected in the ecclesiastical input into the framing of secular law. In the closing two decades of the century, temporal rulers encouraged saints' relics to be carried in procession around the countryside to boost the proclamation of certain laws (and doubtless also to raise church dues in the process as well), and this may have been yet a further factor in increasing the number of reliquaries being made around that time. Co-operation between king and Church went a stage further in 804 when Aedh, king of the Cenél nEógain branch of the Uí Néill dynasty, who controlled most of the northern half of Ireland, had himself 'ordained' (hence his Irish sobriquet Oirdnide) or consecrated, probably by the abbot of Armagh. There are echoes here of Charlemagne's coronation by the Pope in Rome only four years earlier and, according to the Emperor's biographer, Einhard, the Irish kings regarded themselves as Charlemagne's subjects. His expansionist policies may have inspired Máelsechnaill I (846–862), king of the more southerly Clann Cholmáin branch of the southern Uí Néill, to broaden his own horizon and make himself High King of Ireland, which he virtually succeeded in doing.

During the course of the eighth century, too, the Irish monasteries were becoming so laicised that they were even prepared to go to war with one another, as mentioned above (p.68). It is no wonder, then, that such laxity produced a campaign for reform during the last decade of the century which was known as the Céle Dé or Culdee movement. Meaning literally 'Servants of God', this was an appeal to return to the asceticism of the early monastic ideals, and a denunciation of the wealth and worldliness of the monasteries. The Culdee strongholds were 'the two eyes of Ireland', Finglas and Tallaght in Dublin, as well as Terryglass in Tipperary, while Castledermot, Co. Kildare, was another foundation inspired by them. They also had their friendly contact with Columban foundations, particularly Iona, but their relations with the temporal power of Aedh Oirdnide were very much frostier, perhaps all the more so as he held sway over most of the province of Leinster where their monasteries lay. But the rise of Culdees, whose influence lasted until around 900, started only a few years before the arrival of the Norse Vikings, whose independent status in Ireland was to cover approximately the same period. Their first Irish landfall was in 795 on the island of Rechra — either Rathlin, Co. Antrim, or Lambay off the coast of north County Dublin — and for the next quarter of a century they made sporadic raids on Irish monasteries, from which they doubtless took away many of the pieces of religious metalwork which have been discovered in the ground of their homeland in south-western Norway. After 820, their raids became more persistent and penetrated deep inland and even up the Shannon as far as Clonmacnoise. By 841, the Vikings had established a colonial trading post in Dublin, and later they were to found important towns at Waterford, Wexford and other locations along the coast. It is against this background of closer Church-state relations, political expansion, monastic laxity and reform, as well as the frightening initial onslaughts of the Vikings, that we should now try to see the evolution of the Scripture Crosses, which were too heavy to be taken away as booty far across the seas.

Characteristic of many of the Irish High Crosses is the decoration with biblical sculpture and ornamental motifs, together with the ring or wheel which enfolds the junction of arms and shaft. The ring has a structural function on stone crosses in keeping the arms in place and preventing them from snapping off because of the weight — particularly as the arms usually have a notch above and below which weakens their strength at mid-point. The cavity created between ring and arms is not a device likely to have been invented by a stone-mason who would have feared the cracking of his stone as he burrowed deeper and deeper; instead, it is more likely that the ring came into being in some other medium such as metalwork. But the ring must also have had a symbolic significance. A re-vitalisation of the pagan sun motif, and a victory garland for Christ, have been suggested. But, given that the centre of the cross was nearly always occupied by a representation of the Crucifixion which, for early Christians, was the most important event in the whole history of the universe, is it not preferable to see the ring as a cosmic symbol, with Christ at its very centre?

One of the most unusual aspects of the Irish crosses is the application of panels of biblical sculpture to the faces and sides of the cross. It is probably significant that this rare feature is found also on a small enamelled cross in the Vatican Museums, dating from the time of Pope Paschal I (817–824), thus giving us our first hint that Italy had a significant role to play in the development of the Irish High Cross, a suggestion supported by strong emphasis on the iconography of St Peter present on the crosses at Monasterboice, Co. Louth (p.160–2). In contrast to the love of stylization in most early Irish representations of the human figure, as found for instance in manuscripts and the St John's (Rinnagan) Crucifixion plaque (Pl.89), the figure sculpture on High Crosses – often in quite high relief – is seen to be more naturalistic, and likely, therefore, to have been inspired from some source where the classical style of sculpture was practised – be it in Italy or further north in the central European heartlands of the Carolingian empire.

The origin of this sculpture has been the subject of considerable debate – a native development in wood or some other material, images imported through manuscripts or icons, Carolingian ivories, or even ideas brought in by itinerant stucco workers whose work in Ireland, now vanished, was later translated into stone on the High Crosses? Ivories can virtually be ruled out as an immediate source because such valuable objects rarely went beyond imperial or high episcopal courts on the Continent, but the graceful figures in the Tempietto at Cividale in northern Italy, dating perhaps from around the end of the eighth century, support the case for stucco as a contributory source, as this was a material also known to have been used for ecclesiastical and figure sculpture in northern France during Charlemagne's lifetime.

The choice of biblical subjects on the crosses corresponds closely to what we know of cycles painted on the walls of early Christian churches in Rome and from the remarkably well preserved frescoes further north at Müstair in the eastern Swiss canton of Graubünden. What we can glean further from literary sources about the lost frescoes commissioned by Charlemagne's son, Louis the Pious, for his palace chapel at Ingelheim on the middle Rhine, would suggest that the reason for selecting particular subjects among the frescoes also applied to the choice of scenes on the Irish High Crosses. Indeed, the same kind of 'pattern books' which would have been used by the fresco painters may well have served as an inspiration for the sculptural compositions on the Irish crosses – which could once have been coloured like the frescoes, though not a trace of paint remains. In churches, frescoes were there to illustrate the Bible story for those who could not read or to illustrate a point of religious dogma, as well as to induce feelings of piety in the mind of the beholder – and exactly the same motivation could be claimed for the sculptured panels on the Irish crosses. John Higgitt pointed out that the reason why the inscriptions on the Irish High Crosses were on the base of the shaft (rather than higher up, at eye-level, as in England) is that they were to be read by those kneeling in prayer in front of the crosses. This consideration can help to explain why, on some of the crosses, the biblical sequence of pictures is not followed in ascending order up the shaft, but that some particularly important subject that needed to be stressed – such as Christ in the Tomb (Resurrection) or the Baptism of Christ – is placed at the bottom of the shaft.

91   Enamel-decorated hook mount attached to a hanging-bowl
      found in a ninth-century Viking grave at Myklebostad in
      Norway (Historisk Museum, University of Bergen).

92   West face of the ninth-century granite North Cross
      at Castledermot, Co. Kildare.

In the many centuries that have passed since the crosses were carved, knowledge of the identification of many of the individual sculptured panels on the crosses has been lost, so that interpretations of their content vary considerably. Many, however, present no problems. Among the most common are Adam and Eve (Pl.99) and the Crucifixion, so popular because they cover the events from the sin of our first parents to the moment when Christ gave his life on the cross to save mankind from its effects. Sometimes the Old Testament events illustrated on one face of the crosses prefigure events in the life of Christ on the other. One example is Cain slaying Abel, coupled in a single scene with their parents Adam and Eve on Muiredach's Cross at Monasterboice (Pl.105), balancing the first innocent victim of the Old Testament with Christ as *the* innocent victim of the New, though it is curious that nowhere does the scene of Isaac bringing the wood to his own sacrifice find its natural New Testament correspondent in Christ carrying his cross to Calvary, which became standard in later iconography.

The frequency of David's appearance on the crosses reflects both his position as father of the house to which Christ belonged, and the triumph of good over evil, as in his victory over the Philistine Goliath. Another frequent theme is God saving from danger those who are faithful to him and hear his word, as exemplified by his guiding the Israelites through the desert, and providing water for them to drink, or in two events illustrating incidents in the Book of Daniel — Daniel himself in the Lions' Den, and the angel

saving the three Hebrew 'children' from the fiery furnace.

The selection of New Testament stories covers the three cycles in Christ's life – childhood, public ministry, and his Passion, Death and Resurrection. Among the childhood scenes, the most popular is the Adoration of the Magi, Christ's first appearance to the Gentiles in the form of the Magi – four on one occasion, coming each from a different corner of the earth. One childhood scene inexplicably absent on the crosses is the Nativity, so popular in Europe from the fourth century onwards that its omission must say something about the Irish psyche – but what? Equally popular in western art was the Baptism which, as the introduction to the public life of Jesus, was also frequently illustrated on the Irish crosses, while the Marriage Feast of Cana and the Multiplication of the Loaves and Fishes are the only miracles making more than one appearance. With Christ's Crucifixion occupying the central position on the west face of most of the crosses, it is natural that scenes of the Passion and Resurrection are close by, though the absence of the Last Supper surprises even more than the Nativity. Even up to the Carolingian period, artists found it difficult to come to terms with illustrating that incredible moment of the Resurrection, and on the Irish crosses, the nearest approach to the subject is Christ lying in the tomb with a bird breathing into his mouth to signify the moment of his re-awakening to life. Back to back with the Crucifixion, the Last Judgment occupies the east face of a number of the more elaborate crosses, but the Second Coming of Christ and the

Majestas Domini are also occasionally present. Most of the figure sculpture on the crosses illustrates biblical personages, the most obvious recognizable exception being the desert fathers Paul and Anthony, whose communal breaking of bread is a Eucharistic symbol making up for the absence of the Last Supper, but also a memory of two holy men who would have been models for the religious in the monastery where the crosses were erected.

One of the interesting features of the iconography on the Irish crosses is the use of apocryphal material. One example is the scene of Daniel in the Lion's Den on the cross at Moone (Pl.119), where the seven lions shown correspond to the number mentioned only in the apocryphal parts of the Book of Daniel.

Another surprise on the Scripture Crosses is the apparent copying of an unusual John the Baptist cycle on the narrow side of some of the crosses, pointing to the importance of Baptism as a theme on the crosses.

Kells Crosses

In the first millennium, Baptism and the Eucharist were the only two acknowledged sacraments, and the emphasis laid on Baptism as a cleansing from sin is made clear on one of the most interesting of all the crosses from the iconographical point of view, even though only the lower half of it has survived. This is the so-called Broken Cross at Kells (Pl.100). Identification of its panels has long created problems because more than half of their subjects do not appear on any of the other crosses, but the best guess would suggest the following: (see below).

This table shows that eight out of the twelve subjects must have been purposely chosen to include water, in order to stress the importance of the sacrament of Baptism. Noah's Ark and the Passage of the Israelites through the Red Sea, as examples of people saved through water, together with the Samaritan woman at the well, were all symbolically interpreted by the early Church

WEST FACE OLD TESTAMENT	EAST FACE NEW TESTAMENT
The Passage of the Israelites through the Red Sea	The Entry of Christ into Jerusalem
	The Magi questioning Herod
The Pillar of Fire	The Washing of the Christ child
Moses turning the waters of Egypt into blood	The Lame Man at Bethesda + The Samaritan woman at the well
Noah's Ark	The Marriage Feast of Cana
Adam and Eve	The Baptism of Christ

Fathers as parallels to Christ's Baptism. Adam and Eve (Pl.99) may be regarded as the First Generation while the Baptism of Christ back-to-back with it could be interpreted as the Re-Generation of mankind – and it was that very Baptism scene that the pious would have seen on the bottom of the shaft as they sank to their knees to say a prayer in front of the cross. Old and New Testament scenes back-to-back with one another are also contrasted and connected, of which Adam and Eve and the Baptism provide just one example. Another connection is the equine theme at the present top of the shaft, with the horses of the Egyptians perishing in the Red Sea on one face as the Saviour sits side-saddle on his pony entering Jerusalem at the start of his Passion on the other. The panels beneath likewise betray a further interesting parallel between the supernatural light which appeared in the form of a pillar to lead the Israelites through the desert and the star which brought the Magi before Herod, to question him about the whereabouts of the Christ child. This Pillar of Fire and the miracle of the lame man at the pool of Bethesda are both biblical examples of the Lord helping the faithful in their time of travail. This unique and very thoroughly thought-out iconography at Kells shows how crosses such as this can be made to impart a particular message of faith which goes far beyond a simple succession of biblical scenes in approximate chronological order. Even in its broken state, this cross still stands to a height of 2.61m above its base and, when complete, it was probably 5m or more tall, one of the most imposing and mighty of all the Irish crosses.

It is not inconceivable that it was also among the first of the great stone crosses with the main faces decorated with relief sculpture. The series of scripture crosses in general are distributed in the midlands, east and north of the country and, when taken together, they amount to the greatest assemblage of sculpture from the Carolingian period to survive anywhere in Europe. Kells itself has one of the most important collections in Ireland for, in addition to the Broken Cross just mentioned, there are three more. One of these is unfinished, its uncarved bosses standing out in high relief beside others which have been partially finished, giving us an insight into the work-processes involved. The Market Cross has both faces and sides packed with sculpted panels, most presumably biblical in content, though some are difficult to identify, and pageants of horsemen and warriors on the base are not easy to fit into a religious context. Unlike the Broken Cross, it mixes Old and New Testament on one face, placing Christ in the Tomb on the bottom of the shaft with Old Testament figures above. It also has some unusual New Testament scenes – such as the Centurion's Servant and 'Suffer little children to come unto me' – on the other face. A fourth cross (Pl.98, 121), in the shadow of the Round Tower which dominated the old monastery at Kells, does not have its panels so neatly compartmentalized as on the other two, with unframed bands of interlace dividing the individual parts, suggesting that it may be later than the two completed crosses. It is unique among the Irish crosses in having a Latin inscription on the base – *Patricii et Columbae Crux*, 'The Cross of Patrick and

Columba' – which, because it puts the name of Patrick, the national apostle and patron of the Armagh diocese, before that of the founder of the monastic family to which Kells belonged, may signify that Kells was making a gesture of deference or compromise towards Armagh, into whose sphere of influence it came when founded from Iona in 804. A link with Armagh may be found in the iconography of the Kells crosses, as in the presence of Noah's Ark on the Broken Cross and on one cross in Armagh that also shares with it a strict division of Old and New Testament material on the faces. Unusual animal ornament on another cross at Armagh is also very similar to that on south side of SS. Patrick and Columba's cross. Kells and Armagh may have been among the first important Irish centres for the production of High Crosses with scriptural sculpture, but as the Kells crosses act as a link between the biblical material on the northern and other midland crosses which they do not share with one another, it is quite possible that Kells may have been the pivotal distributor or disseminator of iconographical material on the Irish crosses. Wherever it got its inspiration from for these biblical compositions, it seems improbable that it came from the parent monastery at Iona, which does not display the same range of biblical subjects on its crosses. Northern France (Rheims or Corbie?) might be a more fruitful area to search for the origin of the Irish High Cross iconography. The combination of Adam and Eve, their offspring Cain and Abel and the desert fathers Paul and Anthony on the arms of the cross, is a Kells feature found also on the two great crosses at Monasterboice in Co. Louth, which are among the best known and best preserved in the whole country, and to which we must now turn.

Monasterboice Crosses

A twelfth-century *Life* of St Columba tells of his visiting Monasterboice whose founder, Buite, is said to have foretold Columba's birth on the day of his own death. The West Cross at Monasterboice is the tallest in Ireland. The other, lower but more thickset, is called Muiredach's cross, after the man who had it made, according to an inscription on the bottom of the west face. The West cross has the head and shaft carved from two slightly different-coloured stones (which may possibly not even have belonged together originally). The head is one of the most accomplished pieces of early medieval carving to survive in Ireland. Despite exposure to the weather for a thousand years, the rounded, well-modelled faces of the figures attest the high quality of the original carving which – as on most High Crosses – can best be appreciated on the underside of arm and ring, untouched by acid rain (e.g. Pl.106–7). As on the Market Cross at Kells, the east face combines Old and New Testament iconography, the centre of the head (Pl.101) featuring a very curious figure armed with sword and shield and bearing a staff, whom Kees Veelenturf has recently identified as Christ at his Second Coming. Occupying the same position, back-to-back with it, on the west face, is the

Crucifixion surrounded by Passion scenes. The influence of Rome in the iconography of this cross can be sensed through the presence of St Peter in a number of panels on both faces of the head. Some of the bosses on the ring of the west face echo so closely the metal and enamel examples on the Ardagh chalice and the Moylough belt shrine that they — and probably the whole cross — must be a copy of another, smaller prototype designed in other materials. Other interesting iconographical features of this West Cross at Monasterboice are the apparent John the Baptist panels on the narrow south side, and the presence on the bottom of the west face of the shaft of Christ in the Tomb and his Baptism one above the other, suggesting that their messages — the Resurrection of Christ and the significance of Baptism — were among the most important for those kneeling in prayer in front of the cross.

Muiredach's cross (Pl.102) has, in comparison, a much broader shaft which allows for more figures to be portrayed in the four panels on the east face, while the west face confines itself to three, each with a trio of large figures as commonly found in Carolingian compositions. The figures are squat, naturalistic and well modelled with rounded faces and, where male, sometimes with splendid moustaches; it is one of the best-preserved — and crowded — of all the Scripture crosses. The fleshy rotundity of the Adam and Eve/Cain and Abel panel (Pl.105) at the bottom of the east face, when compared to the reduced plasticity of the same panel on the Market Cross and Cross of SS. Patrick and Columba at Kells, shows up the greater mastery of the Monasterboice sculptor. The east face of the Monasterboice shaft exhibits the combination of Old and New Testament, as it bears panels of David's victory over Goliath, Moses smiting the rock to obtain water for the Israelites in the desert, and the Adoration of the Magi, one above the other. At the centre of the head is one of the finest surviving representations of the Last Judgment to survive in European art from the first millennium — Christ standing in the centre with his arms crossed in an Osiris-like pose, flanked immediately by David and his musicians, beyond whom good souls face him on one side while, on the other, the bad souls are banished to their eternal damnation by a trident-holding devil. The bad souls turn their backs on Christ, except for one who tries to turn the clock back, as it were, but too late — as he is swept along the well-worn path to Hell. Beneath is one of the oldest examples of a scene often associated with the Last Judgment in medieval art — The Weighing of Souls. The devil is seen lying on his back trying to upset the balance of the scales bearing a soul in one of its pans, but he is thwarted by St Michael who rams a staff down the devil's throat — all carved with an impish sense of humour also present in the frolicking animals and beard-pulling men (Pl.104) on the base of the shaft. The New Testament figures on the shaft of the west face (Pl.103) have a nobility, deriving partially from the space the carver has allowed between them, but also because the faces — particularly that of Christ as the central person of the trio — show the mason's ability to impart a beatific dignity of expression. Immediately above the cats on the base of the shaft – around whom are woven (secondarily?) the inscription mentioning the Muiredach who commissioned the cross – we find Christ mocked by soldiers as King of the Jews. His cloak (which must surely have once been painted scarlet or purple) is held together on his right shoulder by a penannular brooch of Irish type, showing that these biblical compositions on Irish crosses were no slavish copies of continental models. The various panels on this west face of the cross have been open to a variety of interpretations. The middle panel of the shaft has been seen as Doubting Thomas which, however, is better understood as the non-biblical scene of the Raised Christ (implying his mission to the apostles) as found on the apses of Roman churches of the fifth to eighth centuries. Above this is Christ handing over his ministry by giving the New Testament to St Paul and the keys of the Kingdom of Heaven to St Peter. At the centre of the head (Pl.102) is the crucified Christ accompanied by angels, Stephaton and Longinus, the heads of sun and moon, and also symbolic figures probably the elements Earth and Ocean as sometimes found on Carolingian ivories. Adjoining all of these are representations of the Resurrection and Ascension. Worthy of note, too, on Muiredach's cross is the top, made of a separate stone and carved in the shape of a building with shingles on the roof and bearing figure sculpture on the sides. Its resemblance to both the 'Temple of Solomon' scene in the Book of Kells (Pl.63) and the house- or tomb-shaped reliquary shrines (e.g. Pl.80) has given rise to much discussion as to its significance – *Ecclesia, the* Church – or *a* church, or a stone version of a movable metal shrine which could have been detached from the metal or wooden cross on which the design of Muiredach's cross was presumably based, and it may be noted how the spiral decoration on the south side of the cross (Pl.108) looks like a copy of a metalwork panel.

Durrow and Clonmacnoise Crosses and Inscriptions

Some other features of Muiredach's cross such as the pageant of horsemen and fabulous animals on the base or, more particularly, the snakes intertwining human heads on the underside of the ring (Pl.106–7), are encountered again on crosses at Durrow and Clonmacnoise in the midlands of Ireland, so that one ought to envisage a workshop of masons and designers (probably, though not certainly, monks) travelling from one site to another. Both the Durrow cross and the Cross of the Scriptures at Clonmacnoise share with the West cross at Monasterboice tronco-pyramidal arm-ends which are obviously copied from enamelled metal bosses. The Durrow Cross has one, and probably two, St John the Baptist scenes on the narrow side like the West cross at Monasterboice. With Muiredach's cross (Pl.108), it also shares noticeable horizontal markings on the vertical corner mouldings on the shaft that are best explained as imitating the joints of cylindrical strips of piping used to hide the jagged edges of the sculptured panels on the models on which we must presume these crosses were based. The shaft of the east face of this Durrow cross has what is

East face of the High Cross
at Durrow, Co. Offaly.

probably a Raised Christ panel and a Sacrifice of
Isaac enclosing above and below a field of interlace
which must have had some symbolic significance

is an eschatalogical configuration of figures related
to the Book of Revelations. The west face of the
shaft of the Durrow cross (Pl.109) and the Cross

of the Scriptures in Clonmacnoise (Pl.93 and 95–96) show a marked similarity in their Passion scenes. Other panels on the Clonmacnoise cross have proved difficult to interpret satisfactorily, though a number would appear to be so related to the Passion and post-Crucifixion Gospel narrative that the theme of the whole cross is best understood as illustrating the events between Palm Sunday and Easter. This cross is perhaps the most elegant of the whole series in its tall slender proportions, and graceful uplifting of the arms which are recessed outside the circle (Pl.94).

Without enumerating individual traits, the crosses already mentioned – the Market and Broken crosses at Kells, the two at Monasterboice and the Durrow and Clonmacnoise examples – are sufficiently closely interrelated to form what is perhaps the most important group of High Crosses in the country; it is also the most enterprising in its wide selection of biblical themes. But most of them are also chronologically and historically interesting because of their inscriptions, a number of which have only in recent years been deciphered – at least in part – through the efforts of Liam de Paor and Domhnall Ó Murchadha together with his son Giollamuire. The easiest of these to read is that on Muiredach's cross at Monasterboice (Pl.103), stating that Muiredach had the cross erected, but leaving us tantalizingly ignorant of who he was. Less well preserved, but more informative, is the inscription on two faces of the base of the shaft of the Cross of the Scriptures at Clonmacnoise (Pl.93–94) which can tentatively be reconstructed as 'A prayer for king Fland son of ....., a prayer for

the king of Ireland, prayer' followed on the other face with 'for Colman who made this cross for (?) king Fland'. From this it would appear very likely that the Cross of the Scriptures was erected by Flann (or Fland), son of Máelsechnaill, who reigned as High King of Ireland from 879 until 916. From the fact that the cross (before its recent removal to the nearby Interpretative Centre) stood directly in front of the Cathedral which king Flann had erected with Colman, the abbot of Clonmacnoise, in the year 908, we might derive a neat date for the erection of the cross, which would coincide with the reign of a Muiredach as abbot of Monasterboice from around 891 until 922, thereby placing both crosses in the first quarter of the tenth century. But things are not quite so straightforward because, on another cross (Pl.110) presently at Castlebernard, near Kinnitty in County Offaly, two other inscriptions were deciphered as follows: 'A prayer for King Máelsechnaill, son of Maelruanaidh, a prayer for the king of Ireland' and 'A prayer for Colman who [made the] cross for the king of Ireland, a prayer for the king of Ireland'. This less-accomplished cross was presumably made by a king of Ireland named Máelsechnaill, who happens to have been the father of the Fland named on the Clonmacnoise cross, and he reigned from 846 to 862. But the presence of the name Colman in the Kinnitty inscription must cast some doubt on the identification of the Colman on the Clonmacnoise cross as the abbot of that name, and raise the possibility, aired by Liam de Paor, that he was a master sculptor who could have carved both crosses. If the same Colman created the

Castlebernard cross as well, the 908 date would be too late, and thus the creation of the Cross of the Scriptures in Clonmacnoise might have to be advanced to some time not too long after the start of Flann's reign in 879. But even this is not definite; Colman was a common name in early Ireland, and it is quite possible that the Colman names on the two crosses might refer to two different people. Further complications arise from an inscription on the Durrow cross which, as already mentioned, is iconographically close to the Cross of the Scriptures. One inscription on the west face does not provide a readily identifiable name, but another on the north side, though poorly preserved, can reasonably be reconstructed to include the name of king Máelsechnaill — leaving the options open as to whether it was commissioned by him or was commemorating the achievements of a dead man (which might help to explain why the inscription is on the narrow north side rather than on the broad face). Much more battered is the inscription on another Clonmacnoise cross, the South Cross, with a Crucifixion on the shaft of the west face, but otherwise decorated largely with interlace and trumpet patterns (Pl.III), and also some animal interlace close to that on the ring of the Cross of the Scriptures. Little remains of this inscription but it could well have included the name Máelsechnaill, though this is less certain than on the Castlebernard cross, owing to the bad state of preservation. One way or another, these inscriptions make it very likely that the Castlebernard cross can be dated to the years 846–862, and the Cross of the Scriptures to the period between 879 and 916. It is possible that the Castlebernard cross was an early work, and the Cross of the Scriptures a late work, of the same master mason named Colman. What all the inscriptions do make clear is that the crosses can no longer be seen in a purely religious context. They were commissioned by the highest secular authority in the land, namely the High King, thus giving them a new role as part of a political programme designed to document the importance of the Clann Cholmáin High Kings. They also raise the possibility that the Muiredach who commissioned the Monasterboice cross which bears his name may not have been either of the two abbots known to bear this name, but a king who has not yet been identified. The lack of inscriptions on the northern Irish crosses may be explained by their being erected by the Church authorities who did not feel it necessary to record the fact.

The Ahenny Group of Crosses

Máelsechnaill was one of the first Irishmen who could lay claim to the title 'King of Ireland', which he records obsessively on the crosses. Perhaps imitating Charlemagne, he stretched his conquests beyond his own immediate territory until he became master of virtually the whole of Ireland. One of his victories, though of short duration, involved marching through the southern province of Munster to establish his dominance there in 854 and again in 856. Three years later he followed Charlemagne's treatment of Desiderius by humiliating his rival and brother-in-law Cerball mac Dúnlainge, king of Ossory, whose territory lay just on the far side of the Munster border in the present county of Kilkenny. The creation of an individualistic group of crosses erected on both sides of the dividing line between Kilkenny and the east Munster county of Tipperary may possibly have had something to do with his campaign. They are sometimes called the Ossory group, but are best known from two crosses at Ahenny (Pl.116), on the Tipperary side, which have been widely assigned to the eighth century because of the similarity of their carved ornament to metalwork ascribed, though without reliable evidence, to the same century. More recently, scholars have been introducing novel arguments, including the sophistication of the stonecarving techniques, to suggest that these crosses may be no earlier than the ninth century, potentially even contemporary with some of the great midland crosses, including those probably commissioned by Máelsechnaill. Half a century ago, R.A.S. Macalister believed that he could see the name Máelsechnaill inscribed on one of these crosses (Killamery, Co. Kilkenny) long before the king's name was ever deciphered on any of the midland crosses – but no one since has ever been able to share Macalister's insight. Nevertheless, the possibility that Máelsechnaill's name may appear on the South Cross at Clonmacnoise could support this suggestion, as it and the Ossory crosses are also largely ornamented with interlace and other geometrical decoration, with biblical illustration playing only a minor role.

Ahenny, on high ground overlooking the stream which divides Munster and Ossory, is a site with no apparent monastic tradition. The two crosses there rise from strong bases, while the crosses themselves (Pl.116) are decorated with interlace, spirals and spiralling animal ornament, human interlace, fretwork and other motifs which strongly suggest that both (and others of the group) were copied from wooden crosses with decorated metalwork sheets attached, like that from Tully Lough, Co. Roscommon (p.147). The five bosses on the heads, which doubtless symbolise Christ's five wounds, must also have had metalwork analogues. Those on the South Cross in particular bear comparison with the enamelled bosses on the Northumbrian processional cross now in Bischofshofen in Austria, dating probably from the eighth century. A pair of animal heads trying to bite the lowermost boss on the west face of the South Cross is particularly close to those from Irish metalwork, and the very thick mouldings framing the cross outlines have strong echoes of metalwork. Both Ahenny crosses do, however, have figure sculpture on the base, the South Cross concentrating mainly on horsemen of the kind found on the Scripture crosses of the midlands. The seven figures on the west side of the base of the North Cross correspond closely to those representing The Raised Christ/Mission to the Apostles in the same position on the Cross of the Scriptures at Clonmacnoise, and two of the other sides of the same base may be ornamented with David and Goliath scenes which, though unique, reflect the same iconographical content found on the midland crosses. The large headless body, which may reasonably interpreted as Goliath, is also found on a cross-head at Dromiskin, Co. Louth, which shows close links with metalwork. A cross on the Ossory side of the stream, at a place called Kilkieran, shows similar characteristics, including the unusual tiara-shaped capstones, and horsemen on the base, but lacking biblical sculpture. Another cross of the group is that of Killamery in County Kilkenny, which differs in style, and has what seems to be John the Baptist iconography on the end of one of the arms (and the baptism-related subject of Noah's ark on the other), allowing a further comparison with the midland crosses without, however, proving any contemporaneity. Perhaps a stronger argument for seeing the Ahenny group and the midlands crosses as being of roughly the same period is the triple division of the geometrical ornament on the base of the main cross at Kilkieran finding good parallels on cross-bases at Lorrha, Co. Tipperary and Seir Kieran, Co. Offaly, as well as on the South Cross at Clonmacnoise. The idea of connecting the trail of these crosses — Clonmacnoise, Seir Kieran, Lorrha, Ahenny and Kilkieran — with the advance of Máelsechnaill from his Clann Cholmáin base in Westmeath through Offaly into Munster and on to Ossory is little more than hypothesis, but the notion of paralleling the Ahenny-Ossory group with crosses in the midlands is becoming increasingly more attractive than seeing the former as precocious eighth-century predecessors of the great Scripture crosses of the ninth and early tenth centuries.

Castledermot and Moone Crosses

Another important group of High Crosses of roughly the same period is found spread along the valley of the river Barrow in counties Kildare and Carlow, with an outlier north of the Liffey at Finglas and undecorated examples in Ferns, Co. Wexford. The two most important sites are Castledermot and Moone, close to one another in the southern part of County Kildare. The granite from which the crosses were hewn does not facilitate the rounded modelling achieved in the sandstone of the midland crosses, but has caused the mason to carve his figures and ornaments in a rather shallow and sometimes rough relief. The iconographical programme behind the selection of biblical material on these crosses is not always clear, particularly at Castledermot, but one feature which is common to many of them is the presence of the twelve apostles who are not represented together on crosses of other groupings. This may reflect the adherence to Bible readings practised by the Culdees, one of whose members — Diarmait — was almost certainly responsible for the foundation of Castledermot around 812. He probably came from Tallaght, one of the Culdee centres which is documented as having had contact with Kells in County Meath. This may help to explain a curious coincidence in the iconographical content of the North Cross at Castledermot and the Market Cross at Kells, both of which share an animal-hunting scene on the base (Pl.113), David as harpist and the Sacrifice of Isaac on the head (Pl.115), and an emphasis on the desert fathers Paul and Anthony, whose asceticism would have been a model for the Culdees. Unlike Kells, but paralleled on another Scripture cross at Duleek in County Meath, the back of the South Cross as Castledermot has purely geometrical decoration (Pl.112). The South Cross has its head separate from its shaft – the mortice and tenon construction can be seen through a break in the stone (Pl.115) – but the North Cross (Pl.92 and 114) is monolithic, standing on a base with spiral ornament interspersed with round and diamond-shaped bosses. These look very like imitations of the heads of nails that one can imagine having been used to hammer similarly-decorated bronze panels onto a wooden core of whichever cross stood as model for this one. The North and South crosses have similar biblical content, but one unusual feature of the North Cross is the placing of Adam and Eve at the centre of the head on the west face, stressing more clearly than on any other of the crosses the link between the sin of our first parents and Christ's redeeming death on the cross, portrayed back-to-back with them on the east face. The only other case of an Old Testament scene occupying the central position back-to-back with the Crucifixion is, interestingly, once more the Market Cross at Kells, which has Daniel in the Lions' Den in this position, with arms outstretched like Christ on the cross.

Even more appealing in its stylization than the Castledermot crosses is that at Moone (Pl.119) which has recently been moved into the later medieval church on the site. Unique in Ireland in its tall, slender design, the base and cross combined reach a height of just over 7m. The only biblical figure on the cross itself is the figure of Christ at the centre of the head. Other human figures (including angels?) are not readily identifiable, and animals both real and fabulous occupy much of the remainder of the surface, together with spirals (some with animals uncoiling from them) and a diamond-shape. But the real joy of Moone are the carvings on the base, sculpted by a master stylist who may also have been responsible for another cross displayed in fragments nearby. Except for Adam and Eve on top of the east face of the base, who are portrayed in the round, the figures are in an attractive flat false relief. The base at Moone is one of the rare instances on the Irish High Crosses where the sequence of biblical scenes is to be read from top to bottom, the reason in this case being to allow Adam and Eve be placed back-to-back with the crucified Christ at the top of the west side, as on the North Cross at Castledermot. Beneath the Crucifixion at Moone are the twelve apostles, who are arranged in three rows of four one above the other (Pl.120), with their square bodies reminiscent of the bronze human escutcheon on the bucket from Myklebostad (Pl.91). Beneath Adam and Eve on the east face is old Father Abraham preparing to decapitate his son Isaac when the Lord's angel tells him to sacrifice instead the ram shown above Isaac's back. Beneath this again is Daniel, who was equally saved by the Lord from providing a good meal for the seven ravenous lions flanking him, as the apocryphal story in the Book of Daniel relates. The recognized part of the Book of Daniel continues around the corner on the south face with the three Hebrews (Pl.118) being protected by the Lord's angels from certain death in the fiery furnace. Beneath this is a charming representation of the Flight into Egypt (Pl.117), showing Joseph pulling a pony on which ride the Virgin and child, Christ being represented only by his head, placed at a diagonal to the Virgin's. The remarkable similarity of this scene to one surviving among the Carolingian frescoes at Müstair in Graubünden makes it clear that this panel at Moone must have been painted originally, with Christ's body shown in colour lying across the flat, angular body of the Virgin — one of a number of indications which should convince us that the Irish crosses were once polychrome. At the bottom of the south side of the base is a very graphic demonstration of the Multiplication of the Loaves and Fishes — five flat circular loaves, two flat fish and two eels(?) — which is so striking that it can make its impact and impart its message without even showing Christ who had caused the miracle to happen. These last five scenes were obviously selected to show how the Lord can save the good and the faithful in time of danger — Isaac threatened with death by his father, Daniel and the three Hebrews likely to be killed because their belief in God was forbidden by the Babylonians, the Holy Family being rescued from the peril of Herod by the angel appearing in a dream to Joseph, and finally the faithful listening to the word of God on the mount being sustained from hunger by Christ's miracle. The north side of the base is occupied by two scenes involving the desert fathers Paul and Anthony, and a beast with six heads and legs perhaps of apocalyptic inspiration.

Moone was known as a Columban foundation from at least around 900, if not before, and it was, therefore, probably in contact with Kells, the head of the *paruchia* of Columban monasteries after the first decade of the ninth century. This presumed link with Kells, together with the iconographical similarities between the Market Cross there and the two Castledermot crosses, could suggest that the Barrow valley crosses (and another less decorative example on the important Culdee site of Finglas in the Dublin suburbs north of the Liffey) were derived from Kells. As suggested above, this would help to identify Kells as the pivotal developer of High Crosses, with one branch forming the midland group of Monasterboice, Durrow, Clonmacnoise and others, and a second group spreading southwards along the Barrow valley. The question is best left open whether the northern crosses — well represented by Arboe, Donaghmore, Clones and Armagh — are derived from Kells or have a separate origin. Indeed, there may well have been a number of sources for the iconography of the Irish crosses, as some scenes such as The Adoration of the Magi are represented by two totally different compositions. The cross at Arboe in County Tyrone reaches the impressive height of 5.70m, but it is the only one in the North of Ireland to have remained intact. All its sides and faces are covered with biblical sculpture which, like most of the other crosses in northern Ireland, tend to repeat the same Old and New Testament subjects, and keep them rigorously apart on the individual faces. The Ulster crosses are less adventurous in the extent of their biblical coverage than their counterparts in the east and midlands of the country.

One major difference between the Irish and the British stone crosses of the last quarter of the first millennium is the proliferation of narrative biblical scenes on the former, so obviously visible on the eastern and midland group of Irish crosses, where the greatest innovation and variety is to be

West face of the High
Cross at Arboe, Co. Tyrone.

found. This may well reflect developments which had been taking place on the European continent during the first half of the ninth century, when the representation of biblical narrative cycles held in check by Charlemagne was given free rein under his son Louis the Pious (814–840). His lost

Ingelheim frescoes and those still preserved at Müstair show considerable similarity with the choice of themes on the Irish crosses. Great ninth-century Irishmen such as Sedulius Scottus, who went to Liège around 848, and Johannes Scottus Eriugena who amazed the imperial court at Soissons with his genius, may have been treading paths which, in reverse, could have brought back iconographical innovations from the continent to Ireland. Naturalistic figure sculpture with squat figures like those on the Carolingian ivory diptych in Aachen could have come along the same routes and been adapted by Irish sculptors and stone-masons on the Irish High Crosses, particularly after death of Louis the Pious in 840. By that time Ireland – and the European continent – had been suffering heavily from the incursions of the Vikings. Their spoliation of Irish monasteries had already become intense by 820, causing many metal objects to be taken as booty to Scandinavia (where they were saved for us by being buried in the ground, rather than being melted down as they would have been had they stayed in Ireland). Some of these may have been metal crosses of a kind copied at Ahenny or elsewhere, and the question may be asked whether the need for 'Bibles in Stone' was the reason for creating Scripture Crosses from 850 onwards, or whether their appearance in stone was partially connected with a desire to thwart the Vikings' lust for booty, in addition to allowing Church and state express their new-found confidence in one another by erecting monuments of their patronage?

93 The west face of the Cross of the Scriptures in front of the ruined Cathedral at Clonmacnoise, Co. Offaly, illustrates scenes from Christ's Passion and Resurrection.

94 The east face of the Cross of the Scriptures at Clonmacnoise features Christ in Judgment at the centre of the head.

95 The Cross of the Scriptures at Clonmacnoise: detail of Christ being mocked on the west side.

96 The Cross of the Scriptures at Clonmacnoise: detail of the west face showing soldiers asleep on the stone above the body of Christ in the tomb.

97 Pillar from Banagher, Co. Offaly, now in the National Museum of Ireland, Dublin.

98 The west face of the Cross of SS Patrick and Columba at Kells, Co. Meath, has the Crucifixion placed, unusually, on the shaft of the cross.

99 The Broken Cross at Kells, Co. Meath: the disarmingly naive Adam and Eve on the west face.

100 The theme of the cleansing power of water on the Broken Cross at Kells is epitomised in the Baptism of Christ scene at the foot of the east face.

101 The head of the Tall (or West) Cross at Monasterboice, Co. Louth, is among the finest examples of early medieval stone carving in Ireland.

102 The well-preserved Cross of Muiredach at Monasterboice emphasises Christ's Passion, Resurrection and Ascension on its west face.

103 Muiredach's Cross at Monasterboice is called after an unidentified Muiredach named in an inscription at the foot of the shaft, above which are panels representing Christ being flanked by soldiers and SS Peter and Paul.

104 Muiredach's Cross at Monasterboice: beard-pullers (signifying discord?) on the north side of the shaft.

105 Muiredach's Cross at Monasterboice: Adam and Eve share a panel with their offspring Cain and Abel on the east face.

106 Less affected by wind and rain, the undersides of arm and ring of Muiredach's Cross at Monasterboice best preserve the crispness of the original carving.

107 Snakes and heads surmounted by the Hand of God under the arm and ring of the north side of Muiredach's Cross, Monasterboice.

108 Muiredach's Cross, Monasterboice: 'Inhabited vinescroll' and human interlace separated by a panel of metal-inspired decoration on the south side of the shaft.

109 The High Cross at Durrow, Co. Offaly: the shaft of the west face shares similar Passion scenes with the Cross of the Scriptures at Clonmacnoise (Pl.93).

110 Recent decipherment of the worn inscriptions on the bottom of the cross at Castlebernard, Co. Offaly, has revealed that it was erected by the High King Máelsechnaill I (846–862).

111 Overall ornament on the east face of the South Cross at Clonmacnoise, Co. Offaly.

112 Geometrical ornament on the east face of the South Cross at Castledermot, Co. Kildare.

113 South Cross, Castledermot: a hunting scene on the base.

114 The North Cross at Castledermot has a Loaves and Fishes panel on its base.

115 The South Cross, Castledermot: The Crucifixion is flanked by David the harpist and Abraham about to sacrifice his son Isaac.

116 The North Cross at Ahenny, Co. Tipperary, has many features probably copied from metalwork.

117 The cross at Moone, Co. Kildare: the charming Flight into Egypt panel.

118 The Moone Cross: an angel protecting the three faithful Hebrew 'children' in the furnace illustrates how God can save the good in time of danger.

119 The Moone Cross: the narrative biblical scenes beguilingly carved in flat relief are confined to the base of this unusually tall and slender cross.

120 The Moone Cross: the Apostles in their serried ranks may have had their bodies painted with designs like those on Pl. 91

121 Biblical scenes and interlace merge smoothly on the Cross of SS Patrick and Columba at Kells, Co. Meath, which gets its name from a dedicatory Latin inscription on the base.

122 The twelfth-century cross at Dysert O'Dea, Co. Clare (possibly an assemblage of two separate fragments) demonstrates a wide variety of decorative ornament on the west face.

94

95

96

97

98

99

100

103

104

105

106

107

109

110

112

113

114

117

118

119

8

The Early Churches

■

ABURGEONING REALIZATION OF THE monumental power of stone shown in the High Crosses can also be felt in the slow emergence of stone churches at around the same period. Although the great megalithic tombs scattered around the Irish countryside are clear evidence that pagans used stone in the service of their own religion, it took centuries for Christianity to do the same in Ireland on any widespread basis. The old Irish word for these churches was *damliac*, and one of the earliest indications for their existence is the use of the word in the name of the County Meath village of Duleek, where there was a church dedicated to St Cianán, who is traditionally said to have been a contemporary of St Patrick. Reference in the *Annals of Ulster* to the death of a man in front of a no longer identifiable stone church in Armagh (*in hostio oratorii lapidei*) in 789, shows that there were

stone churches in some of the larger establishments towards the end of the eighth century, but it is only slowly that the number of references to them begins to increase in the course of the following two hundred years. For a country with such missionary and artistic vigour in the seventh and eighth centuries, it comes as something of a surprise to learn that most of Ireland's churches were simple wooden structures even well into the second millennium.

St Bernard of Clairvaux, in the *Life* of his friend, St Malachy, the great Irish church reformer of the twelfth century, refers to him constructing a church (*oratorium*) of smooth planks in a couple of days, which he calls 'an Irish work of sufficient beauty'. How little had changed down the years can be seen from the Venerable Bede's description of the church built five centuries earlier by the Irish saint Finan at Lindisfarne on the east coast of England, which was constructed 'according to the custom of the Irish, not of stone, but entirely of sawn oak', and roofed probably with thatch. The old Irish word for such a church is *dairtheach* (or *duirtheach*), meaning a house of oak, which was presumably the best wood for the purpose. A fifteenth/sixteenth-century manuscript, H.3.17 in the Library of Trinity College, Dublin, reproduces a text written probably three or four centuries earlier, defining the payment for craftsmen building such wooden churches: 'If it be a *duirtheach* of fifteen feet (5m) in length and ten in breadth, he should receive a heifer for every foot in length if the roof be of rushes (or thatch), and a cow for every foot and a half in length if it be of shingles.' The price would go up if the church were more than fifteen feet in length, but would not vary if the church were made of stone. From this, one gets the impression that fifteen feet by ten (4.5 × 3m) must have been the norm for the proportions of such churches. We do have two significant descriptions of wooden churches, both apparently dating from the seventh century. The first comes from the Latin A-Text of the *Hisperica Famina*, a work which far outrivals James Joyce in complexity of meaning. Michael Herren's heroic attempt at its translation produced the information that the church described in it was square, and fashioned from 'candle-shaped beams', suggesting that it was made up of tree-trunks, entire or halved along their length, and presumably placed vertically like those in the Anglo-Saxon church at Greensted in Essex, which has recently been dated to the later eleventh century. It had, furthermore, a vaulted roof, a central altar, a west doorway with a portico in front of it, and four steeples on the top (presumably one for each corner). Square beams were placed in the ornamented roof. The very much later (twelfth-century?) *Life of St Maedoc of Ferns* describes the legendary builder Gobán Saer as having erected a church 'with wondrous carvings and beautiful ornaments'. How sad that none of these carvings survive (if they ever existed in fact), but it is possible that the depiction of Solomon's Temple in the Book of Kells (Pl.63), and the shingled cap-stone of Muiredach's cross at Monasterboice (Pl.102) may give us some inkling of the style of some of the ornament used. Equally sad is that the author of the *Hisperica* gave up the unequal struggle of describing the innumerable objects in the interior, but the Donore handle (p.73 and 83) helps to fill the gap by giving us some idea of the high-quality furnishings which even simple box-shaped churches may have had. But the other seventh-century description is somewhat more specific about the interior. It appears in a *Life of St Brigid*, by Cogitosus, one of the earliest Irish biographies along with Muirchú's *Life of St Patrick* and Adamnan's *Life of St Columba*, and concerns a church in the town of Kildare which, as we have seen (p.34), was an important rival to Armagh. Patroness of Ireland, Brigid herself is a saint often confused with a pagan goddess of the same name, but she must represent a real person whose bones were enshrined in the sarcophagus which her biographer praised for its sumptuousness, and who founded in Kildare what was – for Ireland – a unique double monastery for nuns and monks, which is what gives the church its distinctive character. Cogitosus describes it as follows, in Ludwig Bieler's translation:

Its ground-plan is large, and it rises to a dizzy height, It is adorned with painted tablets. The interior contains three large oratories, divided from one another by walls of timber, but all under one roof. One wall, covered with linen curtains and decorated with paintings, traverses the eastern part of the church from one side to the other. There are doors in it at either end. The one door gives access to the sanctuary and the altar, where the bishop, with his school of clerics and those who are called to the celebration of the holy mysteries, offers the divine sacrifice to the Lord. By the other door of the dividing wall, the abbess enters with her virgins and with pious widows in order to participate in the Supper of Jesus Christ, which is His flesh and blood. The remainder of the building is divided lengthwise into two equal parts by another wall, which runs from the western side to the transverse wall. The church has many windows. Priests and lay persons of the male sex enter by an ornamented door on the right-hand side; matrons and virgins enter by another door on the left-hand side. In this way, the one basilica is sufficient for a huge crowd, separated by walls according to state, grade and sex, but united in the spirit, to pray to the almighty Lord.

Being the centrepiece of one of those rare double monasteries, the church at Kildare must have been very much the exception rather than the rule. But the description certainly makes it clear that its windows let in enough light to appreciate its interior decoration, painted tablets – possibly icons of the kind which Roger Stalley suggested may have been the origin of some of the iconography on Irish High Crosses – tapestries, and perhaps even frescoes, together with the silver and gold sarcophagi of St Brigid and Bishop Conlaed, decorated with precious stones and repoussé figures, and with crowns of precious metals hanging from the ceiling above.

There is a sense of Byzantine richness about the interior of this church, but it must have been larger than the norm if we are to judge by the measurements of the rare traces of wooden churches which have come to light through excavation during the last forty years. The largest, discovered on the island of Inishcealtra in Lough Derg, Co. Clare, was a rectangular building 8 × 5m, consisting of walls about 1m in thickness and made of earth reinforced with wattles, but its excavator, Liam de Paor, found no evidence to provide a date. In County Kerry, two wooden structures have been unearthed beneath stone oratories. One was at Reask on the Dingle Peninsula, where Tom Fanning found that later activity had disturbed all but two of the holes in which the wooden posts had stood. M.J. O'Kelly was more fortunate on Church Island near Valentia on the Iveragh Peninsula, where he recovered six post-holes which suggested the former presence of a wooden oratory 2m wide and 3m long.

What is of particular interest here is that both were built over by oratories of a kind which are emerging as the earliest datable Irish stone churches.

Oratories of Gallarus Type

These stone oratories are called after the finest and best-preserved example at Gallarus (Pl.126) on the Dingle Peninsula in County Kerry. Though comparable to the *bories* in Gordes (Vaucluse), they are probably an independent local development from the beehive huts – small round structures built in the corbel principle and without mortar, of which there are hundreds of ruined examples on the same peninsula, though the best specimens are preserved on the dramatic island of Skellig Michael (Pl.123–4). When the corbel method, ideal for round buildings, is adapted for use in rectangular buildings, there is a danger that the long sides will first sag and then collapse inwards; Gallarus and Skellig Michael are the only places where the long sides have survived intact. Externally, Gallarus looks like an upturned boat, with triangular gables receding like a forehead, and the side walls curving in a gentle parabola until they meet each other in a ridge at the top. About twenty such oratories are known, mainly near the western seaboard, and two have recently provided material for radiocarbon dating.

The first was uncovered by Jenny White Marshall and Claire Walsh on a tiny Co. Kerry island, Illaunloughan near Portmagee, which is only one quarter of an acre in extent. The oratory, measuring 3.2 × 2.20m and now roofless, sat on a *leacht* or stone platform, and was probably preceded by a stone church and, even earlier, by two oratories built of sods. Carbonized material overlying the clay floor of the stone oratory provided a calibrated date of between 640 and 790. Also on the island were a small beehive hut, and a shrine consisting of two large slabs resting together like the sides of a roof, presumably the burial place of an early hermit to whose grave pilgrims would have resorted. The other datable oratory was excavated by Gerry Walsh on the summit of Croagh Patrick in County Mayo and, though now roofless, it shows signs of corbelling. It measures 8.80 × 5m, and a charcoal sample from beneath the interior stone collapse of the oratory gave a calibrated radiocarbon date of between 430 and 890, thus centreing on a date around the seventh century. The presence of this oratory on the top of Ireland's holiest mountain, which pilgrims have climbed annually since time immemorial, supports the suggestion that Gallarus and other similar oratories of the kind in County Kerry ought to be seen in conjunction with a maritime pilgrimage up and down the west coast of Ireland which finds its literary expression in the famous medieval travel tale *Navigatio Brendani*. Radiocarbon dates are suggesting that these corbel-built oratories were built perhaps as much as a century and more before the first historical reference to an Irish stone church in 789, but their distribution along the west coast may mean that they had no direct influence on the development of the normal Irish stone church with upright walls and a roof of thatch or shingles.

How long such corbelled oratories continued to be built we do not know, but it is interesting to note that a curious internal mechanism in Gallarus providing for a door which swings upwards from below finds its only Irish parallel on the external door of the twelfth-century church of St Kevin in Glendalough (p.322) leaving open the possibility of a later date for Gallarus.

Early Churches of Stone

St Columb's House at Kells in Co. Meath (Pl.125) has been equated by some with the church historically recorded as having been founded around 807 for the Columban monks fleeing from the Viking raids on Iona. The two radiocarbon determinations provided by Rainer Berger's Los Angeles laboratory of 650–890 and 654–786 for the mortar in the lower part of this building could support such an identification, while still allowing the upper (and probably later) part with the stone roof to be dated to the twelfth century. Oratories on islands off the west coast – High Island, Co. Galway, Caher Island, Co. Mayo, Teach Molaise on Inishmurray, Co. Sligo, and St Michael's church on Skellig Michael – which have upright walls unlike the corbel-built examples, have provided mortar radiocarbon datings compatible with the last three centuries of the first millennium, thus making them into a second generation of stone churches later than the corbelled oratories built for pilgrimage traffic on these islands. The majestically simple church on St Macdara's Island, Co. Galway (Pl.128) has roof stones imitating wooden shingles suggesting that, even as late as the twelfth century, stone churches were faithfully copying details of earlier wooden oratories on these west coast islands. Another structure that was almost certainly built for pilgrims and provided a radiocarbon date of between 681 and 881 is the miniature St Ciarán's church at Clonmacnoise (Pl.127), the smallest structure on the site and almost certainly the tomb-shrine of the monastic founder, St Ciarán, who died around 549. While showing many signs

of wear and repair down the years, it still retains its basic original shape of a rectangle with an inclining doorway and *antae*, so typical of early Irish stone churches. *Antae* are the projections of the south and north walls out beyond the east and west gables and, as Harold Leask suggested, they are almost certainly a translation into stone of the corner posts of wooden churches. If the date be correct, it suggests that at some time broadly around 800 the first attempt may have been made to copy in stone a wooden shrine which had formerly contained the relics of St Ciarán, possibly to avoid their destruction by fire, or to provide a more sturdy structure for an increasing number of pilgrims coming to venerate them. This small church, and those on the west coast mentioned above, may indicate that increased pilgrimage activity may have been a factor in the gradual change-over from wooden to stone churches before and after 800.

Close to this small shrine at Clonmacnoise, measuring scarcely more than 4m in length, is the Cathedral which, despite having measurements of only 18.8 × 8.7m internally, is nevertheless the largest church known from pre-Norman Ireland (seen in the background on Pl.93). In shape it, too, is a simple rectangle with *antae*, and its west doorway (later replaced by a Romanesque portal around 1200) is off-centre because, as Conleth Manning demonstrated recently, its present south wall lies about 2m inside the line of the original one. If it is identical with the 'great church' which Irish Annals record as having been built around 908 by the High King Flann Sinna and the Clonmacnoise abbot Colman – which is likely but not certain – then the Cathedral could also lay claim to be the oldest identifiable datable church in Ireland. The alignment of the Cross of the Scriptures with the Cathedral's west doorway (Pl.93) tempted Manning to conclude that the cross was contemporary with it. Only slightly smaller in size (14.71 × 9.05m), and with dimensions almost exactly corresponding to those of the Golden Section, is the Cathedral at Glendalough (Pl.130), which has *antae* at both ends, as well as put-log holes in the west gable of the same kind as those found on the original wall of its Clonmacnoise counterpart. Conleth Manning has argued that the rectangular ashlar in the lower courses of the walls of the nave and the rubble masonry above them do not indicate two separate building phases, but that the lower ashlar masonry was taken from an earlier church and

re-used, as were the stones of the doorway. Though the dimensions of the Glendalough Cathedral are only marginally smaller than those at Clonmacnoise, the round relieving arch over its lintelled doorway is so comparable to that of the twelfth-century St Kevin's church nearby that the Cathedral at Glendalough could be considerably later than that at Clonmacnoise. It is of interest to note in both cases that what we may take to be the tomb-shrines of the founding saints were not incorporated into the Cathedrals, but left free-standing not far away, unlike continental churches where the saint's tomb was usually incorporated into the crypt.

These two Cathedrals, with the possible addition of the oldest part of Clonfert Cathedral in County Galway, are the largest stone churches

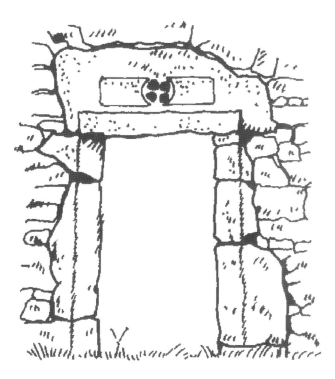

Lintelled doorways of Trinity Church, Glendalough, Co. Wicklow and St Fechin's church at Fore, Co. Westmeath.

known to have been built in Ireland before the 1140s. The church at Trevet, Co. Meath, might be taken to have also been a large church because the *Annals of the Four Masters* record its burning in 860 with the loss of 260 people within but, as Kees Veelenturf has pointed out, because the latest edition of the *Annals of Ulster* reduced the number to 70, our idea of the size of the church must also be amended. That would suggest dimensions corresponding more closely to those of the nave of the Protestant church at Tuamgraney, Co. Clare (Pl.129), which may possibly be identical with the church recorded in the Annals as having been built by abbot Cormac O Killeen who died in 969, thus making it probably the oldest church still used for divine service in Ireland. Even the largest of these churches is devoid of any carved ornament though they may, of course, have made up for this through striking interior decorations that have perished, like those described by Cogitosus in the vanished church at Kildare. Only a very few Irish churches likely to be pre-Romanesque in date bear

any embellishment, and this is in the form of a cross carved above the doorway, as on St Fechin's church at Fore, Co. Westmeath, or the church at Clonamery, Co. Kilkenny (Pl.131) (the saltire cross under the soffit of the lintel of the church of St Mary in Glendalough may be twelfth-century in date). Otherwise, these churches are simple undecorated rectangles, with doorways inclining upwards and often covered with a massive lintel many tons in weight. They normally have only one window, usually round-headed and splaying widely inwards in the east wall. Ann Hamlin's description of wooden churches as 'keeping faith with a deeply revered inherited tradition' also applies to the unadorned box-shaped stone churches which continued to be built as late as the twelfth century in Ireland. That this was due to tradition rather than to an inability to build higher and bigger is shown by the Irish mason's talents in constructing Round Towers which will be considered below (p.246).

123 The breath-taking location of the beehive huts, oratory and church on the island of Skellig Michael off the south-west coast of Kerry.

124 Skellig Michael: the dry-stone beehive huts – one with a cross picked out in white stones over a window – could have served both monk and pilgrim as protection against the wild Atlantic weather.

125 St Columb's House, Kells, Co. Meath: the characteristic stone roofing may have been added in the twelfth century to the building begun some three hundred years earlier to house relics of St Columba.

126 Gallarus oratory, Co. Kerry – an age-old masterpiece of mortarless masonry.

127 Weakened from over-use by pilgrims and, therefore, much repaired down the centuries, the small stone tomb-shrine of the founder, St Ciarán, at Clonmacnoise, Co. Offaly, stands in the shadow of the Round Tower of St Finghin's church (Pl.163).

128 St Macdara's church on an island off Carna, Co. Galway: a monument of timeless simplicity, and noble scion of a conservative Irish building tradition.

129 Tuamgraney, Co. Clare – Ireland's oldest church still in use. The nave, built probably in the tenth century, has an inclining doorway with heavy lintel, and *antae* projecting from the gable – typical features of Ireland's earliest churches.

130 The roofless Cathedral at Glendalough, Co. Wicklow, is the second largest pre-Norman church in the country.

131 Clonamery, Co. Kilkenny: the church dedicated to St Brendan has an equal-armed cross crowning the raised architrave that runs around the sturdily simple doorway.

126

9

Towards the Turn of the Millennium

■

DEBATE HAS RAGED FOR DECADES as to the effect the Vikings had on Irish art, some saying that it was disastrous, others believing that it has been exaggerated. Perhaps there is a bit of both in it. Certainly the illumination of Irish manuscripts takes a down-turn in quality as the ninth century progresses, but it is difficult to put all (or any) of the blame for this directly on the shoulders of the Viking raiders. Other reasons which could be invoked are the destruction of good manuscripts (remember how few large codices survive from the period between the Books of Durrow and Kells in the previous century), the possible dearth of high-quality scribes and the cost of scriptoria after the unique peak of achievement in the Book of Kells, echoing a similar decline in the Imperial Court School at Aachen following Charlemagne's death in 814. After Kells, everything was bound to be an anti-climax, but are we right in assuming that quality subsequently declined to a disastrous level (see p.130)? After all, it is possible that the St Gall 51 and Bobbio/Turin O.IV.20 manuscripts may be later than Kells, and what about the description of a great codex which the twelfth-century Welshman Giraldus Cambrensis saw at Kildare, which makes it sound so like the Book of Kells that some people think it was! One large surviving manuscript probably later than Kells testifies to the apparent continuation of some quality. This is the Macregol (or Rushworth) Gospels bearing the shelf-mark Auct. D. 2. 19 (S.C. 3946) in the Bodleian Library in Oxford. The colophon on the last page indicates that Macregol was both scribe and illuminator of the manuscript. He was an abbot of Birr in County Offaly who died in 822, though how long before his death the manuscript was completed we do not know. While it would

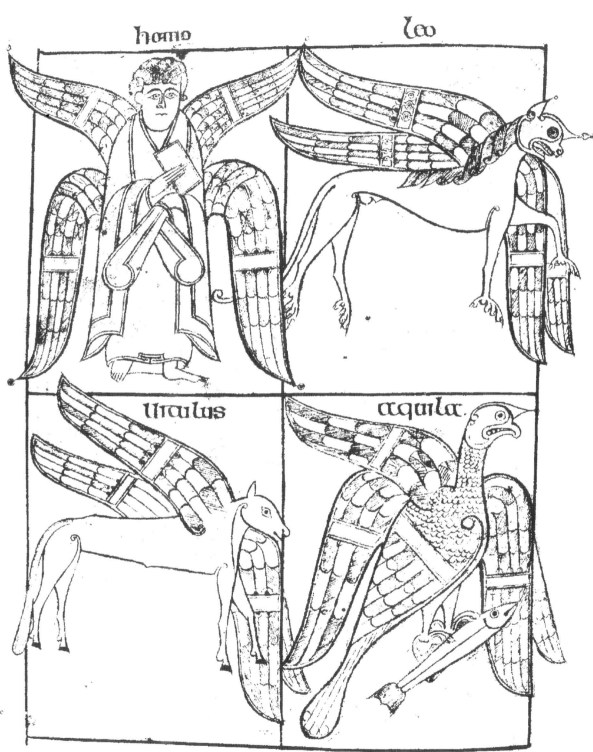

homo

leo

uitulus

aquila

Pen and ink drawings of the four evangelist symbols on Fol. 32v of the Book of Armagh. Ms. 52 in the Library of Trinity College, Dublin.

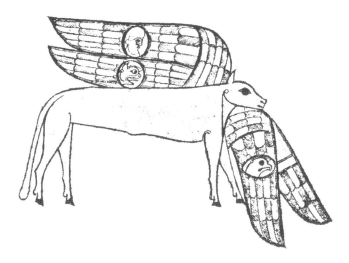

Evangelist symbols in the Book of Armagh.

obviously be unfair to compare his one-man feat with the team-effort of the Book of Kells, Macregol must be credited with producing a fine script. The script, indeed, is better than his decorative work. Pictures of the evangelists, and more particularly their clothing, were not his strongpoint, but he has a happy knack of caricaturing their contented faces with just a few pen-strokes, and further human faces add liveliness to the tops of his otherwise heavy pages of decoration. In them he has, however, managed to show his skills in geometrical patterns and interlace (Pl.134–5), the latter with separate compartments of strongly contrasting colours. Some of his interlace has echoes on one of the High Crosses at Kilkieran, Co. Kilkenny, while his lattice patterns are reminiscent of some of the bronze railings in Charlemagne's Palace chapel at Aachen of *c.* 795–800.

At around the same time, but still before the real onslaught of the Viking invasions, the pen and ink drawings in the Book of Armagh show a more monochrome art being developed. Preserved as manuscript 52 in the Library of Trinity College, Dublin, it was written at the behest of Torbach, abbot of Armagh from 807–808, and is, therefore, one of the few reliably datable early illuminated manuscripts. The lines are drawn with great vigour and sureness in both the individual evangelist symbols and the page (fol. 32v) with the four symbols together, where the eagle (carrying a fish in its claws) bears an uncanny resemblance to its more colourful counterpart on fol. 27v of the Book of Kells. The vogue for pen-and-ink drawing was continued in the mid-ninth century Priscian manuscript, Codex 904, in the monastic library in St Gall, which bears on page 2 an initial P ornamented with a curious cross-legged figure reminiscent of one carved on the North Cross at Clonmacnoise.

The earlier tradition of the pocket Gospel-book is likely to have been kept alive throughout much of the ninth century, as suggested by an example in Lambeth Palace Library in London

(Ms. 1370), which states that Maelbrigit Macdurnan 'dogmatized' the text. He can probably be identified with a man of that name who was abbot of Armagh from around 888 until his death in 927, though it is uncertain whether it was he who actually wrote the text. The Gospel book follows the tradition of the Macregol Gospels in applying the paint thickly like enamel, but here the frames for the evangelists and some of the text pages are not as overpowering as in Macregol. Instead, they are divided up into neat rectangular or L-shaped panels bearing interlace with a broad central band flanked by a narrow one on each side (resembling the Donegal stone examples at Fahan and Carndonagh) but which — unusually for an Irish context — bifurcates in Viking fashion. The interlace is also asymmetrical, and small 'nailheads' within it suggest that it is copied from metalwork, as are the interlocking T-shapes on fol. 172. In addition, there is also an amount of animal interlace forming figures of eight and a variety of fretwork ornament (e.g. Pl.133). Within such frames are the four evangelists, standing frontally in the tradition of the smaller Gospel books. They hold their Gospels, and both Matthew and Luke (Pl.136–7) carry a crook in their right hand. If this manuscript really does date to the period around 900, it shows that scriptoria continued to produce small illuminated pocket Gospel books undeterred by the Viking invasions, but the only two surviving decorated manuscripts which come between it and the later eleventh century are not much more than caricature postscripts, something which could also be said of the roughly contemporary Scottish manuscript known as the Book of Deer,

from a Columban foundation in Aberdeenshire. The first of these two manuscripts is British Library Cotton Vitellius F.XI which was badly damaged by a fire in 1731. A lost colophon, read by Archbishop Ussher before it was burnt, called for a blessing on Muiredach. It is possible, but not provable, that he was the man who erected the cross at Monasterboice, because the first two folios have drawings which do resemble representations on High Crosses (though not at Monasterboice) – the David and Goliath on fol. 1 finding its parallel on the south side of the cross at Arboe, Co. Tyrone, and the David figure seated on the back of an animal as he plays his harp being closely comparable to a panel on the south side of the Cross of the Scriptures at Clonmacnoise. This might place the manuscript within a quarter or half a century on either side of 900 and, as the geometrical decoration of its frames resembles that of the Book of Macdurnan, it helps to support the ascription of the latter manuscript to the abbot of Armagh who died in 927. The final simplification comes with the second of these manuscripts, the so-called Southampton Psalter, Ms. C.9(59) in St John's College, Cambridge (Pl.132 and 138–40), which has narrower frames with simpler geometrical ornament and some well-executed interlacing animals. But its human figures are highly stylized – a Crucifixion on fol. 38v (Pl.140), as well as two David scenes (Pl.138–9) painted with naive charm and a scene of humour, and decorated with compartments of varying colours, as if copying cloisonné enamels. If historical annals are anything to go by, it was only the most important of monasteries, such as Armagh and Clonmacnoise, which retained both scribes (masters of a scriptorium) and a lector (man of learning) by the end of the tenth century, suggesting that the cost of repelling both Viking and Irish marauders had taken its toll on the cultural standards of the old Irish monasteries.

Ninth- and Tenth-Century Brooches

Already in the ninth century, the Vikings were affecting the style of brooches by contributing the material from which many of them came to be made, namely silver. This precious metal had, of course, already been used in major liturgical vessels such as the Ardagh and Derrynaflan chalices, but the material for these may have come from melted-down silver of the late Roman Empire or even Byzantium. But it is hard not to see some Norse trading behind the silver that began to come into fashion for the making of brooches in the ninth century, though analyses have shown that little of it is likely to have come from melting down the Arabic coins which the eastern Vikings had been importing into northern Europe via the Don and the Dnjepr. The same hoard which produced the famous Ardagh chalice also gave us a group of four, later, brooches (Pl.40), which show neatly the transition from the eighth to the ninth centuries in terms of style and ornamentation, though the latest of all, a so-called 'thistle' brooch, may be no earlier than the tenth century. The largest of the Ardagh brooches (Pl.90), perhaps still eighth century, has a semi-circular plate forming one half of the ring and ornamented largely with monotonous interlace, and the pin-

head still retains the triangular shape of the Tara brooch. The sole remaining stud consists of a hemispherical dome of amber covered with a silver sheet cut away to resemble the geometrical designs used in earlier metalwork. On the ninth-century brooches, the semi-circular plate splits down the middle into two almost triangular shapes to be joined only by slender bars. Flat, undecorated silver surfaces form the focal point of these triangles, hemmed in by gilt animals. As we have seen (p.137), brooches from Roscrea, Co. Tipperary (Pl.78) and Killamery, Co. Kilkenny (Pl.144–5), show the gilding fading into the background, and extensive silver surfaces and amber studs coming to dominate the design. Original stamp marks on the pin of the Killamery brooch would seem to be Norse in origin, raising the question whether ninth-century silver brooches could have been made by Norse craftsmen, or were an Irish product. The latter possibility is supported not only by their distribution far inland from the Norse maritime towns, but also by the very Irish-looking animals with their heads turned to look over their backs on the reverse of the Killamery brooch (Pl.145).

Even if originality in the design of brooches did diminish as the decades of the ninth century progressed, as seems also to have been the case with manuscripts, the penannular brooches developed with new styles during the later ninth and earlier tenth centuries. The innovations included the silver 'bossed penannular' brooches (Pl.142, left) which have the expanded, but separated, roughly triangular-shaped terminals each decorated with between two and seven hemispherical bosses, linked by hatched ribbons, and thereby creating panels usually filled with animal ornament. Such brooches have been found not only in Ireland, but also in the North of England and as far away as Iceland and, though there is general consensus that they are of Irish manufacture, there is less agreement whether the impetus for the new style of decoration came from a Norse or an Anglo-Saxon background. Some examples have small bosses incised so as to make them look like blackberries, and these may have contributed to the decoration of the so-called 'thistle' brooches (Pl.142, right) – silver brooches with similarly 'brambled' terminals and also pin-heads which bear a superficial resemblance to thistles. One of these was the latest of the four brooches found with the Ardagh chalice, suggesting that the whole hoard was scarcely deposited much before the year 900. There may well have been a Scottish Pictish element in these, as in other ninth-century brooches in Ireland, but the type with ball-shaped terminations, which grew out of the thistle brooches, became popular all over the Viking world from Ireland to Kiev.

By the tenth century, the fashion in clothes must have been changing among both Norse and Irish, and the brooch gradually gave way to the much smaller ring-pin. But before giving up the ghost, the larger brooch developed along new lines in Ireland and – because half of the examples came to light in Viking towns such as Dublin and Waterford – there must have been a considerable Norse contribution to their development. These are the kite-shaped brooches (Pl.142, centre), consisting of a long pin with a movable kite-shaped part attached to it by hinge. The kite shapes differ, but two well-known examples are

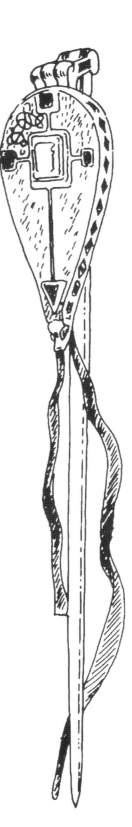

Lost kite-brooch from Clonmacnoise, Co. Offaly.

almond-shaped, one of unknown provenance with panels of animal ornament decorated in a somewhat crude gold filigree, and another from Clonmacnoise, now lost. This provenanced piece may well have been made in the monastery itself, because it has a Latin cross ornamenting both the back and front of the kite. One of these brooches was found in an Irish crannog at Ballinderry, Co. Westmeath and, while it might be thought that this would indicate a native origin, the same site produced a wooden gaming board, long considered to have been of Manx origin, but which James Graham-Campbell now believes to have come from Norse Dublin. Its sides are decorated with Viking-type ring-chain ornament, but also with interlace and fretwork ornament of a kind repeated on an interesting wooden box from the Christ Church Place excavations in Dublin published by James Lang, its own ornament comparable to that of some ninth-century manuscripts.

Crozier Reliquaries – Eighth to Tenth Centuries

Croziers – or, to be more precise, crozier reliquaries – present a series which shows the change in metalworking styles in Ireland over a number of centuries. The typical Irish crozier looks like a walking stick with a shaft between 1m and 1.50m long interrupted by three or four knops or protuberances, and a head very often with a vertical piece – a drop-head – at the extremity. What may be part of one of the earliest known

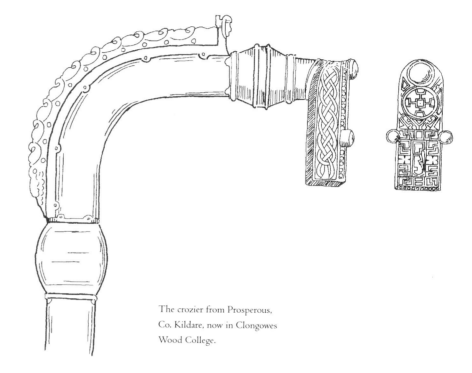

The crozier from Prosperous, Co. Kildare, now in Clongowes Wood College.

examples was found near Stavanger in Norway, and it consists of a piece of bronze tubular casing cast with a spiral and interlace style of the eighth century. What is normally taken to be a rather small crozier-head was found in excavations in Helgö (Pl.143), in the central Swedish parish of Ekerö, where a Viking trading station was importing exotic objects from as far away as Afghanistan (could this possibly be how the Book of Kells got its lapis lazuli?). This 'crozier' has three parts: a rounded knop decorated with linear designs of yellow enamel dominated by settings of blue glass, a middle portion octagonal in cross-section having facets ornamented with similar-coloured enamel inlays forming cross and S-shapes and, finally, a head consisting of a dragon whose jaws open wide to engulf a human head between

Tanq; p̄curtor̄ i debabilone ĩ p̄bo habitancia. polo pelatoꝝ ꝫ tap̄
dicēnꝯ ur hoꝛē īū īt re cuīpꝫ. Expia pōc catione ut y; co̅sacine
t̄illi ꝓ dissecatio�7 p̄ucadoꝛ picuataꝝ ꝫ ag̅ egꝛdī peduls mōcioꝛ
īp̄ta. et ꝭcs ꝭ q̄nere. at uos apoꝛaloꝝ ꝏp̄ta꞊

psalm̄; ĩ confessioe

Ubilate d̄o omnis terra ꞉·
Seꝛuite d̄ño ĩ leticia ꞉·
Inꝺꝛoite ĩ ꝯspectu ꝫ ĩ exultaoe ꞉·
Sciote q̄n d̄ns ipse est d̄s ꞉·
ipse fecit nos ꝫ non ipsi nos ꞉·†
Populus eius ꝫ oues pascue eius ꞉·
Inꝺꝛoite poꝛtas eius ĩ confessioe ꞉·
atria eius ĩ hymnis ꝯfitemini illi ꞉·
lauꝺate nomen ꝫ q̄m suauis est d̄ns ꞉·
ĩ eternum misseꝛicordia eius ꞉·
ꝫ usq; ĩ �580eneracion̄ ꝫ �580eneꝛa꞉ uitas ꞉·

psalm̄; ipsi d̄o

Issericordia ꝫ iudicium cantabo tibi d̄ne ꞉·
psalla ꝫ ĩtelligam ĩ uia
ĩmaculata q̄ño uenies ad me ꞉·
Pambulabam ĩ ĩnocencia coꝛdis mei
ĩ medio domus mee ꞉·
Proponeba ꝼ ꝰ oculos meos rem ĩiustam ꞉·
facientes preuaricationes odiui ꞉·
Non adhesit cor prauum ꞉·
declinante a me malignum ñ cognoscebam ꞉·
Detrahentem secreto proximo suo ꞉·
hunc persequebar ꞉·
Superbo oculo ꝫ ĩsaciabile corde ꞉·
cum hoc non edebam ꞉·†
Oculi mei ad fideles terre ꞉·
ut sederent mecum ꞉·
Ambulans ĩ uia ĩmaculata ꞉·
hic mihi ministrabat ꞉·
Non habitcat ĩ medio domus mee ꞉·
qui facit superbiam ꞉·

Reꝓ̄ ona hiꝛtoꝛ̄ ĩ babi bilone
captiuoꝛū catiuc. poꝛcuntey; ĩ
yꝛ īguloꝛ. ꝑ ꝑ̄ ctia ꝫ uꝛ cuat
ꝝ ue ꝼ tꝛibulacionis te pore
sū̄ma. at uos ecclīa ꝏp̄tū
ꝺ ase ꝑcoꝛ̄꞉

133

god spellep

134

135

136

137

139

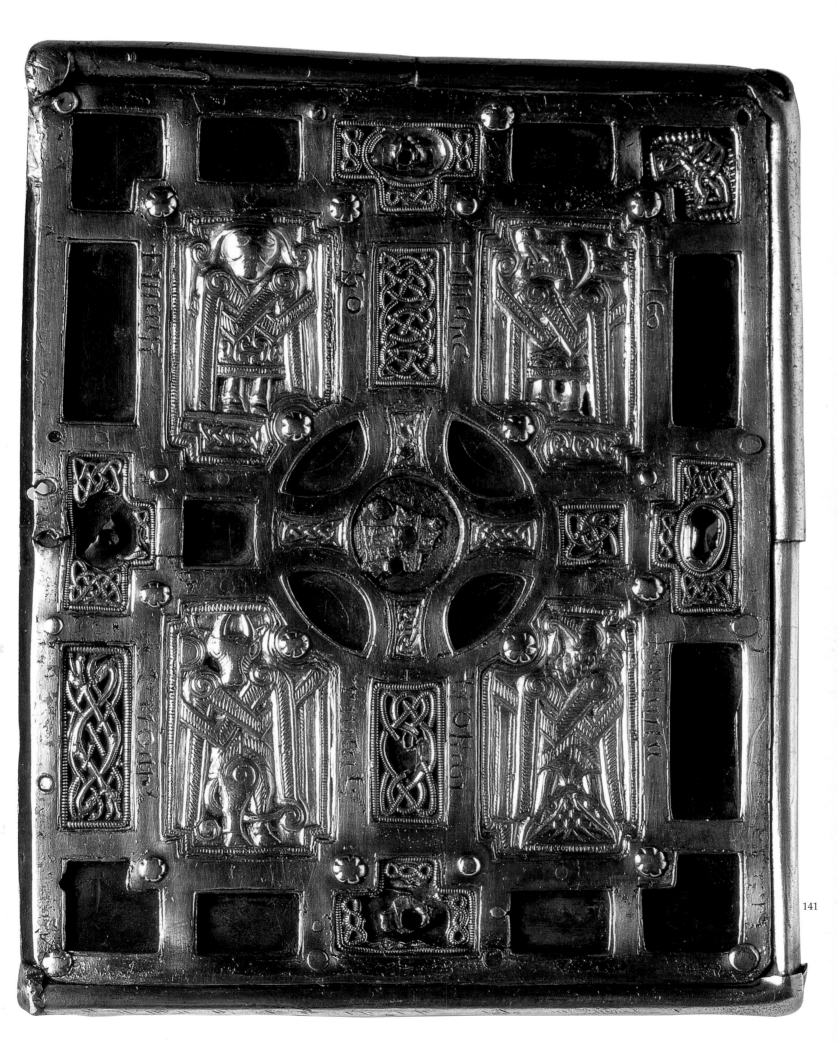

143

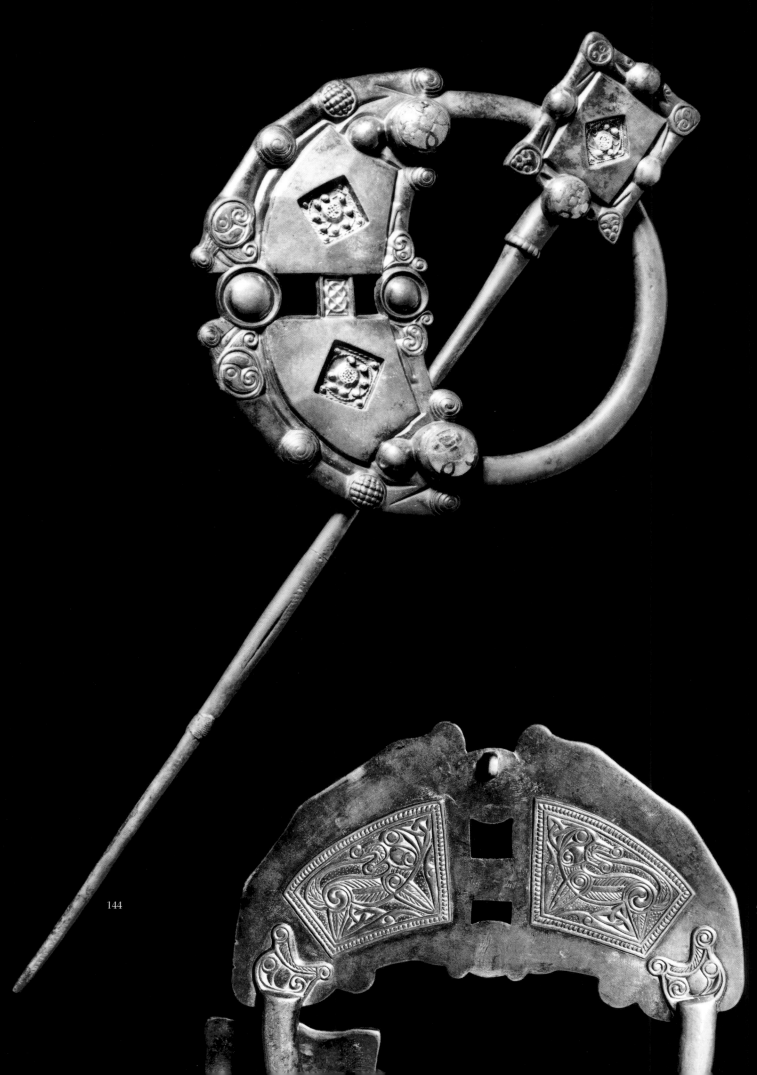

144   145

148

149

150

151

152

153

155

156

157

160

161

its fangs. Where we might have expected an ear, there is an animal head not far removed in style from those in the Book of Kells, and projecting from the curve of the dragon's neck is a further animal head with closed mouth. The craftsman showed off his skill by ornamenting each face of the head differently, with cast herring-bone on one face and scale-like cloisons filled with yellow enamel on the other. The human head – frowning, not unexpectedly in the grip of such a monster – has been tentatively interpreted as Jonah, and the dragon as a whale, reminiscent of scenes on Frankish belt-buckles of the seventh century. But the style of the Helgö 'crozier' would suggest a date closer to 800, and belonging to roughly the same period as the Moylough belt-shrine (p.134–5). Though a similar motif appears on a twelfth-century walrus-ivory crozier from Aghadoe, Co. Kerry (Pl.146), formerly in Stockholm and now in Hannover, no other early crozier can be found to compare with this piece. The possibility that it was not a crozier but was originally mounted on a piece of furniture has been raised by James Graham-Campbell, who points out that its closest parallels are the terminals of chair-backs in eighth-century Hiberno-Saxon manuscripts.

The earliest reasonably complete crozier is that from Prosperous, Co. Kildare, now in Clongowes Wood College (p.215), which still preserves enamel decoration, a feature which disappears on metalwork by the late ninth century when the knops come to be made of cast bronze. By this stage the drop-head has been developed to house a small relic in addition to the enshrined piece of wood which is normally taken to be the staff of an early saint. Typical examples are the croziers of St Dympna of Tedavnet, Co. Monaghan, in the National Museum in Dublin, and of St Mel in the Cathedral dedicated to him in the town of Longford, as well as that from Inishmurray, Co. Sligo, preserved by the Duke of Northumberland at Alnwick Castle. But more impressive is the crozier (Pl.147–52) in the British Museum which has been wrongly linked with Kells in County Meath on the basis of two names on an inscription it bears. Just over 1.30m high, it has a little human head at the top of the drop-front (Pl.151) and, unusually, four knops on the staff (Pl.152). The three lowest (including Pl.147 and 149, bottom) are cast and divided into panels which are round, square or triangular in shape and decorated mostly with interlace and single or double contorting animals. All were originally covered with silver foil which would have made them glisten more brightly than does the exposed bronze. Joining these knops are binding strips, whose purpose was to hide the joint in the bronze tubing of the staff, and they take the form of a ringed cross (Pl.149, centre) standing on a tall stem decorated, in one instance, by interlace and a vertical panel of classical acanthus. Further classical borrowings include an egg-and-dart ornament on the ring of the cross (itself filled with animal interlace) and, on the top of the knop beneath it, a pattern of lozenges divided by bars. How these classical echoes reached Ireland we cannot say. The head of the crozier (Pl.151) also bears panels of animal ornament related to those on the three lowest knops, for which Cormac Bourke's suggestion of a late ninth-century date would seem apposite. The crozier, however, is not all of one period. The uppermost knop at the bottom of the head (Pl.148–50) is very different in style, and outclasses the other three in quality. It, too, has acanthus leaves, but these are now woven into an intricate and ingenious interlace pattern, with both stems and leaves formed of a black substance called niello inlaid with wavy silver lines. Its style places this collar knop in the eleventh century, thus making the crozier a monument which straddles the transition from first to second millennium, as do the Round Towers which have served as nationalistic symbols for Ireland every bit as potent as the High Crosses.

Round Towers

About 65 round towers survive in various states of preservation on Ireland's ancient monastic sites. The tallest, at Kilmacduagh, Co. Galway, reaches a height of 34.28m, and at least nine must have been more than 30m high. Their normal diameter is around 6m and, for structures so tall, their foundations are surprisingly shallow, sometimes no more than 2–3m deep. Resulting instability may have been the cause of a number of them having collapsed and one or two are known to have fallen down so intact that they lay on the ground like a long cannon. Inadequate foundations or disturbed earth may have been the reason why the tower at Kilmacduagh leans more than 60cm out of the perpendicular, but it is now totally stable. The existing tower on Scattery Island (Pl.164) in the Shannon estuary and the demolished example which formerly stood at Downpatrick, Co. Down, both had doorways at ground level, but all other towers have the entrance usually about three metres above ground level. They taper gently upwards from their base, sometimes giving the impression of entasis known from classical columns, to suggest to the eye that the walls were absolutely straight. The building stones, particularly the large ones, are carefully dressed to correspond to the rounded contours of the towers, and the conical caps are built with stones laid flat in the corbel system used in Gallarus oratory. Internally, projecting corbels or a ring of stones jutting out from the surface indicate the former presence of wooden landings, of which there would have been up to seven, each of them pierced so as to allow a ladder to come up from the floor below. Each storey would have been lit by a window, square-, round- or triangular-headed, very much like those in the simple stone churches. No original woodwork survives within the towers, but at places such as Devenish, Co. Fermanagh, Kildare and Kilkenny, modern stairs provide access to the top of the towers, from where a splendid view may be had.

From the days when George Petrie published his extensive study of Round Towers in 1845, considerable discussion has arisen on the purpose and date of these towers, and most would agree with him that they had multiple functions. In the popular mind, they were citadels for the monks against the Vikings, and indeed the very first reference we have to a round tower in Irish historical sources is to one at Slane, Co. Meath, which was burned by the Norsemen in 950. In reality, they would have been impractical as refuges against any approaching enemy, Irish or Viking, because a burning arrow shot into the tower would quickly create such an inferno through internal draughts that people and treasures inside would have been burnt to a cinder, and we know that this actually happened in some cases. Even today, the visitor is struck by the way that these towers are visible from a distance. The first thing one sees approaching Glendalough (Pl.165), Clonmacnoise or Monasterboice today is the tall tower dominating the landscape, reaching heaven-wards above the treetops, informing the traveller that his goal is within reach. When the old monasteries were still operational, the towers must have beckoned like beacons to the weary pilgrim, showing him the location of the saint's relics which he was coming to venerate. But the old Irish word for these towers was *cloictbech* (with different spellings), literally a bell-house, and their tall and graceful shape would lend credence to the comparison with the campanili of medieval Italy and the minarets of the Muslim world. But what kind of bells gave their names to these towers? The *Annals of the Four Masters* record under the year 1552 that the English plundered Clonmacnoise and 'the large bells were taken from the *cloigtheach*. There was not left, moreover, a bell, small or large … which was not carried off'. The tower itself was completed in 1124, and this account would suggest that, at least by the sixteenth century, the bells were large. But, other than this report, there is no indication that such large bells were ever hung or rung in these towers though they could easily have been melted down. Of the surviving bells studied by Cormac Bourke, which are small and were held in the hand, only a few examples – such as those from Lough Lene (Pl.161) in the National Museum in Dublin, and from Cashel in

the Hunt Museum in Limerick – bear decoration which dates them to no later than 900, and thus considerably earlier than our first historical mention of a Round Tower. We cannot, therefore, be sure that our surviving bells were rung in Round Towers. But the presence of a bell on carvings with figures bearing staffs, as at Killadeas (Pl.153) and White Island, Co. Fermanagh, Carndonagh, Co. Donegal and on the pedimented lintel in the Priest's House at Glendalough, suggests the possible use of bells by pilgrims. The Dutch scholar, Professor Koldeweij, has put forward the idea that 'bell house' may mean that the Round Towers were places where pilgrimage bells were stored. Bells may have been kept in them for safe-keeping while pilgrims sojourned on the site, or may even have been on sale as souvenirs of pilgrimage. It is certainly noteworthy that the tower at Armagh was burned 'with its bells' in a major fire in 1020, but perhaps even more significant are the reports that the Slane tower was burned with its founder's staff and the best of all bells, and the one at Monasterboice burned 'with books and treasures' in 1097. Both of these accounts suggest that the items listed – including bells – were valuables. It could be inferred, therefore, that the towers were the monastic treasuries, and that their doors were so high off the ground so as to protect the treasures from acquisitive fingers, rather than from enemy assault.

If the many possible functions of the Round Towers have given rise to much discussion, so too has the question of their origin. By the time the earliest Irish tower is mentioned by an historical source in 950, many towers of a slightly different kind had already been built, or at lest planned, on the European continent. During the tenth century, slender towers were incorporated into the west ends of great Ottonian churches such as St Pantaleon in Cologne, and an even earlier example occurred in the church of St Riquier/Centula, erected by abbot Angilbert in the last decade of the eighth century. The plan of St Gall, of *c.* 820, included two thick-walled round towers, apparently with spiral staircases, attached to the apse of the church possibly by a covered way. But all of these are in pairs. Free-standing campanili at Ravenna could offer a possible origin though, for Maurice Craig, these 'are not really like the Irish towers', and tall slender towers depicted on a fresco in old St Peter's in Rome, usually dated to around 700 though only preserved in a seventeenth-century drawing, do not have the gently tapering walls found in the Irish towers. While vanished wooden examples might have offered a satisfactory explanation had they survived, we might not go too far wrong in seeing the Irish Round Towers as a native expression of the spread of the campanile-idea initially from Italy, and perhaps reaching Ireland's shores through lost examples in the Carolingian lands. Two such Scottish towers, and one on the Isle of Man, are almost certainly derived from the Irish series, while similar towers in East Anglia in southern England are twelfth century in date and appear to be an independent development. But the towers, once introduced into Ireland, continued to be built with little change down to the twelfth century, demonstrating the same conservative approach to architecture shown by the stone churches.

10

The Eleventh Century and the Rise of Dublin

■

MANY THINGS BEGAN TO STIR AND to change with the advent of the second millennium, though Ireland seems to have been largely unaffected by the fear that had gripped many on the European continent that the world would come to an end in the year 1000. Scarcely had the new era dawned when an historically significant event happened at Tara, the sacred site of old Irish high-kingship: Máelsechnaill II, a scion of the Uí Néill dynasty which had been holding onto power in the northern half of Ireland since the time of St Patrick, paid tribute to Brian Boru, initially king of an insignificant sept in County Clare who, having gained control of the southern province of Munster, was now proceeding to subdue the traditional kings of the northern half of the country as well. This was a major political upheaval, proving how the might of an upstart's sword was stronger than any centuries-old right to kingship by lineage, and in 1005, when Brian Boru paid a visit to the primatial see at Armagh and laid twenty ounces of gold upon its altar, he had his secretary record that he was 'emperor of the Irish'. It looked as if Ireland were on the threshold of becoming an island united under one strong monarch, but the king of Leinster was not prepared to accept the yoke – and rebelled. This led to one of the most famous clashes in Irish history, the Battle of Clontarf on Good Friday, 1014, when the Leinster king, backed by the inhabitants of the Norse or 'Ostman' town of Dublin, as it was called, together with their allies from the Western Isles of Scotland and the Isle of Man, fought Brian and whatever Irish support he could muster. Brian won the battle, but lost his life. Clontarf has often been seen as an historic victory of the Irish over the Norse, breaking their power for ever. In reality, the Dublin Vikings' military strength had already been on the wane for some time, and essentially it was a power struggle between rival Irish kings which, through Brian's death, was to usher in a century of political instability. His old adversary, Máelsechnaill II, regained the High Kingship and kept it until his own death in 1022. After that, their respective families, and also the kings of Leinster, settled down to making unsuccessful efforts against each other to gain the High Kingship for themselves in an Ireland that was becoming more and more feudal as the higher provincial kings trampled the lesser kings into virtual servility beneath them.

But the picture had also been changing because Dublin was beginning to take on a new role as an economic power within the land. It was increasingly becoming the prize to play for among the squabbling provincial dynasties and, between 1070 and 1130, the masters of Dublin included two kings from Leinster, two from Munster and one from the rising star of Connacht in the west of Ireland. The reason for this was that, since Dublin had repositioned itself downstream from its original location in the first half of the ninth century, it had gradually been building itself up to become one of the most important trading depots for Viking merchants offering their wares up and down the Atlantic seaboard from Spain to Scandinavia. By the turn of the millennium, and probably long before, its population was not only mixing and meeting with the Irish, but had also become Christian to a large extent, and was probably bilingual also. Its craftsmen had already begun in the tenth century to adopt Irish interlace and geometrical motifs for their own purposes

and, by the early eleventh, they had not only digested these Irish patterns, but had also begun contributing to a new art style which was to become popular throughout the western Viking world. This was the Ringerike style which gets its name from an area north of Oslo where stones were carved with lions, snakes and long, thin tendrils, sometimes interspersed with lobes. English manuscripts illuminated during the reign of the Danish king Cnut, better known as Canute (1016–42), show that Southern England, which formed a part of his kingdom, had contributed details to the development of the style. But excavations in the old Viking city of Dublin during the last three decades have produced evidence that it was already being practised in the city during the first third of the eleventh century, at roughly the same time as the English manuscripts. It would be unjustified to claim that Dublin had invented the style, but the city's craftsmen were certainly involved in its early development, contrary to the older views suggesting that it did not reach Ireland until late in the century. The evidence for its presence in the first few decades of the new millennium in Dublin comes from the decorated wooden pieces published by James Lang. Using the valuable independent evidence provided by the precise stratigraphy observed by the excavator, Dr Pat Wallace, Lang showed how some of the decorated wooden pieces typical of the Ringerike style lay beneath a layer bearing a coin of Sihtric of 1025, and therefore likely (though not certainly) to be before this date. One characteristic piece is a box-lid which shows the grouped tendrils crossing at irregularly-spaced nodal points, suggesting a

Tenth- and eleventh-century bone and wood carvings.

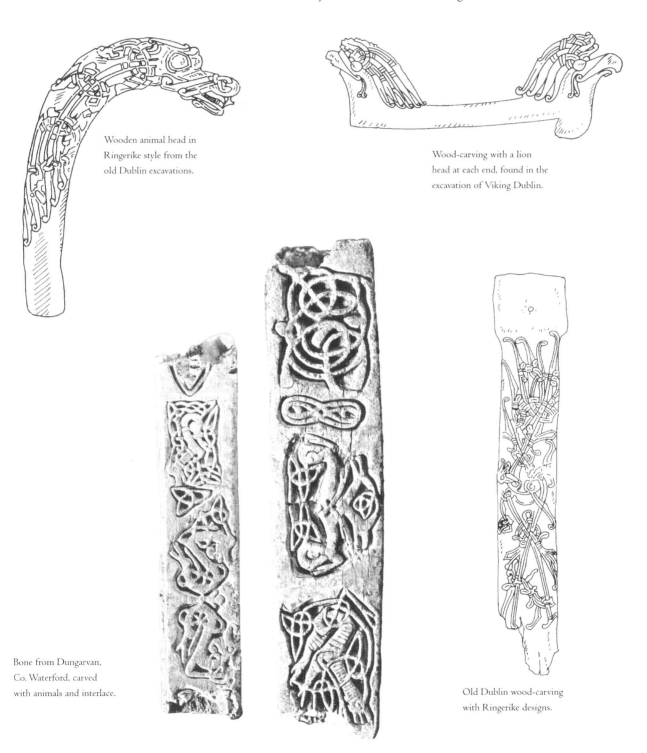

Wooden animal head in
Ringerike style from the
old Dublin excavations.

Wood-carving with a lion
head at each end, found in the
excavation of Viking Dublin.

Bone from Dungarvan,
Co. Waterford, carved
with animals and interlace.

Old Dublin wood-carving
with Ringerike designs.

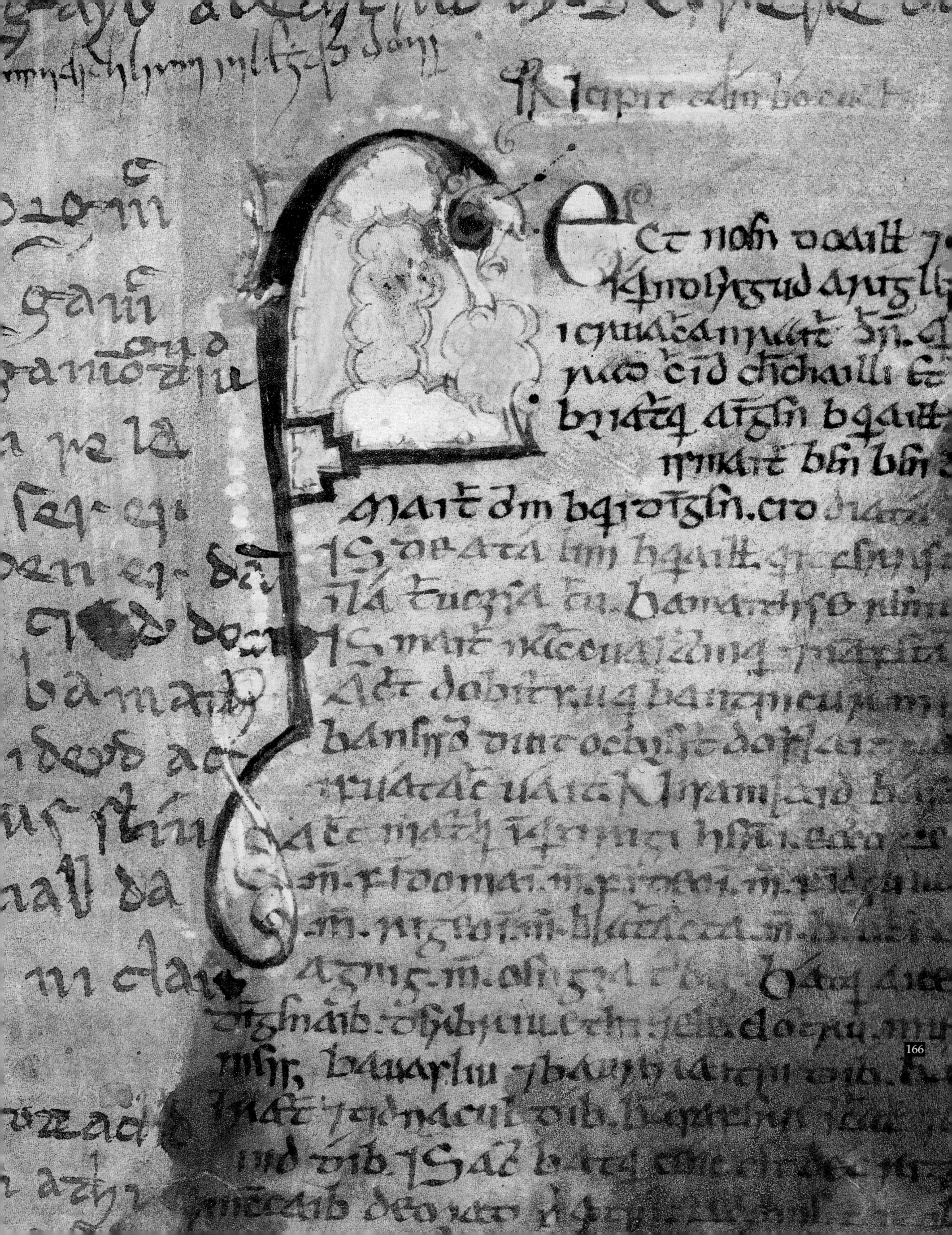

166

ber
ihu xp̄
abrah
isaac
autem: g
tudar lr: g
dechtman: l
cynom lr: ghirun
ammirodab. Ammirodab lr:
lr: ghirint ralmon. Salmo

167

7 tenebutam me

runt mihi hur

thr hiant rlimp

IC es

deduot

ado 2 a

uocaum

thramo

cetr ado vilec

cfii comm̄dam

nf demm̄ me

170

um qui
non abiit
in conſilio
impiorum.

Et in uia peccatoꝛ

ITIUM EUAN
xpi filii di sic
mitto angelum
faciem tuam
nauit uiam tu
Uox clamantis in
nate uiam domini
cite semitas eius
ner in deserto babti
cans babtismum pe
remissionem peccato
diebantur ad illum om
regionis 7 hierosolimit
7 babtizabantur ab illo
flumine 7 confitentes
7 erat iohannes uestitus
7 zona pellicia circa lumbos

knowledge of the Southern English style, but made nevertheless by a Dublin school of carvers. Another is a mount, 26.5cm long and bearing at each end an animal (lion) head whose flowing mane separates into long tendrils (sometimes interwoven across one another), which curl up at the end. An even finer wood-carving is a crook, 16.1cm high, consisting of an animal head and neck with the same curling tendrils visible on the snout and also on the neck, where it is irregularly interrupted by oval-shaped groupings of further interlaced tendrils. Typical characteristics of the style which also appear on some of these pieces are the pear-shaped animal eye with the narrow, pointed part facing forward, and also the asymmetry which differentiates it from the ensuing Urnes style to be discussed below.

Further evidence of artistic activity in Dublin comes from the 'trial-pieces', or 'motif-pieces' as Uaininn O'Meadhra calls them. These are objects of bone, or occasionally of stone, carved with a variety of motifs, including interlace and animals, as found on a bone from Dungarvan, Co. Waterford. Such pieces, rare outside Ireland, have been found in considerable quantities in Dublin, but eighth- or early-ninth century carved bones (Pl.154) from the royal site at Lagore, Co. Meath, and elsewhere, show that the genre predates the foundation of the present city. Eleventh-century Dublin examples of bone include two bearing Ringerike ornament – one (Pl.155) with two interlocking and asymmetrical figures of eight making an animal interlace, and with the ribbons typically interrupted where they cross one another, the other with a design closely resembling one on the book-shrine of the Cathach manuscript (see

below, p.263). Even if it is not possible to define the function of these motif-pieces in relationship to the production of metalwork which we can only presume took place in Dublin, they demonstrate – as do the wooden pieces – an active and inventive community of craftsmen working in the city and keeping in contact with the latest artistic developments in Southern England and Scandinavia.

Eleventh-Century Book-shrines

An interesting link which throws light on the connections between Dublin and the rest of Ireland is a book-shrine which is probably a close contemporary of those Ringerike-carved wooden pieces just mentioned. Corresponding in size to a small pocket Gospel book, this is the *Soiscél Molaisse*, or Gospel of Molaisse, which gets its name from a fragmentary inscription on three edges of the long narrow side of the shrine, and which (in translation) reads: 'A prayer for ...nfailad, successor of Molaisse, who caused this shrine to be made, for ...nlan and a prayer for Gillabaithín, the craftsman who made it'. St Molaisse (or Molaise) was the founder of the famous monastery on the island of Devenish in Lower Lough Erne, Co. Fermanagh, and it was in his honour that the shrine was made by the 'successor of Molaisse', that is, the abbot of Devenish, whose fragmentary name can be reliably completed as Cennfailad, who presumably took up the abbacy on the death of his predecessor in 1001. Raghnall Ó Floinn's suggestion that the incomplete name '...nlan' is that of Scanlan, an *airchinneach*, or functionary, of the same monastery who died in 1011, would narrow the date of manufacture to the years 1001 to 1011. It is marginally too early to show any signs of the Ringerike style, but the back of the shrine does have a Viking-style ring-chain pattern as found on the wooden gaming board from Ballinderry, Co. Westmeath (p.215), now thought to have been made in Dublin. The main face of the shrine (Pl.141) consists of an outer frame enclosing a ringed cross with evangelist symbols in the interstices. The broad outlines consist of a silver sheet partially cut away to provide the compartments decorated on the periphery with cast, filigree and stamped panels, and settings for coloured stones, one of which survives. The arms of the cross are filled with interlace, but the most interesting features of the whole face are the evangelist symbols, identified by carefully engraved Latin inscriptions. The heads of St Mark's lion and St John's eagle are shown in profile on the right, while the other two symbols face the observer. Their respective limbs or wings have spirals at the joints; they are designed like the letter M with the upper diagonals crossing, and are filled with a cross-hatching which echoes Irish metalwork of two centuries earlier. Also rather old-fashioned are the intertwined animals in the panels (Pl.162) surrounding an enigmatic book-holding figure on the side of the shrine who, unusually, is enclosed by a dense menagerie of animals of a somewhat different kind. The box-shape of the shrine with cross-decoration on its main face might seem like a new category of art object, so unusual is its style, but the Lough Kinale

book-shrine (Pl.45) shows that the type already had a long life behind it, and the lost shrines for the Books of Durrow and Kells which preceded this Devenish shrine may well have given it some inspiration. It is important as being the earliest piece of Irish metalwork dated by inscription – the practice of applying inscriptions to shrines having been made popular by the emperors Otto II and III on the continent during the last decades of the previous millennium. But the hinge, which comes from an earlier shrine and was partially decorated with enamel, shows how the main part of the shrine contrasts with earlier metalwork by its greater emphasis on the human figure. It was the first of the shrines which would give fresh impetus to Irish metalwork in the new millennium.

Following it closely in date is another book-shrine with a cross pattern on one face. Designed to contain an eighth- or ninth-century manuscript known as the Stowe Missal now in the Royal Irish Academy, this shrine was manufactured in Clonmacnoise, as the lengthy inscription on one face informs us. It tells us further that the shrine's patrons included Dondchad son of Brian (Boru), king of Ireland and Mac Raíth, king of Cashel – titles more flattering than justified. Other parts of the inscription were long given up as incomprehensible, but Pádraic Ó Riain has recently provided a convincing reconstruction which demonstrates that a third, more local, king was involved in the patronage of this work – Find Ua Dúngallaig, king of Muscraige, a small area in north Tipperary. This would appear to be confirmed by further reconstruction which identifies Mathgamain, abbot of Lorrha in north

Tipperary, as the person who commissioned the shrine, and all of these names combined can now help us to narrow the date of this shrine to the years between 1026 and 1033, rather than the broader dating of 1023–1052 accepted hitherto. The shrine itself is an oak box decorated with silver plates, which are broken through on the back with squares and triangles which reveal a bronze plate underneath. Cross-shapes (like those on the back of the *Soiscél Molaisse*) and plant ornament appear in openwork panels on the side, which is where we also find the far more interesting figural and animal decoration. On the two ends are seemingly winged figures having their heads bitten on either side by quadrupeds who form a neat circular frame (Pl.160). Two of the surviving small compartments at the ends show a

soldier bearing spear and shield (Pl.157), and a deer attacked by dogs (Pl.156). The use of spiral joints and cross-hatched bodies harks back to the style of the *Soiscél Molaisse* and, following its lead, we find further examples of figured scenes. One of these (Pl.159) shows a man about to draw his sword to ward off animals attacking him from the side. Another (Pl.158) shows two figures wearing heavy cloaks, one with a bell and the other with a staff, both flanking a diminutive musician playing what seems to be a lyre who may be compared with David on the Cross of the Scriptures at Clonmacnoise, though stylistically the shrine owes nothing to High Crosses of a century earlier. Iconographically obscure, the cramped squat figures in high relief, with rounded faces and glass eyes, may have an ancestry in lost metalwork of

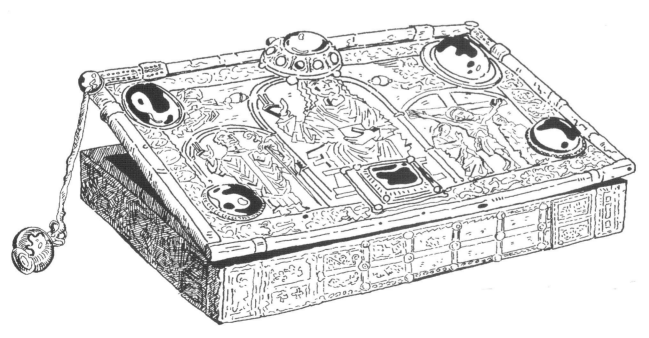

Shrine of the *Cathach* (11th and 15th centuries) in the National Museum, Dublin.

earlier centuries. But they may also owe a debt to contemporary metalwork on the European continent which was reviving an interest in the human figure and applying lengthy inscriptions recording the generosity of regal patrons.

Even if the Ringerike style is equally lacking on the shrine of the Stowe Missal, it does finally begin to make its impact felt in Irish art on a third Irish book-shrine of the eleventh century, that of the Cathach. Like the Stowe Missal, the Cathach (p.27) is preserved in the Royal Irish Academy, but the two shrines — like most of the other reliquaries of the period — are kept in the National Museum in Dublin. The Cathach being an O'Donnell manuscript, it belonged to that family which commissioned the metalwork shrine, probably from a workshop in the monastery at Kells, whose abbot is mentioned in an inscription. The surprise of finding a Scandinavian-style Ringerike design on an Irish monastic metalwork shrine is lessened by the fact that the craftsman, though son of an Irishman, bore the good Norse name of Sitric. If not a Dubliner by birth, he may well have learned his trade there, as the two panels on the shrine with nielloed Ringerike elements are very close to a design on one of the eleventh-century motif-pieces found in the High Street excavations in Dublin. The animals on the shrine have ribbon-shaped bodies forming two irregular and intersecting loops, as in an asymmetrical figure-of-eight. The tendrils, with curled-up ends typical of the style, are interspersed throughout the design. The abbot of Kells mentioned in the inscription reigned from 1062 to 1098 but, as there is a possibility that the plaques have been re-used, we cannot apply this date to them for

certain. A fourth book-shrine known as the Misach also contains Ringerike elements, but here the animals seem to fall apart among a confusion of tendrils.

Eleventh- and Twelfth-Century Manuscripts

Metalwork was by no means the only medium to be affected by a Scandinavian style of animal and interlace ornament. Manuscripts, too, came under its influence. Precisely how this took place is difficult to discern, because we are lacking those generations of decorated manuscripts which would have provided the evidence for the earliest uses of Scandinavian-style ornament by Irish illuminators. Indeed, if we take the Cotton Vitellius F.XI. and Southampton Psalters (p.212) to date from roughly the period around 900, we have a gap of a century and three-quarters before our next group of manuscripts which continue in a remarkably homogeneous fashion for almost another century until shortly before the Norman invasion in 1169. These manuscripts have been largely neglected during the last hundred years, and it is thanks to those two redoubtable friends, Françoise Henry and Geneviève Marsh-Micheli, that we owe their re-emergence from the shadows to claim their rightful place in the history of Irish art.

The first of these manuscripts which can be dated is the Chronicle of Marianus of Mainz (Vatican Library, Ms. Pal. Lat. 830), which was copied in Mainz by an Irish scribe Moel Brigte for his fellow-countryman Marianus Scottus. In a marginal note, he deplores the death of the powerful Leinster king Diarmait son of Mael na mBó, which took place in 1072, and that information and other personal details allows us to ascribe the manscript to the years 1072–73. Some of its initials have quadruped animals performing contortions, and intertwined by vegetal stems which bifurcate before terminating in tendrils curling up at the end. Some of the stems have half-rounded indents which indicate an ancestry in a Scandinavian style akin to the Ringerike, though the decoration is not a true representative of the style. But the manuscript shows that – as with the Kells workshop which produced the metalwork shrine of the Cathach – Scandinavian influence was permeating monastic scriptoria in the third quarter of the eleventh century, although one cannot be sure whether it was coming from Dublin or through manuscripts from the South of England or the continent. The Scandinavian style had certainly come to stay, and it continued little altered in Irish scriptoria for half a century – and in variant forms until around 1150 or later. Good examples are provided by the *Liber Hymnorum* surviving in two related versions, one in the Library of Trinity College, Dublin (Ms. E.4.2) and the other in the Franciscan House of Studies in Killiney (Ms. A.2). Neither can be dated accurately, nor are they necessarily contemporary, but they may span a decade or two on either side of 1100. Each hymn begins with a large initial, its colours now faded but doubtless brilliant originally. The animals, curvaceous and fluid, are more serpentine with long bodies intertwining with themselves and, in turn, being

interlaced with foliate ornament often terminating in a half-acanthus pattern. The style of interlacing with its bifurcation and curving notches is reminiscent of southern English decoration such as that of the Caedmon manuscript (Junius II in the Bodleian Library in Oxford) which is half a century older, thereby underlining the lengthy continuation of this style in Irish manuscripts. Little altered, it recurs again in the second part of one of the great collections of old Irish historical lore and genealogy, manuscript Rawlinson B. 502 also in the Bodleian Library in Oxford, normally dated to around or shortly after 1120, and widely considered to have been produced in Leinster. The first part, totally different in origin, was written partially by the same scribe involved in the compilation of another great, if much mutilated, collection of verse and prose at Clonmacnoise before 1106 – the *Lebor na hUidre*, or Book of the Dun Cow, which bears the shelf-number 23.E.25 in the Royal Irish Academy in Dublin. It has some large initial letters ending in an animal head, and one more elaborate capital letter which reproduces something of the curving rhythms of the *Liber Hymnorum*.

The third great corpus of Irish historical material, the Book of Leinster written probably at Terryglass on the lower Shannon around the 1150s, also bears decorated capital letters (Pl.166) with foliage and animal heads but uses a very different form of ornamental initial. The letter is in the form of an animal or, rather, a beast, whose long ribbon-like body is intertwined with one or more much thinner snakes. The type is seen to better advantage in other manuscripts written earlier in the century, such as the Missal owned by Corpus Christi College, Oxford (Ms. 282). Henry suggested a date for it near the end of the first quarter of the twelfth century; its initials are striking for the large amount of space they occupy on what are rather small pages. The beasts, usually two or more in number and managing to interlock with one another without becoming symmetrical, are of traditional Irish style. But the narrow serpents which writhe around and between their bodies, and whose heads are often seen from above, belong to a much more Scandinavian milieu, related to the style known in the Nordic countries as Urnes. The colours used include brilliant blues, purples and yellows which stand out against a background of startling red. James F. Kenney, in this indispensable *Sources for the Early History of Ireland* (p.706) said that 'it is a reasonable inference that the missal was a product of the reform movement' which had been taking place in the Irish church, and for which the christianized Vikings of Dublin must take some of the credit for initiating. It

comes as no surprise, therefore, to see Scandinavian animal ornament appearing in some manuscripts associated with the reform movement. As we shall see below (p.269), the reform was first tackled in 1101 at the Synod of Cashel where the most monumental use of the great Scandinavian beasts is found on a sarcophagus which John Bradley suggested was made for Cormac Mac Cárrthaigh, builder of Cormac's Chapel (p.301), where it now rests. Cormac's death in 1138 is bewailed by the scribe Maelbrigte hua Maelúanaigh in a note he penned in manuscript Harley 1802 in the British Library in London. This was written in Armagh, where the greatest figure of the Irish church reform, St Malachy, had been bishop until the previous year, 1137, and it is his influence which Françoise Henry saw behind the production of this and certain other manuscripts. Maelbrigte painted some of his initials in the animal-and-foliage style of the *Liber Hymnorum*, but also retained earlier pocket Gospel book tradition in the size of his manuscript as well as in the geometrical frames he provided for his evangelist symbols, two of which survive. The more elegant is the lion of St Mark (Pl.170), part of whose tail curls itself up into a half acanthus. It certainly shows more spirit than the ungainly bovine symbol of St Luke (Pl.169). Another manuscript from the Armagh scriptorium, and preserved in the same Harley collection in the British Library — with the number 1023 — is a small Gospel book written possibly after 1138, and preserving older traditions even more strongly in its two evangelist symbols. The spirited monochrome line-drawing of the lion of St Mark (with a full acanthus at the

The Cashel sarcophagus.

Evangelist symbols and initial letter in the Gospels, British Library, London, Ms. Harley 1023.

end of his tail) and the eagle of St John are the direct descendants of the Book of Armagh symbols produced in the same scriptorium over three hundred years earlier, though they differ somewhat in style. A further manuscript, written probably in Bangor, Co. Down, and perhaps after St Malachy had renewed his connection with the monastery there around 1140, is the Gospel book numbered 122 in Corpus Christi College, Oxford (Pl.167–8 and 172), which reflects an even more remarkable backward look in its use of the Chi-Rho, echoing earlier Gospel manuscripts such as the St Gall 51 Gospels (p.99) or the Maihingen Gosepls now in Augsburg. Its pristine condition helps us to imagine how fresh and colourful its more faded counterparts must have looked, as the blend of blues, purples, oranges and reds outshine

those of the Missal in the same library mentioned above, which also shares similar beasts and snakes. But the Corpus Gospel book also shares the beast-and-foliage style of initial letters with the *Liber Hymnorum*, showing how homogeneous the decoration of many of these manuscripts can be.

Sharing the freshness of the Corpus Christi Gospel book is what is perhaps the latest – and probably also the finest – of all this group of manuscripts, a small Psalter (Pl.171) in the British Library (Add. Ms. 36.929), written by a scribe named Cormac whom we cannot identify. With the Book of Leinster, it may well belong to the third quarter of the twelfth century, but its ornament is incomparably richer. The palette of colours is much the same as those in the Corpus Christi Gospel book (though with a much larger

Decorated initials from
Cormac's Psalter in the British
Library, London.

element of green) and – like the Corpus Christi Missal – the capital letters tend to dominate much of the page they ornament. They present a splendid treasury of beasts, with both foliage and animals intertwining with them, particularly noticeable at the beginning of each of the set of fifty psalms, but the manuscript has echoes of the Book of Kells in the existence of many smaller decorated capital letters throughout the text. With this entrancing little volume, the Irish tradition of illuminated manuscripts going back to the Cathach half a millennium earlier reaches the end of a century-long Indian summer and, like the earlier climax in the Book of Kells, it has no apparent successors. The text of Cormac's Psalter contains a formula of absolution named after St Bernard, the great Cistercian, biographer and friend of St Malachy, and so it can join the Gospel book Harley 1802 and Corpus Christi 122 as having come into being under the aegis of Malachy, the reformer who brought the Cistercians to Ireland. This helps to explain some continental connections both in the texts of these manuscripts (as in Harley 1802) and in their decoration (such as the Canon tables and in the small heads which occasionally appear in the Corpus Christi Gospel book). It is remarkable, however, that these connections are not more in evidence and that the splendid codices being produced by the very active scriptoria in France and Germany in the Romanesque period find so few echoes in Ireland. The most noticeable feature of these Irish manuscripts is the conservative nature of their decoration, which is very traditional, with obvious intentional echoes of the great illuminated codices of three hundred years earlier. The only concession to taste from outside is the use of the beast and foliage motifs which, however, derive probably from some Viking-inspired source which is most likely to have been the city of Dublin.

Some of the simpler forms of decorated initials are found in the manuscripts coming from the old Irish monasteries, and it is significant that these include Rawlinson B. 502, *Lebor na hUidre* and the Book of Leinster, which intentionally gathered up historical, literary and genealogical material compiled over many centuries – lest it get lost or be otherwise destroyed. One gets the distinct impression that, with the advent of the Reform movement and, later, the arrival of the Cistercians and other continental religious orders, the monks of the old Irish monasteries saw the writing on the wall. Being conservatives, they felt the need to preserve old traditions in the face of innovations which they feared would engulf Irish society and destroy what they stood for. They were the last bastions of ancient Gaelic culture, and they demonstrated this by collecting and writing down all the material in these three great codices, reinforcing their role as inheritors of older scriptorial traditions by decorating their manuscripts with designs which echo those of three centuries earlier. Here, a deliberate revival of the ancient was to be pitted against the modern.

Church Reform and its Consequences

Dublin's earliest church – Christ Church – was founded by its Norse king, Sihtric, in 1038 and,

in due course, claimed the status of a Cathedral. Not wanting to have its first bishop consecrated by others in Ireland, the city chose to send him to Canterbury instead. This gave successive archbishops of Canterbury a foot in the Irish door in their efforts to reform the Irish Church which – on matters such as divorce, simony and lay control – was lagging behind the latest improvements in England. The first of the O'Brien kings after Brian Boru to be accepted outside the country as king of Ireland was approached by Canterbury to initiate reforms, but it was not until the reign of his son Muirchertach that the Church in Ireland began to address itself to the problems of reform at the Synod of Cashel in 1101, when Muirchertach took the opportunity of presenting the Church with the Rock of Cashel, former citadel of the kings of Munster. Among other things, the Synod attempted to curb, if not abolish, lay rule over the Irish monasteries, thereby striking at the very heart of these centuries-old foundations. Ten years later, at Rathbreasail, Church authorities divided the country into a number of dioceses, and set about defining their boundaries and organizing their administration along European lines. Gilbert, bishop of the old Norse town of Limerick now under O'Brien rule, presided over the proceedings as papal legate, and his position gave added weight to his thesis that bishops were to have authority not only over parishes – but also over monasteries. This posed a dangerous threat to the independent existence of the Irish monasteries, and began the decline in Irish literature and culture that they had fostered for many generations. These new reformers Donnchadh Ó Corráin describes as having 'destroyed the social, economic and cultural base of Irish learning' and he accuses them of 'asset-stripping', in other words, selling monastic lands to amass money to pay for the administration of the new dioceses. But the old Irish monasteries were not going to give up the ghost so easily, and to earn alternative income, they must have stepped up the practice of pilgrimage which, to judge by the Irish annals, reached its height in the twelfth century, as it did in the rest of Europe. They got royal patronage, where they could, to enshrine the relics of their local saint as a magnet for pilgrims whom they saw as their only means of income. This is probably the best way to explain why the twelfth century provided so many of Ireland's medieval reliquaries; they would probably not exist had the church reform never happened.

Writing at the end of the century, Giraldus Cambrensis noted that the people and clergy of both Ireland and Wales 'have a great reverence for bells that can be carried about, and staffs belonging to the saints, and made of gold or silver or bronze, and curved at their upper ends'. What Giraldus was describing was presumably the relic-shrines rather than the actual bells and croziers of the saints themselves. While book-shrines made up some of the most important reliquaries surviving from the eleventh century, the twelfth century produced a greater variety, as we know from surviving specimens – tomb-shaped shrines, a corporeal reliquary such as St Lachtin's arm, and even a drinking horn preserved as a relic at Tongres in Belgium, and now in the Royal Museum for Art and History in Brussels.

However, the surviving material gives us only a part of the picture, for literary references speak of much greater riches extant in the eleventh and twelfth centuries. For instance, under the year 1129, the Annals of Clonmacnoise recorded the theft from the great altar of a standing cup, three jewels, two cups of silver, a gilt cross, and a chalice, together with what appears to have been a model of Solomon's Temple which king Máelsechnaill had bequeathed to the church.

II

Late Eleventh- and Twelfth-Century Metalwork

■

Croziers and Crozier Reliquaries

The most numerous insignia to have survived from the Irish Church of the early second millennium are croziers and crozier-shrines, whose preservation we owe to their hereditary family keepers who kept them after the old monasteries were deserted in the later Middle Ages. Forming a collection unparalleled in Europe, these crosier-shrines were reputed to have had the power to work miracles and cure the sick. Oaths were sworn upon them, they were used for the collection of church revenues, and they also symbolized the authority of the church or monastery where they were preserved. Earlier croziers have already been discussed (p.215). Of the later group dating from the eleventh and particularly the twelfth century, the finest example is that known as the Crozier of

the Abbots of Clonmacnoise (Pl.175–6), though nothing is known of its early history. It is made up of a straight shaft surmounted by a rounded crook with the typical drop-head. The shaft has three knops, the upper and lower organised in triangular panels with a variety of interlace and geometric patterns interspersed with blue glass studs. Beneath the upper knop are lions (Pl.175) with spiral joints and interlocking legs which have their origin in the Great Beast motif found during the eleventh century in late Viking art both in and outside Scandinavia. Nordic influence is even more to the fore on the crook where elongated beasts have very Scandinavian-looking eyes in the shape of a tear with the narrow point facing towards the turned-up snout. Their bodies, inlaid with silver in niello, interlace with one another, and their junctions are interrupted, as on the

shrine of the Cathach. This animal ornament still echoes the Irish variant of the Ringerike style, but the greater axiality of the loops already shows more than a hint of the symmetry to be found in Ireland's version of the Urnes style which followed it. The silver inlay is also found on another, simpler, crozier which may well have also emanated from Clonmacnoise, and it was a technique typical of this famous midland monastery. But it was, perhaps, also practised elsewhere, as silver was inlaid on other pieces found some distance from the midlands, such as the so-called Inisfallen crozier found in the river Laune near Killarney and now in the National Museum in Dublin. It, too, betrays Ringerike tendencies, though oxydization has robbed it of much of its crisp ornament.

Of the many crozier shrines surviving from around this period, one further splendid example deserves to be mentioned, not only because of the quality of its ornament, but also because it is dated. It was discovered in a blocked-up doorway at Lismore Castle, Co. Waterford, in 1814. An inscription requests a prayer for Nial mac meic Aeducain, who had the crozier made; he became abbot of Lismore in 1090 and died as its bishop in 1113. The inscription also names the craftsman, Neachtain — one of a number mentioned in Irish inscriptions of the eleventh and twelfth centuries, in contrast to the continental tradition where few artificers' names are recorded, showing how highly the Irish regarded them. The hexagonal ferrule at the foot of the crozier bears five horned figures (devils?) between silver motifs at their heads and feet. The knop immediately above them is divided into squares, rectangles and

The Lismore Crozier
(National Museum, Dublin).

Details of the Lismore crozier.

cross-shaped panels bearing animal ornament as well as human figures, some of them forming a four-man interlace harking back to those on the much earlier High Crosses at Ahenny and elsewhere. Another figure bears a satchel on his abdomen, hanging from his neck, which may represent the container of a relic, and appears on twelfth-century High Crosses at Kilfenora, Downpatrick and probably also Cashel (p.308). The middle knop is also divided up into a number of small panels bearing animals, either single or in pairs, interlacing and criss-crossing with one another, and clearly enmeshed by much narrower ribbons, making them look as if they had been caught in a net. The beasts, with a single front leg more noticeable than the hind leg, belong unmistakably to the Urnes style in Scandinavia, which features a Great Beast intertwined with ribbons or a thinner serpent. Curiously, this style was already declining in Scandinavia before it began to influence Irish metal- and stone-work around 1100 and, unlike the preceding Ringerike style, Urnes is not noticeably present in the trial pieces or the decorated woodwork of Dublin, suggesting that it was not Dublin that purveyed the style to Ireland. It should be pointed out that the Irish version of the Urnes style was not particularly close to its Scandinavian parent, and must have come through some other, as yet unlocalized, filter. Though rather different in character, the animals biting one another on the openwork crest of the crozier have long upper snouts and tear-shaped eyes (pointing backwards this time). In such details, they betray their Scandinavian ancestry as much as do the ribbons intertwining among the animals and running amok across the snout of the fine animal head pointing downwards at the end of the crest. The other notable feature of the crook of this crozier is the presence of a number of circular bosses of blue and white *millefiori* glass which, though made of larger coloured rods, are among the earliest examples at this period of an intentional revival of techniques practised in Irish metalwork centuries earlier. The Lismore crozier is, indeed, one of the finest examples of a happy combination of old Irish metalworking techniques and designs of the Scandinavian-inspired animal ornament which are such a feature of Irish art of the eleventh and twelfth centuries.

Bell Shrines

Also sharing with the Clonmacnoise crozier the technique of inlaying strips of silver against a black niello background is a bell shrine now in the British Museum and found some centuries ago, it is said, in a hollow tree beside the well at Kilcuilawn, near Borrisoleigh, Co. Tipperary. It is normally referred to by its Irish name, *Bearnán Cuileáin*. Attached to the bronzed iron bell is a bronze plate incised with a cross-shape having a circular centre and expanding terminals of the kind well-known from memorial slabs at Clonmacnoise and elsewhere. The plate is probably the sole survivor of a total of four – one on each face of the bell, held in place by solid bronze castings above and below. That on top can be divided into two sections. On the extremities of the lower section are downward-looking animal-heads with hairs on the snout curling up at the end in a way which

Detail of the *Bearnán Cuileáin* bell-shrine in the British Museum.

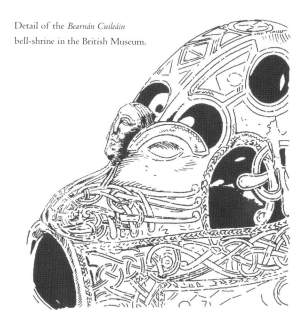

already betrays its roots in the Urnes tradition, while at the same time retaining echoes of the Ringerike style. Emerging like hair from the side of the heads of these monsters is an irregular interlace which terminates in what seems like an attenuated animal head, ornamented with inlaid ribbons of silver. More impressive, and in a splendid state of preservation, is the upper section having on the ends a wonderful animal head resembling a seal just surfacing above the water, more brooding and benign than the combative Urnes beast which must, ultimately, have been its progenitor. The silvery hairs of its 'moustache' flow backwards and curl up in foliate fashion at the ends, and between its prominent eyebrows — decorated with the same wavy silver wire on black niello found on the collar-knop of the British Museum crozier — is a simple but noble face with hair parted in the middle. This is one of the most colourful of all the late Irish reliquaries, and belongs probably to the early twelfth century.

Very fine quality work is also found on parts of the Shrine of St Patrick's Bell (Pl.177–180), now preserved in the National Museum in Dublin. The bronze-coated iron bell is traditionally associated with St Patrick, and is almost certainly centuries older than the shrine which contains it, datable by inscription to the years between 1091 and 1105. The inscription surrounds one face of the shrine which consists of a silver grille made up of openwork crosses, and indicates that one of its patrons was abbot of Armagh and that it was made by a family business comprising father and sons. The other face (Pl.177) is designed as a cross in an almost square frame, both cross and frame divided up into panels of interlace and animal ornament frequently in symmetrical figure-of-eight configurations executed in a complicated filigree technique (Pl.178). Far more eye-catching are the animals on the sides (Pl.179), above and below the cast handle emerging from a cross-in-circle. These animals are long and sinuous, interlacing with one another and with very long jaws curling up at the end. The heads of these animals can be discerned easily because their almond-shaped eyes consist of small blue glass beads. On one side, the lower set of animals forms an equal-armed cross which, though symmetrical, possesses plenty of vitality against the bronze background which gives added relief to the animals. The crest creates an arch terminating in a slender-headed animal from which foliate tendrils curl gracefully backwards to intertwine symmetrically among one another, leaving breathing space between them. One side of the crest (Pl.180) shows two peacocks facing each other and having their wings and tails interleaved with the branches of a Tree of Life which grows up between them. This shrine combines the Scandinavian style of ornament with traditional elements such as filigreed interlace, but our difficulty in finding parallels for it suggests that the other products of its Armagh workshop have not managed to survive.

The Cross of Cong

The use of the Great Beast in the Irish version of the Scandinavian Urnes style reaches a climax in the Cross of Cong (Pl.174) which, together with

St Manchan's Shrine to be discussed below, rivals in vitality and inventiveness the Ardagh Chalice, the Derrynaflan paten and the Tara Brooch of more than three centuries earlier. Its purpose was to enshrine a fragment of the True Cross which was lent to Ireland in 1119. When the High King Turlough O Connor got permission to retain a small portion of the precious relic, he had this processional cross made as a fitting reliquary for it. His patronage is documented in long inscriptions on the narrow sides, which also mention other sponsors as well as the craftsman who made it. It is likely to have been completed around 1127. One of the inscriptions states that 'in this cross is preserved the cross on which the founder of the world suffered' and the rock crystal at the centre of one face was presumably designed to magnify the fragment. It is raised on a conical silver mount, around which are placed bosses of blue and white glass, and ornament of gold filigree as well as niello. Emanating from this central boss out along the arms, and up and down the shaft, is a string of alternating large and small settings of glass linked by strips of silver, their differing sizes – and the cross-shaped lines radiating vertically and horizontally from them – bringing an interesting rhythm into the whole design of the cross. These lines separate panels (Pl.182) bearing one or two great beasts, each subtly different from one another. What makes the cross so attractive at first sight is the gracious undulating curve of the outlines of both arms and shaft. The back (Pl.181) is not formally subdivided into panels, but consists of separated pairs of Great Beasts interlocking with one another in a figure-of-eight, and further interlaced by slender animals who, in themselves, are also subtly asymmetrical (Pl.183). Holding the foot of the cross above a knop are two animal heads with protruding ears (Pl.182–3), and growing up between them on the side is an almost naturalistic piece of foliage with leaves curling up at the end almost reminiscent of the earlier Ringerike style.

Through its subtle variations, the cross avoids the dullness of symmetry ('a fatal sign in any northern animal style' as David Wilson and Ole Klindt-Jensen sagely noted) and shines through the rhythmical movements of the animals which stride and struggle with one another across its surfaces. These add another chapter to the veritable zoo of Scandinavian-inspired animals which dominate much of the ornament of eleventh- and twelfth-century Irish metalwork. But here also there is a definite hint of reviving much earlier techniques through the use of enamel in circular settings along the tubular outline, but with yellow predominating over red – thus reversing the trend used in the eighth century. The complexity and subtlety of its design makes the Cross of Cong one of the last great masterpieces of Irish medieval metalwork. Another recipient of the True Cross in the twelfth century was the abbey which was called after it – Holycross, in County Tipperary. It produced a cast bronze sheet bearing a cross filled with half palmettes, with the area between the arms filled by further interlacing beasts in a subtle low relief which makes it into a minor masterpiece (p.295). Given that it cannot be too far removed from the Cross of Cong in the date of its manufacture, one may well ask if it could have decorated a shrine containing the abbey's True Cross fragment.

173 The portable twelfth-century shrine of St Manchan preserved in the Catholic church at Boher, Co. Offaly, is dominated by a roughly equal-armed cross, and decorated with yellow enamel patterns that hark back to the art of earlier generations.

174 The Cross of Cong in the National Museum of Ireland was made for by the High King Turlough O Connor around 1127 to house a relic of the True Cross, and is one of the last great masterpieces of medieval Irish metalwork.

175 Proud animals beneath the uppermost knop on the Crozier of the Abbots of Clonmacnoise, of c. 1100, preserved in the National Museum of Ireland in Dublin.

176 The crook of the Crozier of the Abbots of Clonmacnoise is decorated with animals of Scandinavian inspiration partially inlaid with silver strips.

177 The shrine made between 1091 and 1105 to house St Patrick's Bell (National Museum, Dublin).

178 Interlace patterns on the Shrine of St Patrick's Bell.

179 Sinuous elongated animals interlace gracefully on the side of St Patrick's Bell Shrine.

180 Haughty peacocks prance on the top of St Patrick's Bell Shrine.

181 The imperfect back of the Cross of Cong is filled with animals forming figures of eight.

182 Great asymmetrical beasts fill the panels on the front of the Cross of Cong, as another holds the base of the shaft firmly in its jaws.

183 The Cross of Cong: floral ornament sprouts unexpectedly between the two large animal heads that grip either side of the shaft.

184 Crossing the palm with silver: foliate tendrils on the hand of the Shrine of St Lachtin's Arm (1118–21), preserved in the National Museum in Dublin.

185 An ingenious tangle of interlace on the Shrine of St Lachtin's Arm.

186 The Shrine of St Lachtin's Arm, which is one of the earliest surviving European examples of its genre, was formerly preserved at Donaghmore, Co. Cork.

187 St Manchan's Shrine: the domed bosses bear 'Great Beast' ornament similar to that on the Cross of Cong (Pl.182).

188 St Manchan's Shrine: the inscrutable bearded and bare-breasted men, each with a different hand-gesture, are comparable to the Romanesque crucifix figures common throughout much of Europe in the twelfth century.

189 The eleventh/twelfth century *Breac Maedhóg* shrine preserved in the National Museum in Dublin. The base is decorated with openwork diaper patterns framed by panels of interlace.

190 The *Breac Maedhóg*: the figures may not have belonged to it originally.

191 The *Breac Maedhóg*: sad and grieving figures attached to the shrine.

192–3 The *Breac Maedhóg*: a single clean-shaven figure with a cross placed third from the left stands out like a true portrait when compared to his more stylized bearded fellows bearing attributes,which could identify some of them as apostles and St Paul.

194 The bronze Crucifixion plaque from Clonmacnoise, Co. Offaly, now in the National Museum in Dublin, shows a Christ more triumphant than suffering and has been variously dated to c. 900 or c. 1100.

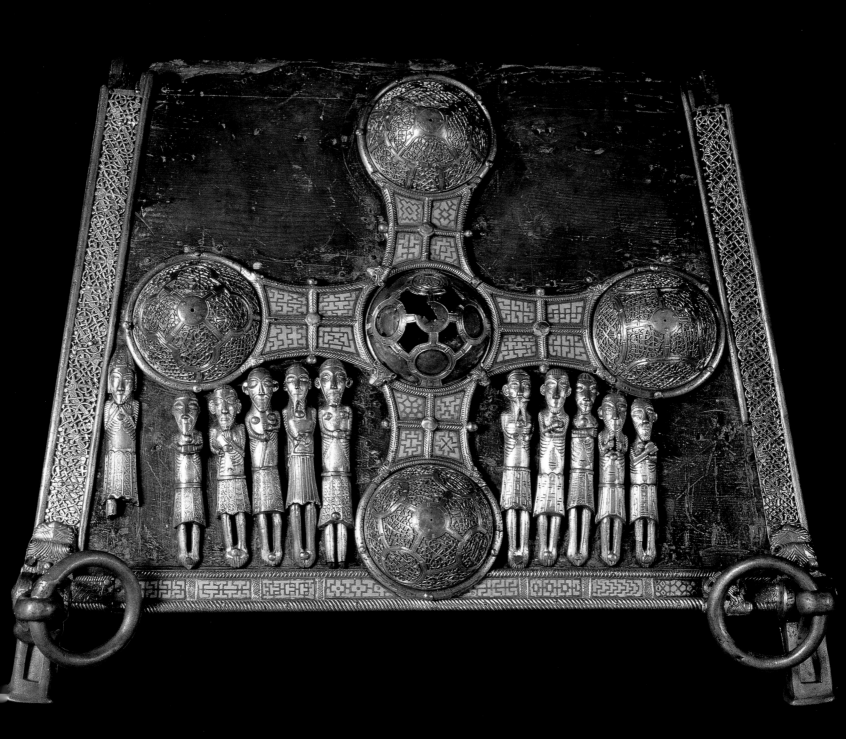

173

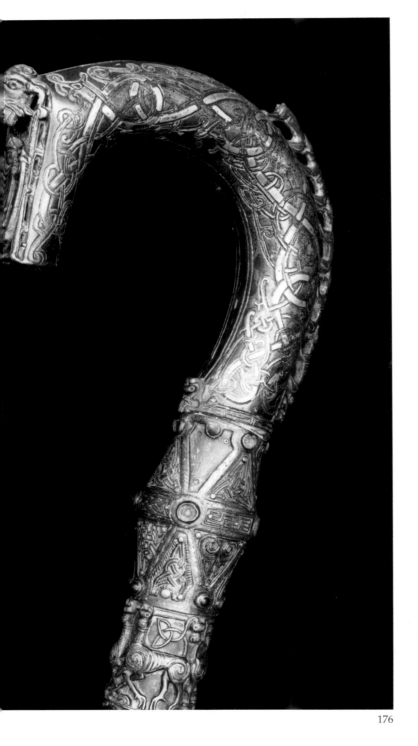

176

177

179

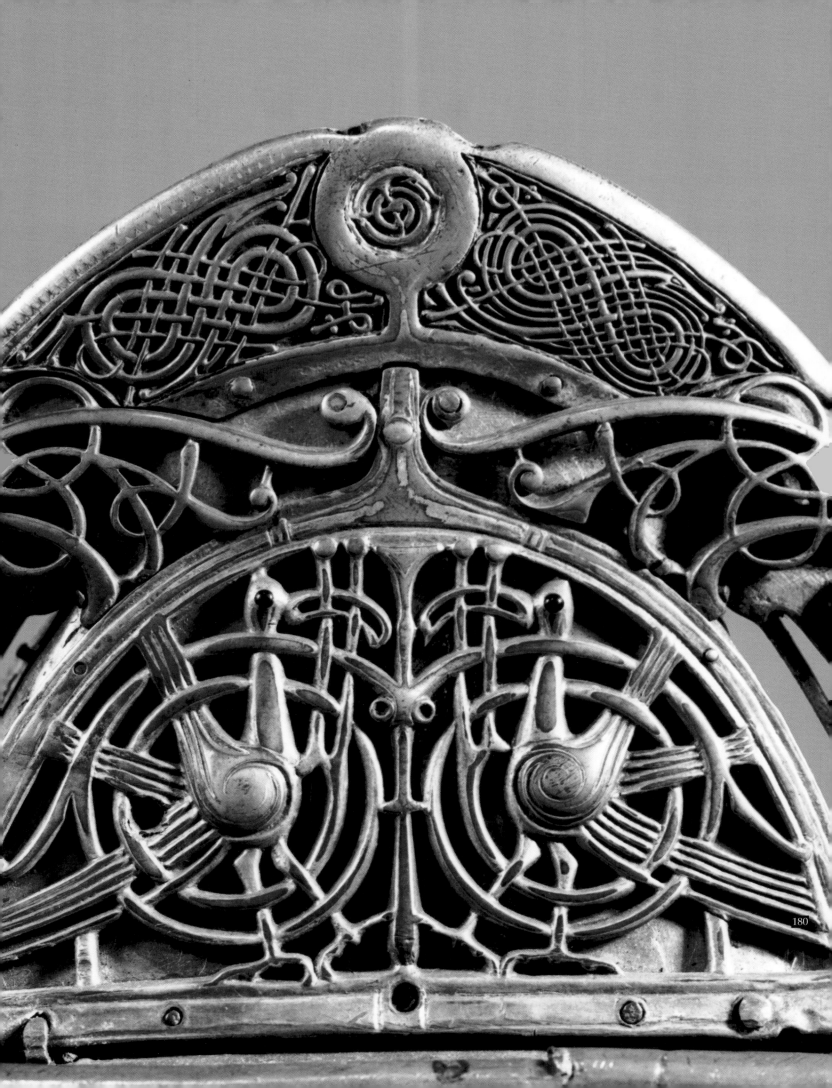

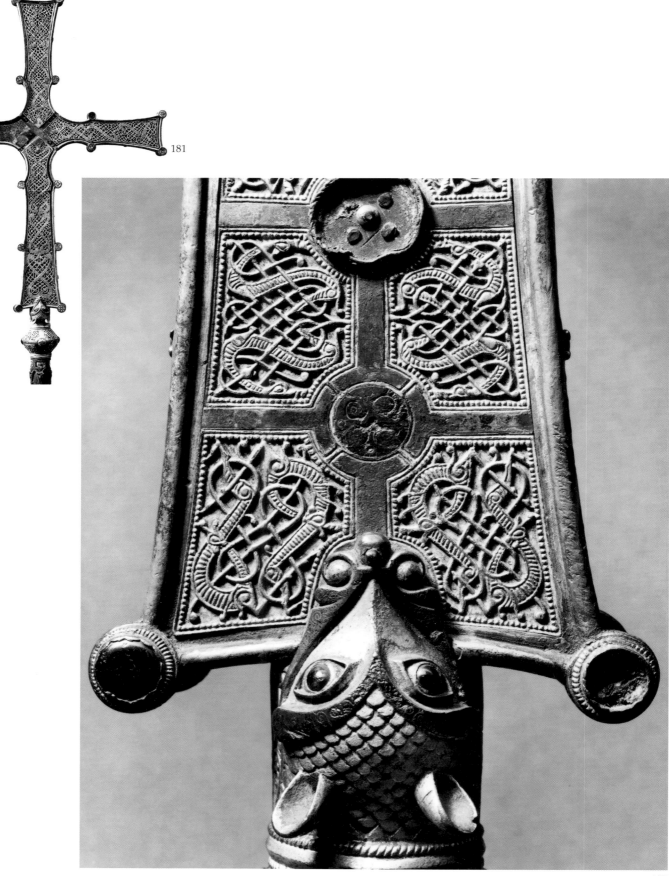

181

182

184

185

186

187

189

190

The Shrine of St Lachtin's Arm

Two further major metalwork shrines with animal ornament remain to be mentioned, both designed to contain corporeal relics of saints. The first of these is the arm-shaped reliquary known as St Lachtin's shrine (Pl.186) – one of the earliest known examples of an arm-shrine surviving anywhere in Europe. The custom of enshrining arm-relics of saints in reliquaries of this kind had already developed on the European continent in the eleventh century, and became more common in the twelfth. This example is in the shape of an upright forearm with fingers clenched. Like the Cross of Cong, it records royal patronage in its inscriptions, which provide a date between 1118 and 1121. It was preserved at Donaghmore, Co. Cork, where a church was dedicated to St Lachtin. However, its inlaid silver links it to the more northerly workshop of the midlands which manufactured the *Bearnán Cuileáin* and the Clonmacnoise crozier. The palm of the hand alone bears foliate ornament (Pl.184), but the eight rectangular panels (Pl.185–6) making up much of the forearm are, once again, decorated with Urnes-derived patterns inlaid with gold and silver in niello, some symmetrical, others clearly not. Further Urnes variants appear on the horizontal binding strip half way along the arm, but some of the animals on the base – including one seen from above, with paws poised at an angle to the body – hark back to animals of the eighth and ninth centuries. Frank Mitchell has pointed to the existence of another echo of previous glories in the former presence of a panel of enamel underneath the base of the shrine.

St Manchan's Shrine

The other important shrine (Pl.173) of a corporeal relic is that associated with a little-known saint named Manchan, which came originally from his monastery at Lemanaghan, Co. Offaly, and is now preserved not far away in the Catholic church at Boher. It differs from the other shrines in having the shape of a gabled roof, probably a variant of the tomb-shaped shrines of three or four centuries earlier. On each corner, it has large rings so that the shrine could be carried – probably shoulder-high – around and beyond the confines of the ancient monastery. The two main faces are dominated by equal-armed crosses consisting of large hemispherical bronze bosses at the centre and extremities, joined by flat arms subdivided into panels with yellow enamel creating different patterns. Each of the large bronze bosses is very different in design but, with the exception of the less-well preserved central boss, they all share subdivision into various shapes

Bronze plaque from Holycross Abbey, Co. Tipperary (National Museum, filled with Urnes-derived quadrupeds (Pl.187), whose details are so similar to those of the Cross of Cong that they may both be products of the same workshop, located in Roscommon. The triangular sides show further examples of high-quality cast animal ornament and yellow enamelled panels. Attached to one face, but not in their original positions, are cast-bronze figures (Pl.188) wearing loin-cloths with facets bearing geometrical, spiral and plant ornament. They vary in size, have long lugubrious bearded faces and high ears, and show stylized ribs and folded arms or joined hands. The only attribute held, other than a stick, is an axe, which prompted David Wilson to identify the figure holding it as the Norse saint Olaf. Apparently, two of the figures did not form part of the shrine, and were forcibly attached to it in the last century. But the others, now lined up in a secondary position on the face, presumably did belong to the shrine originally, and holes in the wooden core suggest that they were formerly arranged in two rows, one above the other. Similar figures now preserved at various locations in Ireland and England may have helped to complement those still on the shrine. Other separate figures with long robes may have come from the same workshop, even if they did not originally form part of the shrine.

The *Breac Maedhóg*

If the curious figures on St Manchan's shrine were arranged in two registers one above the other, they may have been following a precedent created by one of the most unusual and puzzling of the later shrines, that known as the *Breac Maedhóg*, preserved in the National Museum in Dublin. The Saint Maedhóg from which it gets its name was associated with Cavan, and it was for long preserved at Drumlane, the county's most important monastic foundation. The shrine is traditionally said to have got its name Breac, meaning speckled, from the colours of the various relics of saints and martyrs it is said to have contained – Saints Stephen, Laurence and Clement, the ankle of St Martin, and even some of the hair of the Virgin. It is unlikely that any of these saints are represented among the male and female figures which are now attached to the face of this tomb-shaped shrine (Pl.190–3). These are arranged in two, and formerly in three, registers on the face, and are probably not in their original position, that is, if they originally belonged to this shrine at all. Almost all of the males have long beards, and some bear books which could suggest their identification as evangelists. One is balding above the forehead and carries a sword, possibly St Paul, but the other figures – including the ladies – cannot be identified satisfactorily. They have an extraordinary collection of hair styles. Equally bizarre are the birds and feathered figures (angels?) standing on one another between them (Pl.193). The interlace and fret motifs on the hems of the garments echo decoration before the turn of the millennium, and the folds of the figures' garments bear a more than fleeting resemblance to those of the evangelists in much earlier Gospel manuscripts such as the Book of Mulling (p.88). But the figures here are likely to belong to the eleventh or, more probably, the twelfth century, when long, golden sarcophagi with 'weepers' on the sides, and other figures on the sloping roofs, became common on the continent. Yet no obvious parallel for this shrine springs to mind and, while it may reflect knowledge of some French or German shrine, it remains unique, its figures almost overpowering in the treasury of Irish art before the Norman invasion. Together with the figures on St Manchan's shrine, they exemplify a tradition of representing the human figure in Irish metalwork in the first two centuries of the second millennium, showing how the products of metal workshops and manuscript scriptoria go each their own individual ways and have separate sources of inspiration, more so than was the case before the turn of the millennium. In total contrast, the base (Pl.189) consists of bronze panels with open-work cross-decoration framed by panels of interlacing.

Crucifixion Plaques and Crucifixes

Figures of the crucified Christ are found on small, square bronze Crucifixion plaques, of which eight are known. With one exception, all are openwork and conform to a similar formula – a decorated frame enclosing the figure of Christ on the cross, with an angel above each arm and Stephaton and Longinus beneath. Christ is usually clad in a loin cloth but, in two instances, he wears a long-sleeved garment to the feet. In spite of their similarities, no two are made from the same mould. Perforations in the frame make it certain that they were attached to something, but to what is unknown. In many cases, the prominent head has been rubbed smooth, which could argue for the plaques having been repeatedly kissed by the faithful on Good Friday. One of the best-preserved examples (Pl.194) comes from Clonmacnoise (where it may have been made), showing Christ's long robe decorated with half-acanthus and the frame having a repeating pattern of diamond shapes between parallel bars. The presence of these two features on the binding strip of the earlier part of the British Museum crozier (Pl.149) and on the side of the lost kite-shaped brooch from Clonmacnoise illustrated on page 214 is a good argument favouring a date of around 900 for these plaques – and all are so similar that a date for one applies to all. But other cogent reasons can be put forward for a date of around 1100. The half acanthus occurs in a similar form on the crest of an early twelfth-century crozier in the National Museum, and the joyous rather than suffering Christ would conform more to eleventh/twelfth century ideals. One further argument which would sway the evidence more in favour of the latter dating was the presence on a lost example from County Mayo of silver inlay, apparently of the kind found on items datable to around 1100, such as the crozier of the abbots of Clonmacnoise. Christ's hair streaming sideways on an unprovenanced example which shows him wearing a loin-cloth can also be compared to that of the figures on the *Breac Maedhóg*, which are probably either eleventh or twelfth century.

We are on surer ground with the dozen or more Crucifix figures, all of bronze – with one exception, made of silver – which are likely to have an Irish origin. The earliest example is only known through its outline, recognised by Raghnall Ó Floinn on a bronze cross with Ringerike decoration, and therefore probably of the second half of the eleventh century. The surviving examples are not of high quality, and are a pale shadow of their models which survive in hundreds of examples in central Europe. Ó Floinn can scarcely be far wrong in assigning most of the Irish figures to the later twelfth and early thirteenth centuries, when they document clearly a rapid decline in Irish craftsmanship. Our opinion of metalwork in the second half of the twelfth century might have been different, however, had good fortune allowed the survival of three reliquaries mentioned in the Annals as having been executed in the 1160s: one at Clonfert in 1162, another at Mohill in County Leitrim in 1166, and a third at Roscommon in 1170. One rare surviving example of good-quality work in walrus ivory dating probably from the third quarter of the century is the crozier from Aghadoe, County Kerry, now in Hannover (Pl.146). It has echoes of the much older Helgö crozier (Pl.143) in the figure presumed to be Jonah who emerges from the serpent forming the volute of the crozier.

Eleventh- and twelfth-century Irish metalwork can be seen to be idiosyncratically Irish. It combines the dominant Scandinavian-derived animal ornament, traditional native Irish types (such as crozier and tomb-shaped shrines), and a resurgence of techniques and designs practised by Irish craftsmen three or four centuries earlier, such as enamel and *millefiori*. It is, however, also innovative in some of its techniques such as the use of silver and niello. But what is remarkable is that it seems to remain a world apart from the eloquent and imaginative metalwork of the Romanesque period in other parts of Europe, though reflecting its influence in the human figures on the *Breac Maedhóg*, St Manchan's shrine and the separate bronze crucifixes. This is scarcely due to intentional isolationism, or resistance to novel artistic inspiration from abroad, but rather to a conscious programme on the part of the old monasteries to re-inforce the old Irish tradition behind the metalwork enshrining the relics they were using to fight for their very survival. By re-creating older styles and techniques, they were purposely recalling the halcyon days of four hundred years earlier in order to make the point that institutions which had done so much to foster art and culture for centuries should not be made to forego their independence and submit to the reforming party. Their success, at least for a time, may have been due to support from no less a person than the High King, Turlough O Connor (1119–1156), who himself had commissioned the Cross of Cong. It is certainly noteworthy that elements of the reform movement, which had started in Munster with the Synod of Cashel in 1101 and later moved to Ulster under St Malachy, appear to have by-passed O Connor's province of Connacht, despite the fact that he was the most prominent political figure in Ireland during the first half of the twelfth century. Significantly, the Cistercians – the new continental monastic order introduced to promote reform – made little progress in Connacht during his lifetime, moving from one place to another and only finally settling down in Boyle five years after his death. It was towards the end of his life, when archiepiscopal sees were being distributed at the Synod of Kells in 1152, that he clearly co-operated for his own political reasons in order to ensure that one of his bases, at Tuam, would feature as one of the four archbishoprics allotted to Ireland. If we seek a reason why the metalworker's craft would seem to have suffered a decline in Ireland after Turlough O Connor's death in 1156, it is probably best seen not as a result of the reforming movement (which signally failed to produce any fine metalwork of its own) or because of the Norman invasion of 1169, but because largesse from the High King downwards was probably no longer forthcoming. In the second half of the century, financial patronage was probably seen to be more effective if bestowed instead on the new style of Romanesque building and sculpture which had already begun to flourish on the old Irish monastic sites.

12

Twelfth-Century Churches and Crosses

■

Cormac's Chapel and Related Churches

Cormac's Chapel on the Rock of Cashel in County Tipperary (Pl.195) is the most remarkable Romanesque church surviving in Ireland, and its impact must have been startling to those who gathered for its consecration in 1134, most of whom would have grown up with the simple, undecorated rectangular stone churches of earlier Irish generations. It gets its name from Cormac Mac Cárrthaigh, king of Munster from 1123 to 1138, with just one brief interruption when he retired to the reforming monastery of Lismore in County Waterford. There he not only built churches, but also renewed an earlier acquaintance with St Malachy, Ireland's most indefatigable church reformer of the twelfth century. For the Reverend Aubrey Gwynn, Cormac's Chapel was the very embodiment of that reforming

movement, and it must surely have been Cormac's own hand which was responsible for combining together in this one building elements derived from a variety of sources. The almost identical towers rising where other churches would have transepts may well be Bavarian in origin, through connections with Regensburg which may have dispatched a small community of Benedictines to service the new chapel at Cashel. It was probably while the chapel was still being built that a fund-raising group arrived from Regensburg, among whom was probably Christian, a cousin of Cormac's who was later to become abbot of the *Schottenkirche* in Regensburg. The money was being collected for the construction of the church of St Jakob in Regensburg which has similar, though later, towers belonging to a type common in southern Germany.

But, as Roger Stalley has argued, the main influence on the design of Cormac's Chapel comes from the West Country in Southern England, in the area around the Severn estuary. There, the barrel-vaulting of the nave of Cormac's Chapel (Pl.197) and the rib-vaults of its chancel can be found in churches like that at Ewenny in South Wales, while the recently-conserved frescoes in the chancel – possibly depicting Solomon and the Queen of Sheba in front of the buildings of Jerusalem – may be connected in colouring with contemporary fashions in Canterbury. The superimposed series of blind arcades and the corbel-table of heads on the exterior south wall, the scalloped capitals and the chevron ornament widely used inside and out, can all be neatly paralleled in the South-west of England, and fighting the lion on the tympanum of the main, north, doorway (Pl.199) is a centaur who wears a Norman-style helmet with nose-guard, carved before any bellicose Norman baron ever set foot in Ireland. Furthermore, the floral bosses used in decorating the triangular gable above the same north door (Pl.196) are typical of the work of Bishop Roger of Salisbury at Sarum Cathedral, and it may well be that one of the masons working on the chapel may have come from England in the wake of the initial reform movement. One French feature in the Chapel is the series of human, but also animal, heads on the chancel arch (Pl.198), those at the top placed radially, and the others rising up vertically along the curve of the arch to meet them. Such heads are found widely in England, but France has the best parallels for the whole arrangement, as in the church at Bellegarde-sur-Loiret (Loiret). A further feature which is neither French nor English, but appears to be uniquely Irish, is the stone roof and the method of its support. Above the vaults of both nave and chancel there is a chamber or croft with curving sides like the interior of Gallarus oratory, and its walls – partially made of calcareous tufa for lightness – support the carefully-carved roofing stones to prevent them from sagging and falling inwards. Cormac's Chapel, built of a warm-coloured sandstone, may well have been the first of more than half a dozen Irish examples of the same unusual roofing technique, some of which we will encounter below. The amalgam of these various elements into a successful whole makes Cormac's Chapel a totally unique building owing much to England, but which could only have been built in Ireland. Yet this Royal Chapel, as Tadhg O'Keeffe has called it, dating between 1127 and 1134, comes a quarter of a century after the formal launch of the reform movement in Cashel in 1101. Why the lapse of time? We can be fairly sure that, shortly after the Synod of Cashel in 1101, a church was built upon the Rock, a part of which may have been the wall which Brian Hodkinson excavated under the wall of the chancel of the nearby thirteenth-century Cathedral – beneath which he found the walls of an even earlier wooden building. The existence of a stone church older than Cormac's Chapel would help to explain one further unique feature in the Chapel – namely the main doorway being in the north wall of the nave. Cormac's Chapel had three doors, one in the north tower (now blocked), and one on each side of the nave – but none in the west wall, where it would have been expected. That the Chapel's main

The north portal of
Cormac's Chapel, Cashel.

entrance faces north means that it must have
looked out onto an even more important building
on the site of the present Cathedral – possibly the
presumed earlier church towards which the door
of the Round Tower north of the Cathedral is
likely to have faced too. The fact that the chancel
of the Chapel is placed off-centre to the south of
the axial line of the nave could be explained by the
necessity of having had to make room for an
already existing structure, or by having to make a
change in plan during the course of construction.

Liam de Paor described Cormac's Chapel as 'a
piece of Romanesque *architecture*, as hardly any

other Irish Romanesque church is' and, with its
foreign appearance, he put it near the beginning
of the Irish series of Romanesque churches. But
was it the showpiece, uniting elements from
various sources, designed to launch the reform
movement with *éclat* twenty-five years late, or were
there earlier Romanesque churches in Ireland? We
do know that Cormac Mac Cárrthaigh himself
built other churches at Lismore, one of which
contained fresco fragments of a column and
capital which Tadhg O'Keeffe published and
presumed to be contemporary with the Cashel
frescoes. Historically, however, there is no evidence
to prove that any of Lismore's churches were older
than Cormac's Chapel. As there are no decorated
stones which can be associated with the presumed
predecessor of Cormac's Chapel, we may
reasonably infer that Cormac's Chapel was the
first Romanesque stone church on the Rock of
Cashel – but not necessarily the first of Ireland's
Romanesque churches. That distinction may
belong to the lost church of SS. Peter and Paul
consecrated at Armagh in 1126 by Cellach
(Celsus), St Malachy's precursor as a reforming
bishop in the primatial diocese. Its disappearance
may possibly have robbed us of Ireland's first essay
in the Romanesque style, whose dedicatees are the
prime saints of Rome, the centre of that universal
church to which the reformers wanted Ireland to
conform.

Cormac's Chapel did exert architectural and
artistic influence, particularly in Munster where
the reform movement had first taken hold but not,
curiously, in churches directly related to the
O'Brien family which had encouraged it. Another
of Cormac's foundations was Gill Abbey in Cork

city, where the attractive voussoirs published by John Bradley and Heather King and now preserved in St Fin Barre's Cathedral, reveal a quality at least equal to that in Cormac's Chapel, and which show that the latter was by no means alone in its splendour. Gill Abbey was, however, founded after Cormac's Chapel had been completed, and so must be seen as a follower of its style. We are much more uncertain about the date of another Munster church which also shows connections with Cormac's Chapel – that at Kilmalkedar, far away near the end of the Dingle Peninsula in County Kerry. Originally consisting of a nave with a small stone-roofed niche for the raised altar (mostly demolished later to make way for a larger chancel, also stone-roofed), the church shares with Cashel an animal-decorated tympanum, and a series of engaged columns on the nave walls, with recessed blind wall spaces between. A feature shared specifically with the north portal at Cashel is the pattern of interrupted diamonds bearing floral decoration on the underside of the chancel arch. In the Cashel Chapel, the columns in the nave have the function of carrying the ribs of the barrel vault (Pl.197) but, at Kilmalkedar, the colonnade is more decorational and not really necessary to carry the weight of the stone roof starting above them. The stone roof at Kilmalkedar, and the presence at its peak of a finial like that on a Gallarus-like oratory at Teampull Geal nearby, suggests a possible link between the corbelled

Interior blind arcading in the nave of Kilmalkedar church, Co. Kerry.

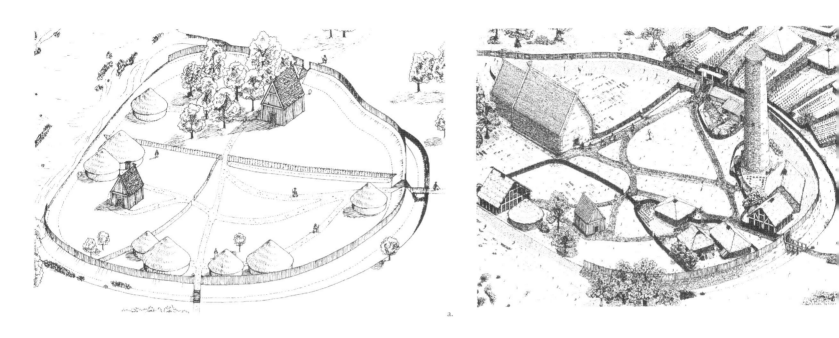

a.

Reconstruction of three stages of development in
the monastery of St Brendan at Ardfert, Co. Kerry:
a. Eighth century, with wooden church
b. 1100–1130, with Round Tower and stone church
c. 1150–1180, imaginary fire with Cathedral and
Romanesque church.

c.

oratories and Kilmalkedar church. But the evidence is not strong enough to prove that Kilmalkedar was a possible conduit for the idea of using a stone roof at Cashel, particularly as the Kerry church lacks the vaulting that helps to support it at Cashel. Kilmalkedar, indeed, incorporates two traditional Irish features which do not appear at Cashel – *antae*, the projections at the corners of the gable walls, and the inclined jambs of the doorway.

In size, Kilmalkedar differs little from other Irish churches without Romanesque decoration, and was much more a station on the pilgrimage road to Mount Brandon in honour of St Brendan than it is ever likely to have been a symbol of the reform movement, more particularly as Kilmalkedar was never in line to become the seat of a bishop. The situation is somewhat different at another Kerry location of Brendan veneration, his birthplace at Ardfert where a Romanesque church built in his honour probably served as a diocesan Cathedral. Most of it was demolished to make way for a larger Gothic successor in the thirteenth century, but the lower portion of its front façade was retained off-centre in the west gable of the new Cathedral. What survives – in the typical warm red sandstone of the Irish Romanesque in contrast with the harder, colder limestone of the Gothic – is a doorway heavily decorated with chevron ornament and flanked on each side originally by at least two blind arcades, those next to the door having a diaper pattern in the lower courses which finds parallels in French Romanesque. The façade may formerly have been framed by *antae* at the corner, like those at Kilmalkedar, and they are present also on another and related Munster church, St Cronan's at Roscrea, Co. Tipperary (Pl.201). Here the *antae* have vertical rolled mouldings at the edges, and both the doorway (Pl.200) and the two flanking blind arcaded arches have pediments in the style of the north doorway at Cormac's Chapel, with which it also shares the use of rosettes flanking the large figure standing out in relief above the doorway. Each of these three churches – Kilmalkedar, Ardfert and Roscrea – has its own links with Cormac's Chapel but seems to adopt only ornamental features rather than developing its whole novel concept, nor do they appear to make any effort towards expanding the size of the churches to scale the heights of those in England or France. Wherever Ardfert and Roscrea got the idea of a double blind arcade flanking the central west doorway, it was not Cormac's Chapel, which had no western doorway, but the source (English or French?) must remain for the present unknown. The retention of traditional Irish *antae* at least at Kilmalkedar and Roscrea, and the continuation of the small size of earlier Irish churches, confirms a conservative reaction to the innovations embodied in Cormac's Chapel and, by implication, to the ideals of reform which lay behind its construction. It was as if the reformers' aspirations were beginning to meet resistance among the older monastic-inspired religious communities, though Ardfert did adopt the new diocesan system during the first half of the twelfth century and Roscrea attempted to do so, while at the same time holding on to a strong monastic tradition.

Even before Cormac's Chapel was completed in 1134, the impetus for getting acceptance of the reforms had moved northwards to Ulster, and

Malachy continued the work zealously when he became bishop of Armagh in 1132. But after five years, he retired to Bangor in County Down where he introduced the Augustinians of Arrouaisian observance in 1140. Of the church which he built there, presumably for them, sadly not a trace remains, but it is likely to have been modelled on the more expansive churches being built in France at the time, an inference supported by a rebuke it drew from an Irishman who, when querying the necessity for such a large church, asked him: 'Good sir, why have you thought good to introduce this novelty into our regions? We are Irish, not Gauls. What is this frivolity? What need was there for a work so superfluous, so proud?'. This comment is contained in the Life of St Malachy by Bernard of Clairvaux, who was obviously trying to demonstrate the conservative nature of Irish church architecture – and how right he was. Malachy persisted, however, and when he brought the Cistercians to Mellifont in County Louth two years later, they brought with them the novel layout of the square or rectangular cloister with a church on one side and domestic structures on the other three. Where Malachy's charisma held sway in Ulster, from his arrival in 1132 until his death sixteen years later, the Romanesque style of ornament does not appear to have flourished greatly, and even subsequent decades failed to produce much more than a handful of Romanesque churches there, to judge by what survives. In the meantime, political power was held by Turlough O Connor of Connacht, High King from 1119 to 1156 and the royal patron of the Cross of Cong around 1127. It was during the period ushered in by the last years of his reign, and particularly in the third quarter of the twelfth century, that most of the Romanesque churches in Ireland would appear to have been built. They are found predominantly on the old monastic sites, and only comparatively few that we know of are located in the new diocesan centres such as Killaloe and Kilkenny. In building such churches which were reverting to old ways in their size as well as in the use of *antae* and west doorways, these monasteries were rejecting the extravagance of Cormac's Chapel, and they decorated just the doorways, chancel arches and occasionally the windows of their churches, in styles which the Irish would have seen spreading along the pilgrim roads of Europe on their way to Rome, Santiago or other shrines. Their small size, in contrast to the grandiose proportions of the glorious Romanesque structures rising in France and England at the time, is another indication of the conservatism of those who built them. Irish Romanesque churches would appear to have been linked with the practice of pilgrimage, probably their monasteries' chief financial resource after the introduction of the reform movement. Where, on the European continent, there were a number of chapels contained within a single large church, the Irish monasteries retained an old native tradition by having a number of separate small churches spread over the site. Each was likely to have been dedicated to an individual Irish saint whose tomb-shrine was involved in a network of pilgrimage traffic. Glendalough had the epithet 'of seven churches', doubtless to imitate the churches on the seven hills of Rome, familiar to Irish pilgrims, demonstrating again the probable link between Romanesque and pilgrimage in Ireland.

Twelfth-Century High Crosses

The twelfth-century High Crosses are very different from the earlier examples. The series of scriptural scenes typical of the ninth- and tenth-century crosses almost entirely disappeared and the Crucifixion and Adam and Eve are among the few biblical subjects continuing in use. What may have been their noblest sculptural expression is a stone head, probably of Christ (Pl.205) and possibly part of a cross — found by Liam de Paor in his excavations on the island of Inishcealtra in Lower Lough Derg, Co. Clare. The same island preserves the earliest datable example of the group, a sandstone cross standing to a height of only 1.60m. Its one visible face is covered all over in low interlacing, and an animal can be seen to devour a human leg on one of the two side panels incorporated into the bottom of the shaft. An inscription on one of the narrow sides, read by Macalister, asks a prayer for Cathasach, *Ardsenoir* or Chief Elder of Ireland, who died in 1111, according to the *Annals of Inisfallen*. Inishcealtra would have been O'Brien territory at the time, and the Ternoc mentioned in another part of the inscription may well have been one of the family associated with king Muirchertach, the advocate of reform who set up the Synod of Cashel in 1101. Interlace is also featured on the two other crosses datable by inscription to the twelfth century, both in the O Connor stronghold at Tuam and now preserved in St Mary's Protestant Cathedral there. Only surviving as shafts, their inscriptions bear the names of the High King Turlough O Connor (1119–1156) and Aedh O'Ossin, abbot of Tuam

from 1126 to 1152, after which he became archbishop. Since the latter is not named as archbishop in the inscriptions, we may take it that both belong to the period of his abbacy. One of the cross-shafts, which adds the name of the mason Gilla Christ U Tuathail, has interlace in rounded relief, and is made up of unframed groups of four knots of either ribbon or animal interlace, though the latter can go off on its own to provide an irregular pattern. One face has a set of four square fretwork patterns of a kind found also on limestone crosses on the Aran Islands in the same county, and also at Kilfenora, thus providing us with a rough chronological framework for them.

The other datable cross-shaft formerly stood in the Market Square at Tuam until 1992 when it was brought into the Cathedral — hence its name, the Market Cross. Its shaft is divided into numerous panels richly decorated with animal interlace in a flat relief. The interlace is sometimes tight and sometimes loose, like that on the same patron's Cross of Cong of *c.* 1127. The designs are based on fatter beasts criss-crossing one another in figures-of-eight, with a narrower animal interlacing itself among their limbs. The uppermost panel on one face of the Tuam Cross shaft has woven into the interlaced animals an ingeniously carved cross with a sunken square at the centre. The base of the cross which bears the inscription is also decorated with animal interlacing in relief. It has, in addition, two figures standing out from it in high relief, one with a crozier, the other without, suggesting that they may represent the abbot and the king mentioned in the inscription beneath their feet. One curious feature on the sides of the base is a circular holder for a (metal?) upright support for the lost head of the cross. A wooden model is likely for the cross (Pl.207) on the Rock of Cashel (now in the Hall of the Vicars' Choral there), where the differently-shaped supports are tied horizontally to the centre of the shaft in what looks like a carpentry technique. This Cashel Cross sits on a contemporary base bearing on one face a copy of openwork cross designs found on metalwork, and on another a panel of 'inhabited vine-scroll' having antecedents centuries older in both Ireland and Britain, while a third features an animal in a pattern of interrupted concentric circles. Evidence for the system of side supports for the arms of crosses is also found on two earlier crosses of a different kind, one at Drumcliff, Co. Sligo and the other at Boho, Co. Fermanagh, but there is still debate whether these two belong to the ninth/tenth century group of crosses, or act as intermediaries between them and the twelfth-century crosses.

On the Cashel cross, each face has a long and graceful figure standing out in very high relief — one a bishop, normally taken to be St Patrick, holding a crozier and clad in formal vestments, the other (Pl.207) long-robed and with outstretched arms, presumably Christ, bearing a rectangular object on the breast which probably represents a satchel for relics. Standing on top of the shaft of the Market Cross in Tuam Cathedral is a cross-head which has a similar combination of figures — a crowned Christ wearing a loin-cloth and with arms outstretched on one face, and a bishop or abbot in full canonicals on the other, where he carries a staff and is flanked by two much smaller figures on each side. This cross-head clearly does not belong to the shaft on which it stands, so that the inscription on the base of the latter cannot be used to date the cross-head, where the Christ figure is clearly modelled on one of the many bronze crucifix figures still surviving in many parts of Europe, including Ireland. The nearest parallels for the triangular decoration on the loin-cloth are south-eastern English or northern French, whereas the long-robed Christ figure at Cashel resembles the great English stone roods, though ultimately derived from the Volto Santo in Lucca.

The combination of Christ and an abbot or bishop is also typical of a number of other twelfth-century crosses, of which the finest was probably Roscrea. With its surface now much pitted by weather, this was obviously once a fine piece of sculpture, with interlaced animal ornament on the underside of the surviving ring. Unusually, the narrow sides of the shaft bore long-robed (secular?) figures, one perhaps female, while one of the faces clearly bears a representation of Adam and Eve. Not far away, and re-erected close to a small but very attractive Romanesque church at Monaincha, is a further cross with the figure of Christ on one face, animal interlace on the other, and the heads of two unidentified (biblical?) figures on one side. Cross and church are on what was once a small island in the middle of a lake, now dried up, and a much-frequented place of pilgrimage down to the seventeenth century. Another important place of pilgrimage (until 1862) is Glendalough where a much smaller Market Cross sharing many features with its counterparts west of the Shannon is kept in the Interpretative Centre. Each side is filled with a single panel of Scandinavian-style Great Beast animal ornament and, as at Tuam, there are two figures standing in high relief on the front of the base. Above one another on the main face of the cross are the figures of Christ and a bishop or abbot – probably, in this instance, the monastic founder, St Kevin. He is on a much smaller scale than the emaciated figure of the crucified Christ above, who wears an undecorated loin-cloth, though in equally high relief. The volutes on the arms of the cross, the rows of pelleted decoration on the edges of the shaft and the placing of the two figures one on top of the other, are also found on one of the most striking of the twelfth-century crosses, well-preserved because carved in hard limestone. This is the cross at Dysert O'Dea, Co. Clare, where head and shaft – though closely fitting – may not have originally been designed for one another, as the two figures differ considerably in the height of their relief. The head (Pl.203), bearing the long-robed figure of Christ with outstretched arms, may show the Saviour wearing a crown, demonstrating that he is the all-merciful judge, fitting in with the twelfth-century ideal, rather than the suffering Crucified Christ of the Carolingian period. On the west face (Pl.122), back-to-back with Christ, is a cross of five conjoined diamonds in relief bearing floral motifs in the same position as on the Glendalough cross. The shaft presents us with an abbot figure in very high relief and further variants of the fighting beasts, back-to-back or forming figures-of-eight, but in a style less animated than on the Market Cross at Tuam. This Dysert cross may be marginally later than the Tuam cross, possibly

bringing us into the second half of the twelfth century. On the base, it has – like the shaft at Roscrea – a rather stylized Adam and Eve and what may be another Old Testament subject, Daniel in the Lions' Den.

At the centre of the Burren, some 15km north of Dysert O'Dea, is Kilfenora, which originally had at least seven crosses, all carved out of the local limestone. One standing in a field to the west of the Cathedral is decorated with interlacing and geometrical patterns resembling those on the Tuam shaft carved by Gilla Christ. On the present east face is the figure of Christ in high relief (Pl.202), wearing a satchel as at Cashel, and standing on a little platform supported by a rope-moulding which runs out into a triangular shape at the bottom. Fergus O'Farrell made the interesting suggestion that this triangle may have had a sarcophagus-shaped shrine placed up against it, like the sole surviving twelfth-century stone example at Clones, Co. Monaghan. The link between cross and shrine is further strengthened by another Kilfenora example in the Cathedral grounds, known as the Doorty Cross. On its east face, there are three figures (Pl.204), one a bishop, and each with a different type of crozier (volute, drop-head and T-shaped), but near the bottom of the west face (Pl.206), beneath the figure of Christ on the head, there is a horseman riding above the shingled roof of what must be a tomb-shaped shrine of the kind known from eighth- and ninth-century metalwork. The rider could well be a mounted pilgrim coming to venerate the relics of the local saint, Fachnan, contained in the shrine, the original of which has long since vanished. This consideration of relics leads us back to the Dysert

195 Cormac's Chapel on the Rock of Cashel, Co. Tipperary, built by Cormac Mac Cárrthaigh between 1127 and 1134, is Ireland's only true piece of Romanesque architecture.

196 Cormac's Chapel, Cashel: the tangent gable over the main doorway, unusually in the north wall of the nave, may have been copying wooden models in the west of England.

197 Cormac's Chapel, Cashel: in the nave, engaged columns carry a barrel vault which supports a small chamber beneath the stone roof.

198 Cormac's Chapel, Cashel: the arch decorated with human heads leads to the chancel which still retains traces of Romanesque frescoes.

199 Cormac's Chapel, Cashel: on the tympanum above the north door, a helmeted centaur fires his arrow at a lion rampaging behind him.

200 St Cronan's Church, Roscrea, Co. Tipperary: the tangent gable above the west doorway frames a figure standing out in relief which is flanked by rosettes similar to those on the north door gable of Cormac's Chapel (Pl.196).

201 The west front is all that remains of St Cronan's Church in Roscrea, with its characteristic gabled blind arcades between the central doorway and the traditional Irish *antae* at the sides.

202 The West Cross at Kilfenora, Co. Clare: the figure of Christ with outstretched hands seems to bear a square reliquary on the front of its garment.

203 The twelfth-century limestone cross at Dysert O'Dea, Co. Clare: in contrast to the west face (Pl.122), the east face bears a high-relief figure of Christ at the top of the cross (possibly with a replacement head).

204 The east face of the so-called 'Doorty' cross at Kilfenora, Co. Clare, is remarkable for its striking variety of crozier-shapes and the enigmatic figures on its lower shaft.

205 Dignified resignation is portrayed in this noble twelfth-century head, of the dead Christ, found in the excavations at Inishcealtra, Co. Clare. It may once have formed part of a High Cross (National Museum, Dublin).

206 The 'Doorty' Cross, Kilfenora: a horseman riding on what seems like a shingled roof at the bottom of the shaft on the west face may represent a pilgrim approaching a shrine formerly on the site.

207 The twelfth-century St Patrick's Cross on the Rock of Cashel, Co. Tipperary, bears a figure of Christ on one face, and had side-supports which suggest copying of wooden carpentry models.

208 The miniature round tower and the sacristy would both appear to be additions to the original twelfth-century stone-roofed church of St Kevin at Glendalough, Co. Wicklow.

209 The Nuns' Church at Clonmacnoise, Co. Offaly, is typical of the small size of twelfth-century monastic churches in Ireland, and demonstrates clearly how the west doorway and chancel arch were their main bearers of Romanesque ornament.

197

198

199

200

201

202

205

206

O'Dea cross where the bishop or abbot – presumably St Tola, the eighth-century founder of the monastery – holds a volute crozier in his left hand, while his right, where now there is nothing but a gaping hole, was probably originally an arm-shaped reliquary raised in blessing, but fashioned in bronze to contain a relic, and removable so that it could be brought on tour and returned, a suggestion supported by the existence of the metalwork shrine of St Lachtin's arm of *c.* 1120 (p.295). Kilfenora and Dysert O'Dea clearly demonstrate a link between their High Crosses and reliquaries, making it likely that highlighting the local abbot or bishop along with Christ on the twelfth-century crosses was designed to generate pilgrimage traffic and to increase the financial rewards which accompanied it. Seen in this light, the twelfth-century High Crosses can be understood, like the metalwork shrines, to have played a role in helping to keep alive the old Irish monasteries and the age-old tradition which they fostered. Perhaps the later Romanesque churches fulfilled the same function.

Later Romanesque Churches

Close to the High Cross at Dysert O'Dea is a church much altered since first built in the twelfth century, and best known for the Romanesque doorway (Pl.210) which was probably re-assembled in its present form in the south wall sometime around the 1680s. The three inner orders of the arch seem to have belonged together originally, and consist of chevron ornament and an unusual cut-out pattern of almost Moorish appearance in the middle order. The series of heads in the outermost order of the arch, and the jambs and columns of the doorway, are in a state of considerable confusion. The columns can be cylindrical in shape or facetted into six or eight sides and decorated with floral motifs, while others are twisted and bear pelleted rope-moulding and chevron work which has echoes in a doorway at Clonkeen, Co. Limerick. The jambs consist of different groups of stones decorated with flat animal interlace reminiscent of that on the shaft of the Market Cross at Tuam, while the capitals are carved in the form of human heads, with animals whispering into their ears. But the most fascinating feature of the doorway is the disparate collection of animal and human heads forming the outermost order of the arch. Animal heads, one comparable to those holding up the metalwork Cross of Cong (Pl.182–3), hold a roll in their mouths in a style so similar to the portal at Bellegarde-sur-Loiret that some French connection must be postulated – a link which has also been suggested for a curious seated figure built into the wall of the church at Rath, just over a mile away. The human heads vary from the narrow, thin and clean-shaven to the oriental mandarin, bearing various hair-styles and one even wears a cap. These have counterparts in the Burren area to the north, particularly in the small church at Templecronan, where both human and animal heads decorate the underside of projecting corbels which held the wooden barge-boards of the gables.

Similar, though undecorated, corbels are found in one place in the eastern part of the country, namely Glendalough, whose Market Cross has already shown interesting parallels with Dysert O'Dea and Tuam. Glendalough (Pl.2) has among its seven churches a number of Romanesque elements, including the so-called Priest's House with its blind external Romanesque arch forming the gable of a small building. Rachel Moss has recently suggested that it may have been concocted in its present form only two centuries ago and is unlikely therefore, in her view, to have served as the tomb-shrine of St Kevin. But as it is located in an anciently enclosed area marked by a now almost imperceptible irregularly-shaped bank, with an entrance indicated by a tall granite cross, it may well replace an earlier tomb-shrine on the site in which the Romanesque arch may have played a role. Other than the addition of a twelfth-century chancel to the earlier Cathedral (p.196), the main Romanesque decoration in Glendalough is to be found in the Priory of St Saviour (Pl.211), located about a mile away from the main cluster of monuments in the valley. Unusual in having a domestic building attached, this is a nave and chancel church with entrances in the north and south walls (reminiscent of Cormac's Chapel) and a window in the east gable with stones inside and out carved with chevrons, rosettes and other elements, but all wrongly re-assembled by the Board of Works in the last century. The scallop shape of decoration is found on an exterior capital and also in inverted form on two of the bases of the columns in the chancel arch. The main capital on the south side of the arch bears a human head on each corner, a feature found already in Cormac's Chapel and which we shall meet again shortly on other Leinster sites.

The building of this church has often been associated with the second great saint associated with Glendalough, Laurence O'Toole, who was abbot here from 1154 until he was transferred to the archbishopric of Dublin in 1162. Documentary evidence is lacking for the connection, but ascribing the church to the period of his abbacy is quite acceptable.

One feature noticeable on this and on other Romanesque churches from the second quarter of the twelfth century onwards is the way in which the stones have been finished with tool marks at a diagonal to the main edge of the stone. The presence of this stone finish on at least one of the stones of the west end of another church at Glendalough, St Kevin's (Pl.165 and 208), shows it also to belong to the twelfth century, even though there are no indications of carving in the Romanesque style. It shows how careful one must be with the dating of undecorated stone churches in Ireland, which cannot be labelled automatically as 'pre-Romanesque'. Two cases in point are other churches in Glendalough, Trinity and Reefert, both of which are nave-and-chancel churches with rounded, smooth but otherwise unornamented chancel arches. We cannot say when these churches were constructed, but there is nothing against considering them as being either eleventh century or possibly even as contemporary with those bearing Romanesque ornament. The twelfth-century date suggested above for St Kevin's on the basis of the diagonal tooling on its west gable is borne out to a considerable extent also by the mortar age determination carried out by Rainer Berger's Los Angeles laboratory, giving a calibrated date of between 1000 and 1280. Originally, the church was a simple rectangle having a doorway with inclining jambs, a relieving arch over it akin to that on the nearby Cathedral, and also with a mechanism for an exterior clap-door of wood which opened upwards, as with the internal arrangements at Gallarus Oratory. St Kevin's has a stone roof supported by a vault as in Cormac's Chapel, and it was later extended by the addition of a chancel (now disappeared) and, much more strikingly, a round tower which, as it were, grows out of the stone roof above the west doorway. The aforementioned Trinity Church was another Glendalough example of this unusual combination, and there the tower rose above a porch at the western end of the church, but was blown down by a storm in 1818. A further surviving specimen is St Finghin's Church at Clonmacnoise (Pl.163), where the tower rises from the ground upwards to the south of the junction of nave and chancel. St Columb's House at Kells (Pl.125), for the lower part of which a ninth-century date has been proposed (p.195), also has a stone roof with a chamber above the nave vault, as at St Kevin's in Glendalough, so that it is likely to have been part of a twelfth-century renovation of the House. Other examples of stone roofs occur in St Mochta's House at Louth, and St Doulogh's near Malahide, Co. Dublin, which – though lacking datable ornament – may also be dated with probability to the twelfth century. Likely to be roughly contemporary are two island churches with stone roofs, St Macdara's off the coast of Connemara, Co. Galway (Pl.128), and St Patrick's near Skerries, Co. Dublin, the latter imitating Cormac's Chapel in its use of tufa and possibly completed for a synod there in 1148. We are on

surer dating ground with three other stone-roofed churches – apparently a particularly Irish contribution to European architecture. One is St Flannan's oratory at Killaloe, which has a well-preserved roof and simple Romanesque doorway. The second is the larger church at Rahan, Co. Offaly, where ruined stairs must have led to a small chamber above the chancel which probably bore a stone roof. The chancel arch has interesting bulbous bases and finely-carved Romanesque capitals with heads on either side of a floral pattern related to the palmette. The third church has largely disappeared, but eighteenth-century illustrations show it as having had a steep stone roof. This is St Molaisse's House on the island of Devenish which, though now roofless, still retains traces of palmette decoration on its corner bases. Further ornament may have included some of the well-carved Romanesque fragments bearing plant and Urnes-style animal ornament now displayed in the site museum.

Besides St Molaisse's House, which was presumably a tomb-shrine containing his relics, Devenish has one other building with Romanesque decoration, and that is the extremely well-preserved Round Tower. A pair of binoculars will help the viewer to appreciate the heads (some bearded) and a wave-like ornament on a frieze running around the top of the tower just below the conical roof. The Round Tower at Kildare has an apparently original Romanesque doorway (not very well preserved) and the slender tower at Ardmore in County Waterford has animal-headed corbels which would permit an ascription to the twelfth century. But the finest Round Tower with Romanesque ornament is undoubtedly that at

Timahoe in Co. Laois. Here, more than 4m above the ground, is a stepped doorway or, more correctly, two doorways one behind the other, with hour-glass bases and – its most notable characteristic – well-preserved capitals with single heads, or twin heads with hair and beards intertwined with one another. These heads were carved in all probability by a master mason who also worked on one of the most attractive of all Irish Romanesque portals, that at Killeshin, Co. Laois (Pl.213). Its combination of two very different hues in the yellowing granite and brown sandstone could suggest that it was originally painted, and its decoration is in such subtle and light relief that it may well have needed colour to make its effect felt. The doorway splays shallowly and is topped by a tangent gable, the whole giving

the impression of a welcoming porch. The gable looks re-set and, at least in part, modern, and the outermost order of the arch also appears to have been re-assembled at some time, as the splendid, if worn, head forming the keystone is marginally off-centre. It is one of a total of eleven heads used on the Killeshin doorway, of which those on the pilaster capitals of the outermost order are also bearded, with their hair and beards intertwined, as at Timahoe. Very different in style, and somewhat more portrait-like, are the single-head capitals of the two middle orders (Pl.212), which have softly-rounded, shaven, youthful faces, with high ears typical of Irish Romanesque, and carefully-carved eye-lids. Less to the fore here than on many other Irish Romanesque portals is the presence on the capitals of fleshy plant decoration and of animal ornament in the usual Irish version of the Urnes style, though there are some small animals in the chevron triangles of the arch which seem to go back to older metalwork styles.

One of the remarkable features of the Killeshin doorway is the prominence of an inscription running along the abacus above the head-shaped capitals, together with another one incised on the north jamb, giving the name of an otherwise unknown mason, Cellachan. Sadly, the main inscription has been badly defaced, but the word LAGEN, the Irish word for the province of Leinster, stands out clearly, and the letters D.AR followed after an interval by the letter I before the word Lagen could reasonably be reconstructed as Diarmaid Rí, Dermot, king of. The most obvious person to fit this inscription is Diarmaid or Dermot McMurrough, king of Leinster from around 1133 until his death in 1171, the man

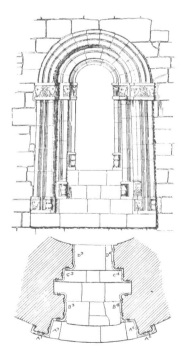

Doorway of the Round Tower at Timahoe, Co. Laois.

who brought about the Norman invasion of Ireland after he was banished from the country for having abducted the lady Dervorgilla, wife of Tighernan O'Rourke, king of Breifne. Diarmaid was also involved in founding the Cistercian abbey at Baltinglass in 1148, and the presence there of bulbous column-bases similar to those at Killeshin would strengthen the notion that his patronage was paramount to the creation of this portal, a gesture which he would surely have wanted to be recorded on the doorway. Baltinglass had an English mother house at Louth Park in Lincolnshire and, if the masons who carved the bulbous bases there had come with the monks from England, the Killeshin portal could be ascribed to sometime around the 1150s. The tangent gable is one of the dominant features of this doorway, but is not directly derived from an earlier example on the north doorway at Cormac's Chapel.

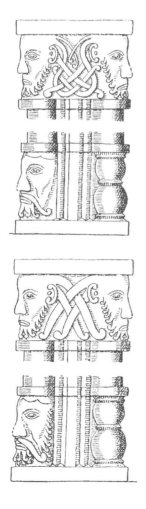

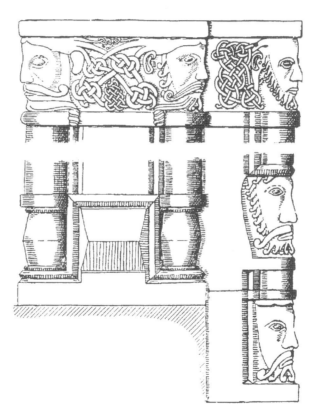

Capitals and bases of the Round Tower doorway at Timahoe, Co. Laois.

Twelfth-Century Architectural Sculpture

The porch element, which recedes shallowly into the wall at Killeshin, stands out much more strongly from the gable at Freshford in County Kilkenny. There too the portal bears an inscription, which has not yet been deciphered, but it also introduces us to full figure sculpture on an Irish Romanesque doorway, even though the horseman on one side and the two standing figures on the other side of the doorway have yet to be identified. More striking is the sculpture surviving at Kilteel, Co. Kildare, where there are head-capitals (Pl.214) even bolder than those at Killeshin, and where Diarmaid MacMurrough may also have contributed to the church decoration as his mother came from here, according to Francis John Byrne. The sculpture is at present re-assembled as forming part of a chancel arch, but Conleth Manning has argued cogently that the individual stones may have been distributed between the doorway and the chancel arch of a demolished church, the original location of which is unknown. The context of the figures is very different from that of the large head-capitals in that some have clearly recognizable biblical subject-matter; they stand out in high relief mostly flanked by vertical architectural roll-mouldings, and are not accompanied by the geometrical, animal or vegetal ornament so frequently found on other Irish Romanesque work. The Old Testament scenes include Eve handing the apple to Adam under the spreading branches of fruit-laden tree (Pl.215), and David (or Samson?) and the Lion. David, however, is certainly identifiable as the long-robed figure (Pl.216) holding the head of the vanquished Goliath on top of a pole which he carries over his right shoulder, an unusual rendering of the scene which harks back to some panels on the older High Crosses, such as that on the Tall (West) Cross at Monasterboice. Further figures, one holding a staff, another a tumbling acrobat, and two bearded men embracing one another on top of a rosette (Pl.217), have not yet been fitted into a scriptural context. Whatever its precise source may have been, the sculpture probably comes from a tradition of English or French origin, where it was common to carve figures illustrating biblical scenes on the exposed surfaces of churches, inside or out.

The apparent concentration on Old Testament subject-matter recurs in one of the most important collections of Irish Romanesque sculpture, now built into the western gable of Ardmore Cathedral in County Waterford (Pl.218). This is clearly not its original position, as the individual carved stones have been jumbled together incoherently into a row of thirteen arcades (some empty) above two much larger lunettes, each of which has a further set of arcades within it. Here, again, the two most immediately recognizable subjects are both Old Testament scenes – Adam and Eve in the centre of the left-hand lunette and the Judgment of Solomon in the upper part of the right-hand lunette, with a harper (David?) behind the second lady approaching king Solomon with his sword raised. Beneath this latter scene are three figures carrying staffs and wearing long robes with broad, straight folds to just above the knee and, as they find interesting comparisons among the two embracing figures at Kilteel, one may well ask if the same hand were not at work in both places. The right-hand lunette may contain a Virgin and Child, but the identity of the other figures remains uncertain, though the suggestion has been made that they may include parts of a David and Solomon cycle. Solomon the Temple-builder would certainly be a suitable subject for illustration on a Cathedral erected presumably to serve as the diocesan centre of a new bishopric set up under the Synod of Kells in 1152, though it only lasted a little more than fifty years. The carving may have been associated with the church recorded in the Annals as having been built by Mael Etain O Duib Ratha, who died in 1203, but it should possibly also be linked to a bishop of Ardmore named Eugene who witnessed a charter in Cork between 1172 and 1179. He seems to have spent some time in northern Britain in the mid–1180s, giving us a possible chronological peg and perhaps providing also some indication of where Eugene may have recruited some of his sculptors for Ardmore.

Northern Britain may also have had some influence on two other important sets of sculptures in the north of Ireland, both of which appear to have been lintels. What they have in common is that the New Testament moves to the forefront because the centrepiece is the Crucifixion – two rare instances in twelfth-century Europe where this subject appears over the west doorway of a church. The lintel at Raphoe, Co. Donegal, is broken into two fragments, one in the porch of the Protestant Cathedral, and the other built into the outer north wall of its nave. When united together in a picture, a small piece can be seen to be missing in the middle, suggesting that the lintel may have cracked under the weight of the masonry above it. The resulting loss of parts of the Christ figure means that we can say little more about the Saviour on the Cross other than that there is an angel present on each arm. To the left, as we see it, St Peter cuts off the ear of Malchus who is shown as one of those come to arrest Christ. On the right side, two figures appear to be holding the seamless garment – paradoxically also cracked down the middle in a scene meant to symbolize the unity of the church. On the extreme right is a dome topped by a cross, presumably Christ's tomb, with the angel sitting on a flat stone outside it being approached by a single lady. In comparison to the Ardmore figures, the persons forming this brief Passion cycle are tall and thin, suggesting to Françoise Henry such a close comparison to the earlier High Crosses that she dated this lintel to the ninth/tenth century. But while there are no clear indications that it is twelfth-century in date, this becomes much more likely when it is compared with the other Crucifixion lintel at Maghera, Co. Derry, where the accompanying decoration – including Urnes-style ornament, foliage and a crozier-bearing mitred figure as on the later High Crosses – clearly shows it to belong to the twelfth century. Christ wears a loin-cloth, and his emaciated arms are stretched out along the elongated arms of the cross, above each of which are two angels. Flanking Christ are Stephaton and Longinus, as on the earlier High Crosses, and the blood of Christ spurts from his right side on to the torso, rather than the eyes, of Longinus. On each of their heads stands a thief, whose bodies

210 The south doorway of the church at Dysert O'Dea, Co. Clare, with its curious collection of heads, was re-assembled in its present form probably in the seventeenth century.

211 The Romanesque church of St Saviour's Priory at Glendalough, Co. Wicklow, was probably built by the abbot St Laurence O'Toole in the 1150s.

212 The twelfth-century church at Killeshin, Co. Laois: above the capitals with clean-shaven heads rise the orders of the arch decorated with pelleted chevron, as well as animal and floral ornament.

213 Killeshin church: the difference in the colour of the stones used in the west doorway may have been disguised originally by the use of paint.

214 Kilteel church: a head capital with moustache, beard and hair interlacing profusely on either side, is an Irish Romanesque speciality.

215 Kilteel church: Eve handing the apple to Adam.

216 Kilteel church: David with the head of Goliath on a pole.

217 Kilteel church: two figures embracing.

218 Ardmore, Co. Waterford: twelfth-century sculpture fragments re-assembled under arcades on the west wall of the Cathedral. Adam and Eve are identifiable in the lower left lunette, and the Judgment of Solomon is visible in the upper part of the right lunette.

219 St Mary's Cathedral, Tuam, Co. Galway, erected probably shortly after 1184. The span of its chancel arch is the largest of any Romanesque church in Ireland.

220 St Mary's Cathedral, Tuam: a Silenus-like face on a capital of the chancel arch.

221 St Mary's Cathedral, Tuam: a mason's jovial invention on a capital of the chancel arch.

222 St Brendan's Cathedral, Clonfert, Co. Galway: glum lion on a capital of the doorway.

223 Clonfert Cathedral: the late twelfth-century west doorway, with its tangent gable, is the high point of Irish Romanesque stone carving.

224 Clonfert Cathedral: the Irish *horror vacui*, or fear of empty spaces, seen sometimes in the Book of Kells, is also palpable in the west doorway of the Cathedral which is exuberantly decorated with a variety of motifs including animals biting a continuous roll-moulding on one of the inner orders of the arch.

225 Clonfert Cathedral: The florally-decorated triangles in the tangent gable leave recesses for human heads – some stylized, others more realistic, as one might expect from a Romanesque masterpiece teetering on the threshold of the Gothic.

226 St Flannan's Cathedral, Killaloe, Co. Clare: the doorway rescued from an earlier church and later built into a corner of the Gothic cathedral is probably Ireland's last purely Romanesque portal, of *c.* 1200, decorated with a wide variety of animal and foliate motifs.

210

214

217

219

220

222

223

224

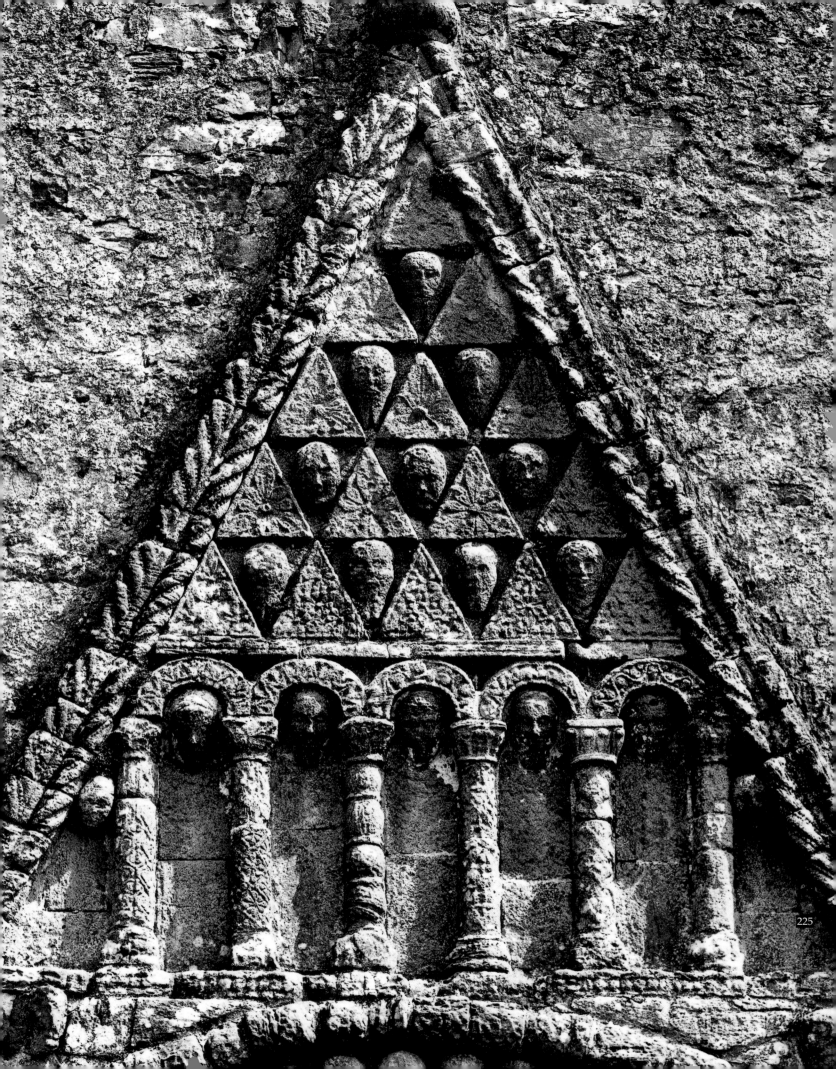

rise upwards between Christ's arms and the cross. Under the cross-ends are what we may take to be the Virgin on the left and the Centurion on the right. The figures standing at each end of the lintel are not easy to identify, but they may represent the Mocking of Christ on the left and possibly variations of the same grouping as found on the right at Raphoe – a soldier holding the seamless garment and three ladies attending the standing angel. These two unusual Crucifixions were carved by different hands – witness the differing length and styles of the clothing worn – and both reflect throwbacks to the iconography of the High Crosses. As an instance, the blood of Christ spurting on to Longinus is found seemingly on the South Cross at Clonmacnoise. Yet the composition of the scenes is totally different, as demonstrated by the ladies approaching the angel beside the tomb, and the shape of the tomb itself. Figure-sculptured lintels may have become something of a speciality in the northern half of Ireland during the twelfth century, as there is another with a Crucifixion at Dunshaughlin, Co. Meath and two further examples in County Donegal, including one at Clonca which seems to bear Christ in Majesty flanked by six apostles on each side. As both Raphoe and Maghera were listed as suffragan bishoprics of Armagh in the list which the Papal Legate, Cardinal Paparo, brought back to Rome after the Synod of Kells in 1152, we should perhaps see these two lintels as belonging to churches trying to demonstrate their worthiness to achieve Cathedral status, and built by two men vying with one another to succeed the ageing Gelasius as Archbishop of Armagh – which

Gilbert of Raphoe finally did in 1175. The most likely date for these two lintels, therefore, is the third quarter of the twelfth century, and not too far removed in time from the sculptures at Ardmore, which are perhaps marginally later.

The Nuns' Church, Clonmacnoise – Tuam – Clonfert – Killaloe

During the very same period, the *Annals of the Four Masters* reported that, in 1167, Dearbhforgaill, otherwise Dervorgilla, the lady abducted (perhaps willingly) by Diarmaid McMurrough, finished the Nuns' Church at Clonmacnoise (Pl.209), which is normally identified as the church bearing that name today and located a considerable distance to the east of the main complex of monastic buildings. But the local *Annals of Clonmacnois* insert the same notice under the year 1180 – probably by mistake, but possibly not, as the differing styles of the Romanesque decoration of the church could fit in with both of these dates. The building history of the church is complicated by the reconstruction worthily carried out by James Graves and the Kilkenny Archaeological Society in 1866. It left out one carved stone (displayed at the Rosc Exhibition of 1967) which has its virtual twin in the doorway as they reconstituted it, suggesting that the portal is either incorrectly reconstructed, or that its stones come from two different churches – or both. But the chancel arch brings us more clearly to the nub of the problem, recognized by Brash in 1875 when he pointed out the incongruity between the capitals and the arch. The jambs consist of engaged columns bearing capitals which fit uncomfortably into the general series of Irish chancel-arch capitals. They are decorated with a tangle of animal interlace alongside fretwork motifs and serpents, together with plant ornament and human masks, including one looking like the so-called mask of Agamemnon from Mycenae. The work is carried out in the low relief more at home on the geometrical panels of western High Crosses of the twelfth century, and which may have required colouring to achieve its effect. The comparison with the fretwork on the datable Tuam cross-shafts would suggest a date not much later than the 1150s, while the bulbous bases when compared to those at Killeshin could lend support to a similar conclusion. The light relief decoration is in complete contrast to the deep-cut carving of the chancel arch, which has an undecorated area at the bottom of each order looking as if it were designed to have been embedded more deeply in the jambs of some other church. The low relief of the capitals is repeated on some of the diaper patterns on the voussoirs, but the high relief chevron ornament of the arch with its characteristic pellet ornament, and its regularly interrupted rhythm allowing a central arris roll to expand into a lozenge, bring the style much closer to the chancel arch at Monaincha, normally dated to around 1180, and the earliest parts of Christ Church Cathedral in Dublin, built probably in the following decade, suggesting the introduction of new ideas from England at the time. The animals biting a roll forming the middle order of the portal arch come close to Clonfert, which is widely seen as the apogee of the style in Ireland, bringing

us nearer to the end of the century. Dervorgilla's completion of the church, historically recorded as having taken place in 1167, might possibly be equated with the jambs of both doorway and chancel arch, but not necessarily with the voussoirs of the doorway and chancel arch, which should be dated closer to 1180, making it difficult to adhere to one of the few chronological anchors in the Irish Romanesque which Dervorgilla might seem to have offered us.

Perhaps marginally later than the second phase of the Nuns' Church is the Romanesque part of Tuam Cathedral. It was Roger Stalley who pointed out the significance of an entry in the *Annals of Loch Cé* for the year 1184 stating that the great church of Tuam 'fell in one day, both roof and stone', as it almost certainly provides us with a date *post-quem* for the construction of the surviving parts of the Cathedral. Only the original chancel remains, but this has ample evidence to show that, even after Rory O'Connor, son of Turlough, had lost most of his power as High King, Tuam was still able to command high quality workmanship in its Cathedral building. More than 5m wide, the chancel arch (Pl.219) has the largest Romanesque span in Ireland and, though the western part was exposed to the elements for decades after a fire in 1787, the original crispness of the carving is still very apparent. The pelleting and deeply-cut chevrons find companions in the Nuns' Church, and some sides of the box-shaped capitals show how the Urnes-style animal ornament continues into the last quarter of the twelfth century. But the real joy of these capitals are the smiling bearded human masks (Pl.220–221), with bulging eyes and decorative eyebrows ending in a floral motif, one of the figures having animal ears giving it almost the appearance of a classical Silenus face. The carver of the masks was also responsible for much, if not all, of the ornament on the internal jambs of the east window of the chancel, as elements of a similar mask appear on the top of a vertical panel also containing a Great Beast with human head, and intertwined beasts of Urnes derivation. These latter also make other appearances on the jambs where they tussle in ferocious combat and form a complex interweave leaving no surface uncarved in a design showing a remarkable capacity for innovation in what might otherwise have been considered a tired and overworked genre of animal interlace. Unique is the scene of a man sinking his sword into the gullet of a serpent beneath him as he is tempted from the side by a hideous devil. Also making a refreshing, if occasionally repetitive, appearance is foliage, including a running vine scroll. Foliage also features prominently among the fine late-twelfth century fragments at Annaghdown, Co. Galway, a site associated with St Brendan whose burial place at Clonfert in the same county is heralded by a doorway which, in every sense, is one of the high points of Irish Romanesque.

Clonfert doorway (Pl.223), probably an insertion into an older church with *antae*, has one old-fashioned feature in the inclined jambs of the doorway which is emphasized by the contrast with the straight sides of the innermost order inserted in the fifteenth century. Both jambs and arch present a riot of baroque exuberance, every surface covered tightly with ornament of very considerable variety. Classical palmettes and anthemion

luxuriate alongside tightly-meshed interlace, chevrons and conjoined circle-motifs on the jambs. Above the capitals (Pl.222), from which animal-heads of different kinds emerge, there are smaller and friendlier variations of the same theme, where the carver leaves it to the fancy of the observer whether they should be seen as canine, feline or leonine — or just the product of his lively imagination. In the orders of the arch above (Pl.224), somewhat similar animals hold roll mouldings like those on the Nuns' Church doorway, a rope-moulding is supported by floriated lozenge panels deeply hollowed out behind, and circular bosses appear in many guises — flat with floral motifs, round-backed with serpent-like surrounds, or domed in high relief with geometric, plant and interlace ornament.

Chancel arch of Monaincha.

Even more memorable is the tangent gable above all of this (Pl.225). At the peak is a pyramid of triangles, those to the forefront with petalled flowers alternating with others which recede, each containing a human head, some stylized and bearded, but with one row of shaven heads which look more portrait-like. Beneath these triangles within a triangle is a tall-columned narrow colonnade with heads at the top, and the spaces beneath now empty but probably once painted – as they are the only uncarved part of the whole doorway. This unique *tour de force* cannot be dated by itself but, on the basis of its rich foliage and hollowed-out ornament, a date late in the twelfth century is the most probable.

Dating to somewhere around 1200, according to Tessa Garton, is a late Romanesque doorway (Pl.226), presumably part of a former Cathedral at Killaloe, Co. Clare, demolished to make way for a larger, Gothic structure, into the south-west corner of which the doorway has been inserted. Like Clonfert, it too is exuberant in its ornament, but it brings in new animal elements in high relief. Its use of interrupted chevron shows a link with the Nuns' Church, and indeed its profuse use of chevron is one of its most remarkable features. The portals of Clonfert and Killaloe bring us appropriately to the end of our chosen time-span but, while the Transitional style of architecture with its incipient pointed arches was already being introduced by the Normans into the eastern half of Ireland, most notably at Christ Church Cathedral in Dublin, the familiar Romanesque style continued in the western province of Connacht for another three decades. There it is found being used in Augustinian foundations at Ballintober and Cong, as well as in Cistercian churches at Abbeyknockmoy, Boyle and Corcomroe. The Cistercians had put Romanesque ornamentation to good use already in the middle third of the twelfth century, and it was they who introduced the Gothic style at places such as Inch in County Down – but that would take us beyond the bounds of the present volume.

Epilogue

■

SPIRITUALLY, IRELAND HAS ALWAYS BEEN A PART OF EUROPE — but a very individualistic one. Nowhere can this be seen more clearly than in its art of the early medieval period which we have been studying here. Much of its inspiration comes ultimately from the European continent, but Ireland digests thoroughly what it receives, and coalesces disparate material into new and ingenious combinations to create a refreshingly new style. It shares with other areas of northern Europe a fascination with animal ornament, it revitalizes pagan Celtic spirals, and blends these with interlace and geometry to produce an anti-classical art full of vitality and longevity. Renaissances of the antique came and went without leaving any great impression, as Ireland remained preoccupied with variations on old themes marked with the stamp of quality and individuality frequently shared with northern Britain. Though the treasury of these decorative, abstract motifs shows nothing particularly Christian to the modern eye, early medieval art in Ireland was essentially a church art, and its main producers — often doubtless with secular patronage — were the

349

monasteries, which fostered the independent tradition of Irish art illustrated in this volume. Conservative these monasteries may have been, but the very fact of their existence and ubiquity throughout the country set Ireland and its art apart from most of the rest of Europe. It is thanks to them that Ireland is such a storehouse of an absorbing collection of manuscripts, metalwork and stone-carving so full of inventive imagination and strange, but wonderful, fantasy. We cannot but be eternally grateful to them for their considerable, if often somewhat neglected, contribution to the corpus of European art.

Bibliography

■

Abbreviations

JRSAI Journal of the Royal Society of Antiquaries of Ireland

PRIA Proceedings of the Royal Irish Academy

Bibliographies

Werner, Martin. *Insular art: an annotated bibliography*. Boston 1984.

Harbison, Peter. 'Arts bibliography'. In Dáibhí Ó Cróinín (ed.), *A new history of Ireland*, vol. I (forthcoming).

General works

Bede, The Venerable. *A history of the English church and people*. Harmondsworth 1955.

Berger, Pamela. The Ardagh Chalice, Numerology and the Stowe Missal *Eire – Ireland*, Fall, 1979, 6–16.

Bieler, Ludwig. The island of scholars. *Revue du moyen âge latin* 8, 1952, 213–31.

_____ *Ireland: harbinger of the Middle Ages*. Oxford 1963.

Bourke, Cormac. *Patrick: the archaeology of a saint*. Belfast 1993.

Byrne, Francis John. *Irish kings and high-kings*. London 1973.

Cone, Polly (ed.) *Treasures of early Irish art 1500 B.C. – 1500 A.D.* New York 1977.

De Paor, Liam. *The peoples of Ireland*. London and Indiana 1986.

De Paor, Máire and Liam. *Early Christian Ireland*. London 1958.

Edwards, Nancy. *The archaeology of early medieval Ireland*. London 1990.

Graham-Campbell, James. Irish monastic art, 5th to 8th centuries. *Monastic Studies* (Montreal) 14, 1983, 225–45.

Grosjean, Paul. Sur quelques exegètes irlandais du VIIe siècle. *Sacris Erudiri* 7, 1955, 67–98.

Gwynn, Aubrey. *The Irish church in the 11th and 12th centuries* (ed. Gearóid O'Brien) Dublin, 1992

Harbison, Peter. *Ancient Irish monuments*. Dublin 1997.

_____, Homan Potterton and Jeanne Sheehy. *Irish art and architecture*. London 1978.

Haseloff, Günther. Irland. In Helmut Roth (ed.), *Kunst der Völkerwanderungszeit*. Propyläen-Kunstgeschichte, Supplement Band IV, Frankfurt, Berlin and Vienna, 1979, 223–43.

Henry, Françoise. *La sculpture irlandaise pendant les douze premiers siècles de l'ère chrétienne*, 2 vols. Paris 1933.

_____ *Early Christian Irish art*. Dublin 1954.

_____ *Irish art*, 3 vols. London 1967–70.

Hughes, Kathleen. *Early Christian Ireland: introduction to the sources*. London 1972.

_____ and Ann Hamlin. *The modern traveller to the early Irish church*. London 1977.

Laing, Lloyd. *The archaeology of late Celtic Britain and Ireland c. 400–1200 A.D.*, London 1975.

Lucas, A.T. *Treasures of Ireland: Irish pagan and early Christian art*. Dublin and New York 1973.

Mahr, Adolf and Joseph Raftery. *Christian art in ancient Ireland*, 2 vols. Dublin 1932 and 1941.

Megaw, Ruth and Vincent. *Celtic art from its beginnings to the Book of Kells*. London 1989.

Moody, T.W. and F.X. Martin (ed.) *The course of Irish history*. Cork 1967.

O'Brien, Jacqueline and Peter Harbison. *Ancient Ireland*. London and New York, 1996.

Ó Corráin, Donncha. *Ireland before the Normans*. The Gill History of Ireland 2, Dublin 1972.

_____ *Prehistoric and early Christian Ireland*. In R.F. Foster (ed.), *The Oxford History of Ireland*. Oxford and New York, 1989, 1–43.

Ó Cróinín, Dáibhí, *Early medieval Ireland, 400–1200*. London 1995.

Raftery, Joseph and William O'Sullivan. *Artists and craftsmen: Irish art treasures*. Dublin 1980.

Ryan, Michael (ed.). *Treasures of Ireland: Irish art 3000 B.C. - 1500 A.D.*, Dublin 1983.

_____ The Sutton Hoo ship burial and Ireland: some Celtic perspectives. In Robert Farrell and Carol Neuman de Vegvar (ed.), *Sutton Hoo: fifty years after*. American early medieval studies 2, Oxford (Ohio), 1992, 83–116.

Stokes, Margaret. *Early Christian art in Ireland*. London 1894.

Stokstad, Marilyn. The art of prehistoric and early Christian Ireland. In Harold Orel (ed.), *Irish history and culture: aspects of a people's heritage*, Lawrence (Kansas) and Portmarnock, 1979, 43–78.

Thomas, Charles. *Britain and Ireland in early Christian times, A.D. 400–800*, London 1971.

Wilson, David and Ole Klindt-Jensen. *Viking art*. London 1980.

Collected essays – general and personal

Bourke, Cormac (ed.). *From the isles of the North: early medieval art in Ireland and Britain*. Belfast 1995.

_____ (ed.). *Studies in the cult of St. Columba*. Dublin 1997.

Bradley, John (ed.). *Settlement and society in medieval Ireland. Studies presented to F.X. Martin, o.s.a.* Kilkenny 1988.

Erichsen, Johannes (ed.). *Kilian, Mönch aus Irland, aller Franken Patron. Aufsätze*. Munich 1989.

Henry, Françoise. *Studies in early Christian and medieval Irish art. Vol. 1 – Enamels and metalwork*, London, 1983; *Vol. II* (with Geneviève Marsh-Michéli) – *Manuscript illumination*, London, 1984; *Vol. III – Sculpture and architecture*, London, 1985.

Herity, Michael. *Studies in the layout, buildings, and art in stone of early Irish monasteries.* London 1995.

Higgitt, John (ed.). *Early medieval sculpture in Britain and Ireland*. BAR British Series 152, Oxford 1986.

Hughes, Kathleen. *Church and Society in Ireland A.D. 400–1200* (ed. David Dumville) London 1987.

Karkov, Catherine E. (ed.). *The Insular tradition*. SUNY series in medieval studies. Albany, N.Y. 1997.

_____ and Robert Farrell (ed.). *Studies in insular art and archaeology*. American early medieval studies 1, Oxford (Ohio) 1991.

King, Heather (ed.). *Clonmacnoise studies*, Vol. 1 Dublin 1998.

Löwe, Heinz. (ed.). *Die Iren und Europa im früheren Mittelalter*, 2 vols. Stuttgart 1982.

Mackey, James P. *An introduction to Celtic Christianity*, Edinburgh 1989.

MacNiocaill, Gearóid and Patrick F. Wallace (ed.). *Keimelia. Studies in medieval archaeology and history in memory of Tom Delaney*. Galway 1988,

Manning, Conleth (ed.). *Dublin and beyond the Pale. Studies in honour of Patrick Healy*. Bray 1998.

Ní Chatháin, Próinséas and Michael Richter, *Irland und Europa. Die Kirche im Frühmittelalter / Ireland and Europe. The early Church.* Stuttgart 1984.

Ryan, Michael (ed.). *Ireland and insular art A.D. 500–1200.* Dublin 1987.

_____ (ed.). *Irish antiquities. Essays in memory of Joseph Raftery.* Bray 1998.

Rynne, Etienne (ed.). *North Munster Studies. Essays in commemoration of Monsignor Michael Moloney.* Limerick 1967.

_____ (ed.). *Figures from the past. Studies on figurative art in Christian Ireland in honour of Helen M. Roe.* Dun Laoghaire 1987.

Spearman, R. Michael and John Higgitt (ed.). *The age of migrating ideas. Early medieval art in northern Britain and Ireland.* Edinburgh and Stroud 1993.

Stalley, Roger. *Ireland and Europe in the middle ages. Selected essays on architecture and sculpture.* London 1994.

Whitelock, Dorothy, Rosamund McKitterick and David Dumville (ed.). *Ireland in early mediaeval Europe. Studies in memory of Kathleen Hughes.* Cambridge 1982.

Youngs, Susan (ed.). *'The Work of angels': masterpieces of Celtic metalwork 6th–9th centuries A.D.* London 1989.

Manuscripts

Alexander, J.J.G. *Insular manuscripts, 6th to the 9th century: a survey of manuscripts illuminated in the British Isles Vol. 1.* London 1978.

Alton, Ernest Henry and Peter Meyer. *Evangeliorum quattuor codex Cenannensis,* 3 vols. Berne 1951.

Bober, Harry. On the illumination of the Glazier codex: a contribution to early Coptic art and its relation to Hiberno-Saxon interlace. In *Homage to a bookman: essays on manuscripts, books and printing written for Hans P. Kraus on his 60th birthday, Oct. 12, 1967,* Berlin 1967, 101–19.

Brown, Peter. *The Book of Kells.* London and New York, 1980.

Brown, T.J. Northumbria and the Book of Kells. *Anglo-Saxon England* I, 1972, 219–46.

Calkins, Robert G. *Illuminated books of the Middle Ages.* London 1983.

De Paor, Liam. The world of the Book of Kells. In Liam

de Paor, *Ireland and early Europe.* Dublin 1997, 147–59.

Dodwell, C.R. *The pictorial arts of the West, 800–1200.* New Haven and London, 1993.

Duft, Johannes and Peter Meyer. *The Irish miniatures in the abbey library of St Gall.* Berne, Olten and Lausanne, 1954.

Farr, Carol. *The Book of Kells; its function and audience.* London and Toronto, 1997.

Fox, Peter. *The Book of Kells, MS 58, Trinity College Library, Dublin. Facsimile and commentary.* Lucerne 1990.

Friend, A.M. The canon tables of the Book of Kells. In Wilhelm R.W. Koehler (ed.). *Medieval studies in memory of Arthur Kingsley Porter.* Cambridge (Massachusetts), 1939, 611–641.

Great Books of Ireland, Thomas Davis Lectures. Dublin 1967.

Guilmain, Jacques. The forgotton medieval artist. *Art Journal* 25, 1965, 32–42.

Haseloff, Günther. Die insulare Buchmalerei. In Heinrich Beck, Herbert Jankuhn, Kurt Ranke and Reinhard Wenskus (ed.), *Reallexikon der germanischen Altertumskunde* IV, Berlin, 1979–80, 74–85.

Hemphill, Samuel. The gospels of Mac Regol of Birr; a study in Celtic illumination. *PRIA* 29 C, 1911–12, 1–10.

Henderson, George. *From Durrow to Kells: the insular gospel-books, 650–850.* London 1987.

Henry, Françoise. *The Book of Kells.* London 1974.

_____ and Geneviève Marsh-Michéli. A century of Irish illumination (1070–1170). *PRIA* 62 C, 1962, 101–64.

Koehler, Wilhelm. *Buchmalerei des frühen Mittelalters: Fragmente und Entwürfe aus dem Nachlass* (ed. Ernst Kitzinger and Florentine Mütherich). Munich 1972.

Lawlor, H.J. The Cathach of St Columba. *PRIA* 33 C 1916, 241–443.

Lowe, E.A. *Codices Latini Antiquiores, Part II, Great Britain and Ireland.* Oxford 1935 (compare also the second edition, 1972).

Luce, A.A. *et al. Evangeliorum quattuor codex Durmachensis.* Olten, Lausanne and Freiburg. i. Br., 1960.

McGurk, Patrick. Two notes on the Book of Kells and its relation to other insular gospel-books. *Scriptorium* 9, 1955, 105–7.

_____ The Irish pocket gospel book. *Sacris Erudiri* 8,

1956, 249–70.

_____ *Latin gospel books from A.D. 400 to A.D. 800.* Les publications de Scriptorium, vol. 5 Paris, Brussels, Anvers and Amsterdam, 1961.

Meehan, Bernard. *The Book of Kells.* London 1994.

_____ *The Book of Durrow: a medieval masterpiece at Trinity College, Dublin.* Dublin 1996.

_____ 'A melody of curves across the page': art and calligraphy in the Book of Armagh. *Irish Arts Review Yearbook* 14, 1998, 90–101.

_____ The Book of Kells and the Corbie Psalter. In Dáibhí Ó Cróinín, Katharine Simms and Toby Barnard (Eds). *'A Miracle of Learning', Studies in manuscripts and Irish learning. Essays in honour of William O'Sullivan.* Aldershot 1998, 29–39.

Meyvaert, Paul. The Book of Kells and Iona. *The Art Bulletin* 71, 1989, 6–19.

Nees, Lawrence. Ultán the scribe. *Anglo-Saxon England* 22, 1993, 127–46.

_____ The Irish manuscripts at St. Gall and their continental affiliations. In James C. King (ed.), *Sangallensia in Washington: the arts and letters in medieval and baroque St Gall viewed from the late twentieth century.* New York 1993, 95–132 and 314–24.

Nordenfalk, Carl. An illustrated Diatesseron. *The Art Bulletin* 50, 1968, 119–40 (see also 55, 1973, 532–46).

_____ *Celtic and Anglo-Saxon painting. Book illumination in the British Isles 600–800.* New York 1977.

_____ Another look at the Book of Kells. In Friedrich Piel and Jörg Träger (ed.), *Festschrift Wolfgang Braunfels,* Tübingen 1977, 275–79.

Ochsenbein, Peter, Carl Schmuki and Anton von Euw. *Irische Buchkunst: die irischen Handschriften der Stiftsbibliothek St. Gallen und das Faksimile des Book of Kells.* St Gall 1990.

Ó Cróinín, Dáibhí, Pride and Prejudice, *Peritia* 1, 1982, 352–62

_____ Rath Melsigi, Willibrord, and the earliest Echternach manuscripts. *Peritia* 3, 1984, 17–42.

O'Mahony, Felicity (ed.). *The Book of Kells: proceedings of a conference at Trinity College, Dublin, 6–9 September, 1992.* Dublin and Aldershot, 1994.

O'Reilly, Jennifer. The Hiberno-Latin tradition of the evangelists and the gospels of Mael Brigte. *Peritia* 9, 1995, 290–309.

O'Sullivan, William. The Lindisfarne scriptorium: for and against. *Peritia* 8, 1993, 17–42.

Rickert, Margaret. *Painting in Britain: the middle ages.* Harmondsworth 1954.

Roth, Uta. Studien zur Ornamentik frühchristlicher Handschriften des insularen Bereichs: von den Anfängen bis zum Book of Durrow. *Bericht der Römisch-germanischen Kommission* 60, 1979, 5–225.

Rynne, Etienne. The art of early Irish illumination. *Capuchin Annual* 36, 1969, 201–22.

Schauman, Bella. The Irish script of the MS. Milan, Biblioteca Ambrosiana, S. 45 sup. (ante *ca.* 625). *Scriptorium* 32, 1978, 3–18.

Simms, G.O. *Irish illuminated manuscripts.* The Irish Heritage Series, 29. Dublin 1985.

_____ *Exploring the Book of Kells.* Dublin 1988.

Stevick, Robert D. *The earliest Irish and English book arts: visual and poetic forms before A.D. 1000.* Philadelphia 1994.

Sweeney, James Johnson. *Irish illuminated manuscripts of the Early Christian period.* New York 1965.

Warner, George F. *The Stowe Missal, Ms. D.II.3 in the library of the Royal Irish Academy, Dublin,* 2 vols. London 1906 and 1915.

Werckmeister, Otto-Karl. Three problems of tradition in pre-Carolingian figure style: from Visigothic to insular illumination. *PRIA* 63 C, 1962–4, 167–89.

_____ *Irisch-northumbrische Buchmalerei des 8. Jahrhunderts und monastische Spiritualität.* Berlin 1967.

Werner, Martin. The Book of Durrow and the question of programme. *Anglo-Saxon England* 26, 1997, 23–39.

Whitfield, Niamh. Brooch or cross? The lozenge on the shoulder of the Virgin in the Book of Kells. *Archaeology Ireland* 10(1), 1996, 20–23.

Wright, David H. The tablets from Springmount bog: a key to early Irish palaeography. *American Journal of Archaeology* 67, 1963, 219.

_____ *Sutton Hoo and the Book of Durrow: the Hiberno-Saxon illuminator's dependence upon a living tradition of metalwork in the seventh century*. British Museum seminar lecture, May 1977.

Zimmermann, E. Heinrich (ed.). *Vorkarolingische Miniaturen*, Berlin 1916.

Metalwork and other crafts

Armstong, E.C.R. and H.J. Lawlor. The Domhnach Airgid. *PRIA* 34 C, 1917–19, 96–126.

Blindheim, Martin. A house-shaped Irish-Scots reliquary in Bologna, and its place among other reliquaries. *Acta Archaeologica* 55, 1984, 1–53.

Bourke, Cormac. Early Irish hand-bells. *JRSAI*, 110, 1980, 52–66.

_____ Irish croziers of the eighth and ninth centuries. In Michael Ryan (ed.), *Ireland and insular art A.D. 500–1200*, Dublin 1987, 166–173.

_____ The Blackwater shrine. *Dúiche Néill: Journal of the O'Neill Country Historical Society* 6, 1991, 103–106.

_____ Further notes on the Clonmore shrine. *Seanchas Ard Mhacha* 16(2), 1995, 27–32.

Crawford, Henry S. A descriptive list of Irish shrines and reliquaries. *JRSAI* 53, 1923, 74–93 and 151–76.

Dunraven, earl of. On an ancient chalice and brooches lately found at Ardagh, in the county of Limerick. *Transactions of the Royal Irish Academy* 24, 1874, 433–54.

Elbern, Victor H. Eine Gruppe insularer Kelche. In Ursula Schlegel and Claus Zoege von Manteuffel (ed.), *Festschrift für Peter Metz*, Berlin 1965, 115–23.

Fuglesang, S.H. *Some aspects of the Ringerike style*, Odense 1980.

Graham-Campbell, James. Two groups of ninth-century Irish brooches. *JRSAI* 102, 1972, 113–28.

_____ The initial impact of the Vikings on Irish art. *Viking Society for northern research: Saga book* 20, 1978–9, 42–8.

_____ *Viking artefacts*. London 1980.

Harbison, Peter. The Antrim cross in the Hunt Museum. *North Munster Antiquarian Journal* 20, 1978, 17–40.

_____ A lost crucifixion plaque of Clonmacnoise type found in County Mayo. In Harman Murtagh (ed.), *Irish midland studies: essays in commemoration of N.W. English*, Athlone 1980, 24–38.

_____ The date of the Moylough belt shrine. In Donnchadh Ó Corráin (ed.), *Irish Antiquity. Essays and studies presented to Professor M.J. O'Kelly*. Cork 1981, 231–39.

_____ The bronze Crucifixion plaque said to be from St John's (Rinnagan), near Athlone. *Journal of Irish archaeology* 2, 1984, 1–17.

Haseloff, Günther. *Email im frühen Mittelalter: frühchristliche Kunst von der Spätantike bis zu den Karolingern*, Marburg 1990.

Holmquist, Wilhelm. An Irish crozier-head found near Stockholm. *Antiquaries Journal* 35, 1955, 46–51.

Hunt, John. On two 'D'-shaped bronze objects in the Saint Germain museum. *PRIA* 57 C, 1956, 153–7.

Johansen, Olav Sverre. Bossed penannular brooches: a systematization and study of their cultural affinities. *Acta Archaeologica* 44, 1973, 63–124.

Kelly, Eamonn P. The Lough Kinale book-shrine. In T. Michael Spearman and John Higgitt (ed.), *The Age of migrating ideas. Early medieval art in northern Britain and Ireland*, Edinburgh and Stroud 1993, 168–74.

Kendrick, T.D. and Elizabeth Senior. St. Manchan's shrine. *Archaeologia* 86, 1937, 105–18.

Kilbride-Jones, H.E. *Zoomorphic penannular brooches*. Reports of the Research Committee of the Society of Antiquaries of London 39, London 1980.

Lang, James T. *Viking-age decorated wood: a study of its ornament and style*. Medieval Dublin Excavations 1962–81, ser. B. vol. 1. Dublin 1987.

Mac Dermott, Máire. The Kells crozier. *Archaeologia* 96, 1955, 59–113.

Michelli. Perette E. The inscriptions on pre-Norman Irish reliquaries. *PRIA* 96 C, 1996, 1–48.

Mitchell, G.F. The cap of St. Lachtin's arm. *JRSAI* 94, 1984, 139–40.

Newman, Conor. Notes on some Irish hanging bowl escutcheons. *Journal of Irish Archaeology* 5, 1989–90, 45–8.

Ó Floinn, Raghnall. Irish Romanesque crucifix figures. In Etienne Rynne (ed.), *Figures from the past. Studies on figurative art in Christian Ireland in honour of Helen M. Roe*, Dun Laoghaire 1987, 168–88.

_____ The Soiscél Molaisse. *Clogher Record* 13(2), 1989, 51–63.

_____ A fragmentary house-shaped shrine from Clonard, Co. Meath. *Journal of Irish Archaeology* 5, 1989–90, 49–55.

O'Kelly, Michael J. The belt-shrine from Moylough, Sligo. *JRSAI* 95, 1965, 149–88.

O'Meadhra, Uaininn. *Early Christian, Viking and Romanesque art: motif-pieces from Ireland: an illustrated and descriptive catalogue of the so-called artist's trial pieces ...* Stockholm, 1987.

Organ, Robert M. Examination of the Ardagh chalice: a case history. In William J. Young (ed.), *Application of science in examination of works of art*, Boston 1973, 238–71.

Ó Riain, Pádraig. The shrine of the Stowe missal, redated. *PRIA* 91 C, 1991, 285–95.

Ryan, Michael (ed.). *The Derrynaflan hoard I. A preliminary account*. Dublin, 1983.

_____ The Donore hoard: early medieval metalwork from Moynalty, near Kells, Ireland. *Antiquity* 61, 1987, 57–63.

_____ The formal relationships of insular early medieval eucharistic chalices. *PRIA* 90 C, 1990, 281–356.

_____ Decorated Irish metalwork in Bobbio. *Archaeology Ireland* 5(2), 1991, 17.

_____ Ten years of early Irish metalwork. *Irish Arts Review Yearbook* 10, 1994, 153–6.

_____ The Derrynaflan hoard and early Irish art. *Speculum* 72, 1997, 995–1017.

_____ and Eamonn Kelly. New finds at the National Museum of Ireland. *Ireland of the Welcomes* 36(5), 1987, 22–5.

Smith, Reginald A. Irish brooches of five centuries. *Archaeologia* 65, 1914, 223–50.

Somerville, Orna. Kite-shaped brooches. *JRSAI* 123, 1993, 59–101.

Stevenson, Robert B.K. The Hunterston brooch and its significance. *Medieval Archaeology* 18, 1974, 16–42.

_____ Further notes on the Hunterston and 'Tara' brooches, Monymusk reliquary, and Blackness bracelet. *Proceedings of the Society of Antiquaries of Scotland* 119, 1983, 469–77.

_____ Further thoughts on some well known problems. In R. Michael Spearman and John Higgitt (ed.), *The age of migrating ideas: Early medieval art in northern Britain and Ireland*. Edinburgh and Stroud 1993, 16–26.

Stokes, Margaret. Observations on two ancient Irish works of art known as the Breac Maedhog, or shrine of St Moedoc of Ferns, and the Soiscel Molaise or gospel of St Molaise of Devenish. *Archaeologia* 43, 1871, 131–50.

_____ *Early Christian art in Ireland*. London 1894.

_____ *Notes on the Cross of Cong*. Dublin 1895.

Swarzenski, Georg. An early Anglo-Irish portable shrine. *Bulletin of the Museum of Fine Arts, Boston* 52, n° 289, 1954, 50–62.

Wamers, Egon. Some ecclesiastical and secular insular metalwork in Norwegian Viking graves. *Peritia* 2, 1983, 277–306.

_____ *Insularer Metallschmuck in wikingerzeitlichen Gräbern Nordeuropas*. Neumünster 1985.

Werner, Joachim. Jonas in Helgö. *Bonner Jahrbücher* 178, 1978, 519–30.

Whitfield, Niamh. The original appearance of the Tara brooch. *JRSAI* 106, 1976, 5–30.

_____ The Waterford kite-brooch and its place in Irish metalwork. In Maurice F. Hurley, Orla M.B. Scully and Sarah W.J. McCutcheon, *Late Viking age and medieval Waterford, Excavations 1986–1992*, Waterford 1997, 490–517.

_____ and Elizabeth Okasha. The Killamery brooch: its stamped ornament and inscription. *Journal of Irish Archaeology* 6, 1991–92, 55–60.

Wilson, David M. An early representation of St Olaf. In D.H. Pearsall and R.A. Waldron (ed.), *Medieval literature and civilization: studies in memory of G.N. Garmonsway*, London 1969, 141–45.

Youngs, Susan. The Steeple Bumpstead boss. In R. Michael Spearman and John Higgitt (ed.), *The age of migrating ideas. Early medieval art in northern Britain and Ireland*, Edinburgh and Stroud 1993, 143–50.

_____ Enamelling in early medieval Ireland. *Irish Arts Review Yearbook* 13, 1997, 43–51.

Architecture and architectural sculpture

Barrow, G.L. *The Round Towers of Ireland*. Dublin 1979.

Berger, Rainer. Radiocarbon dating of early medieval Irish monuments. *PRIA* 95 C, 1995, 159–74.

Bradley, John. The sarcophagus at Cormac's Chapel,

Cashel, Co. Tipperary. *North Munster Antiquarian Journal* 26, 1984, 14–35.

_____ and Heather King. Romanesque voussoirs at St Finbarre's cathedral, Cork. *JRSAI* 115, 1985, 146–51.

Brash, R.R. *The ecclesiastical architecture of Ireland to the close of the twelfth century*. Dublin 1875.

Champneys, A.C. *Irish ecclesiastical architecture, with some notice of similar or related work in England, Scotland and elsewhere*. London 1910.

Craig, Maurice. *The architecture of Ireland from the earliest times to 1880*. London and Dublin 1982.

Crawford, H.S. The Romanesque doorway at Clonfert, *JRSAI* 42, 1912, 1–7.

_____ and H.G. Leask. Killeshin church and its Romanesque ornament. *JRSAI* 55, 1925, 83–94.

Crotty, Gerard. A Romanesque fresco in Cormac's Chapel. *Tipperary Historical Journal* 1988, 155–8.

De Paor, Liam. Cormac's Chapel: the beginnings of Irish Romanesque. In Etienne Rynne (ed.), *North Munster Studies. Essays in commemoration of Monsignor Michael Moloney*, Limerick 1967, 133–45.

Garton, Tessa. A Romanesque doorway at Killaloe. *Journal of the British Archaeological Association* 134, 1981, 31–57.

Hamlin, Ann. The archaeology of the Irish church in the eighth century. *Peritia* 4, 1985, 279–99.

_____ The study of early Irish churches. In Próinséas Ní Chatháin and Michael Richter (ed.), *Ireland und Europa. Die Kirche im Frühmittelalter / Ireland and Europe. The early Church*, Stuttgart 1984, 117–26.

Harbison, Peter. How old is Gallarus oratory? A reappraisal of its role in early Irish architecture. *Medieval Archaeology* 14, 1970, 34–59.

_____ The Romanesque Passion lintel at Raphoe, Co. Donegal. In Agnes Bernelle (ed.), *Decantations: a tribute to Maurice Craig*, Dublin 1992, 72–7.

_____ Architectural sculpture from the twelfth century at Ardmore. *Irish Arts Review Yearbook* 11, 1995, 96–102.

Hare, Michael and Ann Hamlin. The study of early church architecture in Ireland: an Anglo-Saxon viewpoint with an appendix on documentary evidence for round towers. In L.A.S. Butler and R.K. Morris (ed.), *The Anglo-Saxon church*. Council for British Archaeology Research

Report 60, London 1986, 131–45.

Herren, Michael W. *The Hisperica Famina 1. The A-text*. Toronto 1974.

Hodkinson, Brian. Excavations at Cormac's Chapel, Cashel, 1992 and 1993: a preliminary statement. *Tipperary Historical Journal* 1994, 167–74.

Horn, Walter, Jenny White Marshall and Grellan D. Rourke. *The forgotten hermitage of Skellig Michael*. Berkeley, Los Angeles and Oxford, 1990.

Leask, Harold G. Carved stones discovered at Kilteel, Co. Kildare. *JRSAI* 65, 1935, 1–8.

_____ *Irish churches and monastic buildings, I: the first phases and the Romanesque*, Dundalk, 1955.

McNab, Susan. The Romanesque figure sculpture at Maghera, Co. Derry, and Raphoe, Co. Donegal. In Jane Fenlon, Nicola Figgis and Catherine Marshall (ed.), *New Perspectives. Studies in art history in honour of Anne Crookshank*, Blackrock 1987, 19–33.

_____ The Romanesque sculptures of Ardmore Cathedral, Co. Waterford. *JRSAI* 117, 1987, 50–68.

_____ From Tomregan to Inishcealtra: Irish twelfth century sculpture. *Irish Arts Review Yearbook* 13, 1997, 32–4.

Manning, Conleth. Clonmacnoise cathedral: the oldest church in Ireland? *Archaeology Ireland* 9(4), 1995, 30–33.

_____ Kilteel revisited. *Journal of the Kildare Archaeological Society* 18(3), 1996–7, 296–300.

O'Keeffe, Tadhg. La façade romane en Irlande. *Cahiers de civilisation médiévale x–xii siècles* 34(3–4), 1991, 357–65.

_____ Lismore and Cashel: reflections on the beginnings of Romanesque architecture in Munster. *JRSAI* 124, 1994, 118–52.

O'Kelly, Michael J. Church Island near Valencia, County Kerry. *PRIA* 59 C, 1958, 57–136.

Perry, Mark. The Romanesque frescoes in Cormac's Chapel, Cashel. *Ireland of the Welcomes*. 44(2), 1995, 16–19.

Petrie, George. The ecclesiastical architecture of Ireland anterior to the Norman invasion, comprising an essay on the origin and uses of the round towers of Ireland. *Transactions of the Royal Irish Academy* 20, 1845, 1–521.

Radford, C.A.R. The earliest Irish churches. *Ulster Journal of Archaeology* 40, 1977, 1–11.

Rynne, Etienne. The round towers of Ireland: a review article. *North Munster Antiquarian Journal* 22, 1980, 27–32.

Stalley, Roger. The Romanesque sculpture of Tuam. In Alan Borg and Andrew Martindale (ed.), *The vanishing past. Studies of medieval art, liturgy and metrology presented to Christopher Hohler*, BAR International Series 111, Oxford 1981, 179–95.

_____ Three Irish buildings with west country origins. In Nicola Coldstream and Peter Draper (ed.), *Medieval art and architecture at Wells and Glastonbury*, London 1981, 62–80.

_____ *The Cistercian monasteries of Ireland.* London and New Haven, 1987.

_____ Hiberno-Romanesque and the sculpture of Killeshin. In P.G. Lane (ed.), *Laois: history and society* (forthcoming).

Stokes, Margaret. *Early Christian architecture in Ireland.* London 1878.

Veelenturf, Kees. Vroege kerkelijke architectuur in Ierland: het material in de geschreven bronnen. In D.R. Edel, W.P. Gerritsen and K. Veelenturf (ed.), *Monniken, ridders en zeevarders*, Amsterdam 1988, 61–81.

Walsh, Gerry. Preliminary report on the archaeological excavations on the summit of Croagh Patrick, 1994. *Cathair na Mart* 14, 1994, 1–10.

White Marshall, Jenny and Claire Walsh. Illaunloughan: life and death on a small early monastic site. *Archaeology Ireland* 8(4), 1994, 24–28.

High Crosses and cross-decorated slabs

Crawford, H.S. A descriptive list of early cross-slabs and pillars. *JRSAI* 43, 1913, 326–34 (see also 46, 1916, 163–7).

De Paor, Liam. The limestone crosses of Clare and Aran. *Journal of the Galway Archaeological Society* 26, 1955–56, 53–71.

_____ The high crosses of Tech Theille (Tihilly), Kinnitty, and related sculpture. In Etienne Rynne (ed.), *Figures from the past. Studies on figurative art in Christian Ireland in honour of Helen M. Roe*, Dun Laoghaire 1987, 131–58.

Edwards, Nancy. An early group of crosses from the kingdom of Ossory. *JRSAI* 113, 1983, 5–46.

_____ Some observations on the layout and construction of abstract ornament in early Christian Irish sculpture. In F.H. Thomson (ed.), *Studies in medieval sculpture*, London 1983, 3–17.

_____ The origins of the free-standing stone cross in Ireland: imitation or innovation?. *Bulletin of the Board of Celtic Studies* 32, 1985, 393–410.

_____ Some crosses in County Kilkenny. In William Nolan and Kevin Whelan (ed.), *Kilkenny: history and society*, Dublin 1990, 33–61.

Fanning, Thomas. Excavation of an early Christian cemetery and settlement at Reask, County Kerry. *PRIA* 81 C, 1981, 67–172.

_____ and Pádraig Ó hÉailidhe. Some cross-inscribed slabs from the Irish midlands. In Harman Murtagh (ed.), *Irish midland studies. Essays in commemoration of N.W. English*, Athlone 1980, 5–23.

Hamlin, Ann. Early Irish stone carving: content and context. In Susan M. Pearce (ed.), *The early church in western Britain and Ireland. Studies presented to C.A. Ralegh Radford ...*, BAR British Series 102, Oxford 1982, 283–96.

Harbison, Peter. Early Carolingian narrative iconography: ivories, manuscripts, frescoes, and Irish High Crosses. *Jahrbuch des Römish-germanischen Zentralmuseums* 31, 1984, 455–71.

_____ A group of early Christian carved stone monuments in County Donegal. In John Higgitt (ed.), *Early medieval sculpture in Britain and Ireland*, BAR British Series 152, Oxford 1986, 49–85.

_____ *The high crosses of Ireland: an iconographical and photographic survey*, 3 vols. Bonn 1992.

_____ A high cross base from the Rock of Cashel and a historical reconsideration of the 'Ahenny group' of crosses. *PRIA* 93 C, 1993, 1–20.

_____ The extent of royal patronage on Irish high crosses. *Studia Celtica Japonica* 6, 1994, 77–105.

_____ *Irish high crosses with the figure sculptures explained.* Drogheda 1994.

Henry, Françoise. *Irish high crosses.* Dublin 1964.

Hicks, Carola. A Clonmacnoise workshop in stone. *JRSAI* 110, 1980, 5–35.

Higgitt, John. Words and crosses: the inscribed stone cross in early medieval Britain and Ireland. In John Higgitt (ed.),

Early medieval sculpture in Britain and Ireland, BAR British Series 52, Oxford 1986, 125–52.

Horn, Walter. On the origin of the Celtic cross: a new interpretation. In Walter Horn, Jenny White Marshall and Grellan D. Rourke (ed.), *The forgotten hermitage of Skellig Michael*, Berkeley, Los Angeles and Oxford 1990, 88–97.

Kelly, Dorothy. Irish high crosses: some evidence from the plainer examples. *JRSAI* 116, 1986, 51–67.

_____ The heart of the matter: models for the Irish high crosses. *JRSAI* 121, 1991, 105–45.

Lionard, Pádraig. Early Irish grave-slabs. *PRIA* 61 C, 1960–61, 95–169.

Macalister, R.A.S. *The memorial slabs of Clonmacnois, King's County*. Dublin 1909.

_____.The history and antiquities of Inis Cealtra. *PRIA* 33 C, 1916, 93–174.

_____ The inscriptions on the slab at Fahan Mura, Co. Donegal. *JRSAI* 59, 1929, 89–98.

_____ *Corpus inscriptionum insularum celticarum*, 2 vols. Dublin, 1945 and 1949.

MacLean, Douglas. The origins and early development of the Celtic cross. *Markers: Journal of the Association of Gravestone Studies* 7, 1990, 232–75.

McNab, Susanne. Styles used in twelfth-century Irish figure sculpture. *Peritia* 6–7, 1987–88, 265–97.

_____ Early Irish sculpture. *Irish Arts Review Yearbook* 1990–1991, 164–71.

O'Farrell, Fergus. 'The cross in the field', Kilfenora: part of a 'founder's tomb'? *North Munster Antiquarian Journal* 26, 1984, 8–13.

Ó Murchadha, Domhnall. Stone sculpture in pre-Norman Ireland. *Capuchin Annual* 1969, 172–200.

_____ Rubbings taken of the inscriptions on the Cross of the Scriptures, Clonmacnois. *JRSAI* 110, 1980, 47–51.

_____ and Giollamuire Ó Murchú. Fragmentary inscriptions from the West Cross at Durrow, the South Cross at Clonmacnois, and the Cross of Kinnitty. *JRSAI* 118, 1988, 53–66.

Porter, Arthur Kingsley. *The crosses and culture of Ireland*. New Haven 1931.

Richardson, Hilary and John Scarry. *An introduction to Irish high crosses*. Cork 1990.

Roe, Helen M. An interpretation of certain symbolic sculptures of early Christian Ireland. *JRSAI* 75, 1945, 1–23.

_____ *The high crosses of western Ossory*. Kilkenny 1958.

_____.*The high crosses of Kells*. 1959.

_____ The Irish high cross: morphology and iconography. *JRSAI* 95, 1965, 213–26.

_____ *Monasterboice and its monuments*. 1981.

Seaborne, Malcolm. *Celtic crosses of Britain and Ireland*. Shire Archaeology, Aylesbury, 1989.

Sexton, Eric. *A descriptive and bibliographical list of Irish figure sculptures of the early Christian period*. Portland (Maine) 1946.

Sheehan, John. A Merovingian background for the Ardmoneel stone? *Journal of the Cork Historical and Archaeological Society* 99, 1994, 23–31.

Stalley, Roger. European art and the Irish high crosses. *PRIA* 90 C, 1990, 135–58.

_____ *Irish high crosses*. Dublin 1991 and 1996.

Stevenson, R.B.K. The chronology and relationships of some Irish and Scottish crosses. *JRSAI* 86, 1956, 84–96.

_____ Notes on the sculptures at Fahan Mura and Carndonagh, County Donegal. *JRSAI* 115, 1985, 92–95.

Stokes, Margaret. *The high crosses of Castledermot and Durrow*. Dublin, 1898.

_____ Notes on the high crosses of Moone, Drumcliff, Termonfechin, and Killamery. *Transactions of the Royal Irish Academy* 31, 1896–1901, 541–78.

Veelenturf, Kees. *Dia Brátha: eschatological theophanies and Irish high crosses*. Amsterdam 1997.

Waddell, John and Patrick Holland. The Peakaun site: Duignan's 1944 investigations. *Tippeary Historical Journal* 1990, 165–86.

Wallace, Patrick F. and Timoney, Martin A. Carrowntemple, Co. Sligo, and its inscribed slabs. In Etienne Rynne (ed.), *Figures from the past. Studies on figurative art in Christian Ireland in honour of Helen M. Roe*, Dun Laoghaire 1987, 43–61.

Werner, Martin. On the origin of the form of the Irish high cross. *Gesta* 29(1), 1990, 98–110.

Acknowledgments

■

Photo Credits

AKG, Paris: 59, 67, 68, 69.

Belzeaux-Zodiaque: 4, 5, 6, 7, 8, 9, 10,
11, 12, 14, 15, 16, 17, 18, 19, 21, 22,
34, 36, 42, 43, 47, 52, 53, 58, 60, 61,
62, 63, 64, 65, 66, 72, 73, 74, 75, 76,
77, 78, 81, 82, 84, 85, 88, 89, 90, 91,
93, 94, 95, 96, 97, 98, 101, 102, 103,
104, 106, 107, 108, 109, 111, 112,
113, 114, 115, 116, 117, 118, 120,
130, 131, 132, 133, 134, 135, 136,
137, 138, 139, 140, 144, 145, 146,
147, 148, 149, 150, 151, 152, 154,
156, 157, 158, 159, 160, 162, 163,
166, 167, 168, 169, 170, 171, 172,
175, 176, 177, 178, 179, 180, 181,
182, 183, 184, 185, 186, 187,
188, 189, 190, 191, 192, 193,
194, 195, 196, 197, 198, 199,
200, 201, 202, 203, 204, 206,
207, 208, 210, 211, 212, 213,
214, 215, 219, 220, 221, 222,
223, 224, 225, 226.

Bord Failte: 79 (N.M.I. Dublin).

Paul Caponigro: 128, 218.

Dieuzaide-Zodiaque: 51, 54, 55, 56, 57.

Dúchas, The Heritage Service: 2 (Con
Brogan), 3, 121, 122, 123, 124, 125,
127, 153, (Wiltshire Collection) 209.
Peter Harbison: 1, 23, 24, 25, 26, 27,
29, 30, 31, 33, 35, 37, 38, 86, 87, 99,
100, 105, 110, 119, 126, 129.

Arnold Hintze, Kirchen-Sieg,
Allemagne: 28.

Jacqueline O'Brien: 32, 141, 142, 164,
165, 173.

John Kennedy, The Green Studio:
20, 70, 71.

Moira Concannon (Ulster Museum,
Belfast): 13.

Museum of Fine Arts, Boston
(Theodora Wilbour Fund in Memory of
Charlotte Beebe Wilbour): 80.

National Museum of Ireland: 39, 40, 41,
44, 45, 46, 48, 49, 50, 83, 155, 161,
174 (Photo Valerie Dowling), 205.

The Photographic Archives,
Françoise Henry. Department of
Archaeology, University College,
Dublin: 216, 217.

The Slide File: 92.

Antikvarisk-topografiska arkivet,
Stockolm: 143.

Drawings and plans by
Brother Noël Deney

Drawings not by Brother Noël Deney:
    Page 71: both drawings after
    R.B.K. Stevenson.
    Page 72: by kind permission of
    Dr Sue Youngs, British Museum.
    Page 251: after Jim Lang, by kind
    permission of Dr Pat Wallace and the
    National Museum of Ireland.
    Page 305: reconstructions drawn by
    Dan Tietzsch-Tyler, reproduced
    by kind permission of Dúchas,
    © The Heritage Service.

Designed by Pascale et
Jean-Charles Rousseau

The plates reproduced in gravure and in
colour were selected and printed by the
Ateliers de La Pierre-qui-Vire

Project manager: Jacques Collin

Index

■